Controlling Capital

T0304067

Controlling Capital examines three pressing issues in financial market regulation: the contested status of public regulation, the emergence of 'culture' as a proposed modality of market governance and the renewed ascendancy of private regulation.

In the years immediately following the outbreak of crisis in financial markets, public regulation seemed almost to be attaining a position of command – the robustness and durability of which is explored here in respect of market conduct, European Union capital markets union and US and EU competition policies. Subsequently there has been a softening of command and a return to public–private co-regulation, positioned within a narrative on culture. The potential and limits of culture as a regulatory resource are unpacked here in respect of occupational and organisational aspects, stakeholder connivance and wider political embeddedness. Lastly, the book looks from both appreciative and critical perspectives at private regulation, through financial market associations, arbitration of disputes and, most controversially, market 'policing' by hedge funds.

Bringing together a distinguished group of international experts, this book will be a key text for all those concerned with issues arising at the intersection of financial markets, law, culture and governance.

Nicholas Dorn, a sociologist, is associated with the School of Advanced Legal Studies, University of London, having previously researched for Cardiff University and taught at Erasmus School of Law, Rotterdam. He is the author of *Democracy and Diversity in Financial Market Regulation*.

Controlling Capital

Public and Private Regulation of Financial Markets

Edited by
Nicholas Dorn

Routledge
Taylor & Francis Group

LONDON AND NEW YORK

First published 2016
by Routledge

2 Park Square, Milton Park, Abingdon, Oxfordshire OX14 4RN
711 Third Avenue, New York, NY 10017

a GlassHouse book

Routledge is an imprint of the Taylor & Francis Group, an informa business

First issued in paperback 2017

British Library Cataloguing in Publication Data
A catalogue record for this book is available from the British Library

Library of Congress Cataloging-in-Publication Data
Controlling capital : public and private regulation of financial markets /
Edited by Nicholas Dorn.
pages cm
Includes bibliographical references and index.
ISBN 978-1-138-94312-4 (hbk) – ISBN 978-1-315-67272-4 (ebk) 1.
Financial services industry–Law and legislation. 2. Financial services
industry–Government policy. 3. Banking law. I. Dorn, Nicholas
(Professor), editor.
K1066.C66 2016
346.07–dc23
2015034076

ISBN: 978-1-138-94312-4 (hbk)
ISBN: 978-1-138-57007-8 (pbk)

Typeset in Baskerville by
Servis Filmsetting Ltd, Stockport, Cheshire

Contents

Notes on contributors

John Biggins previously worked as a researcher on transnational private regulation in the over-the-counter derivatives markets at the Centre for Regulation and Governance, University College Dublin, as part of a broader research initiative funded by the Hague Institute for the Internationalisation of Law: *Transnational Private Regulation – Constitutional Foundations and Governance Design*.

Olha O Cherednychenko is Associate Professor of European Private Law and Comparative Law at the University of Groningen, and Director of the Groningen Centre for European Financial Services Law, the Netherlands.

Brett Christophers is Associate Professor, Department of Social and Economic Geography, Uppsala University and author of *The Great Leveler: Capitalism and Competition in the Court of Law*.

Jay Cullen is Lecturer in Corporate and Banking Law in the School of Law, University of Sheffield. His most recent book, on banking regulation, corporate governance and financial market theory, is *Executive Compensation in Imperfect Financial Markets*.

Nicholas Dorn, a sociologist, is associated with the School of Advanced Legal Studies, University of London, having previously researched for Cardiff University and taught at Erasmus School of Law, Rotterdam. He is the author of *Democracy and Diversity in Financial Market Regulation*.

Richard H Hansen is an associate at NautaDutilh NV in Amsterdam who specialises in international commercial and investment arbitration, which is also his main area of recent publishing.

Ron Kerr is Senior Lecturer at University of Edinburgh Business School. Recent publications include (with Sarah Robinson) 'From symbolic violence to economic violence: the globalizing of the Scottish banking elite'.

Gerard J Meijer is a partner at NautaDutilh NV in Amsterdam and head of the firm's (international) arbitration practice. He is also Professor of Arbitration and Dispute Resolution at Erasmus University in Rotterdam.

Justin O'Brien is Professor of Business Law and Ethics in the School of Business Administration, American University of Sharjah, United Arab Emirates and Director of the Centre for Law, Markets and Regulation at the Faculty of Law, University of New South Wales, Sydney. He is the author of *The Triumph, Tragedy and Lost Legacy of James M. Landis: A Life in Full.*

Dieter Pesendorfer is Senior Lecturer in Regulation in the School of Law, Queen's University Belfast. His main areas of publishing are risk regulation and regulatory reforms in finance.

Sarah Robinson is Senior Lecturer at the School of Management, Leicester University. Recent publications include 'In search of an international experience: towards a "Bildung" understanding of MBA learning'.

Colin Scott is Principal of the College of Social Sciences and Law and Professor of EU Regulation & Governance, University College Dublin. He is co-editor of *Transnational Private Regulation: Conceptual and Constitutional Debates.*

Sally Wheeler is Professor and Head, School of Law, Queen's University Belfast. She has interests in corporate governance, corporate social responsibility and human rights. She is the author of 'Global production, CSR and human rights: the courts of public opinion and the social license to operate'.

Introduction: questions asked

Nicholas Dorn

Financial market misconduct and its attendant reputational and financial risks have joined contagion and instability risks as priorities for action through public policy and market compliance. The concerns over instability have by no means gone away; rather, 'post crisis' regulation is now double-hatted, being concerned with both sets of issues. In addressing this widened agenda, both public policy and private regulation are explicitly interlocking their actions. The book explores the cognitive, cultural, legal and political means through which this 'post crisis' agenda is constructed and asks about possible consequences. This introductory chapter presents themes, summarises chapters and raises questions about the relations between public and private regulation.

We start with some inconvenient truths. After the initial shock of the 2007–2009 crisis, public regulators adopted a more active and commanding stance. Yet, from the early 2010s onwards, financial market participants' manipulation of benchmarks – on interbank borrowing rates, foreign exchange and other important market reference points – repeatedly announced itself, being evidenced by the gleeful remarks of traders on telephones and in internet chat-rooms. Should regulators have known; indeed, how many junior or medium-level officials did know about something that was said to be an open secret in the markets, yet did not forward their concerns to management level; did some senior regulators know, deciding not to respond; worse, did some respond in such a manner as to imply assent (*Economist* 2012)? A crisis of credibility slowly built up, through press commentary, an internal report into the Bank of England (Grabiner 2014), and parliamentary hearings that were far from cosy (House of Commons Treasury Select Committee 2015). 2015 then saw an 'unprecedented' criminal investigation by the Serious Fraud Office into the Bank's liquidity operations during 2008 (Binham 2015). All of these caused the Bank of England to look again at its procedures, whereupon it 'spotted 50 instances of potential market abuse that in the past it might have missed' (ibid). The public and political debates that ensued arrived at the broad conclusion that, just as managers of the manipulation-happy traders should have known – unless the culture supported looking away – so it was with the Bank of England. Deniability, a stock-in-trade in finance, appears to be running out of credibility as an account for failure.

These and other events discussed in this book suggest several things. Whatever claims may be made for private regulation, under certain circumstances it can turn out to be an ugly thing: benchmark-setting had been under the nominal purview of the British Bankers' Association. Equally, public regulation is a work still in progress. The Bank of England did not exactly cover itself in glory, after it picked up regulatory responsibilities from the discredited Financial Markets Authority. Pushing regulatory responsibilities 'upwards', to the highest technocratic level, is no guarantee of alertness or performance. Clearly, however, upwards is the current direction of evolution of public regulation, within national, regional and international *fora*.

This ascent is paralleled by the increasingly internationalised nature of private regulation. Between public and private, in place of the behind-closed-doors collusion that was characteristic of the pre-crisis years, from the mid-2010s onwards there has been an explicit strategy of public–private interlocking and cooperation. What are the prospects for this public–private regulatory compact? Will it be seen over future years as having 'worked' from the points of view of immediate and wider stakeholders – or as a reprise of historical error, with better separation being needed between public authority and private regulation?

These themes run throughout the book, the three parts of which address: first, issues of state/market balance-of-power and ability to command (previously old-fashioned but now somewhat rehabilitated considerations); secondly, the development of shared cognitive and cultural spaces (now more in open *fora*, less behind closed doors); and, thirdly, the dynamism of and some quandaries raised by private regulation. In addressing these 'macro' issues, one should also keep in mind the situation of both public and private regulators as human beings who, in order to know some things, may have let others slip into their blind spots, a theme returned to in the Afterword of the book.

Themes and chapters

Command

Many commentators have found in the crisis and in its *sequelae* clear and vivid confirmation of the harms that arise from the dominant position of these markets within the political economy. That not only economic harm has resulted but also institutionalised wrongdoing – gleeful traders, eye-averting managers, boards blessed with deniability and regulators until recently either tolerant or compromised – underlines the need not only to de-risk and clean up these markets but also to down them in size (Wolf 2015).

Against that, other commentators, having overcome their brief surprise, have reconfirmed themselves as true believers in these markets, on the grounds that unwise state actions distorted and up-ended markets, not vice versa. If public regulators would give up remaining pretensions of command regulation, and if private regulation can expand not only internationally but also horizontally to cover more or perhaps all regulatory issues, then the markets could do the job that public regulators – sometimes referred to as *The Taliban* – cannot do.

Certainly, crisis, crisis management and its institutionalisation have resulted in much cognitive jostling over these two well established positions. For readers who find themselves spoken to by oppositionalist readings of the relationships between financial markets and public politics, the book title *Controlling Capital* reflects a state of tension, between the control of capital and control by it. In other words, a tension is experienced between (a) a statist project of not simply sustaining public authority over markets but also fundamentally remaking them (not only for *their* own good but also for *our* good) and, (b) a post-statist or anti-statist project of accepting, championing and enlarging private governance (let market self-understanding flow unimpeded, from market associations, through technocrats and into the international policy space). Such claims and counter-claims can be found aplenty in this book, sometimes explicit and otherwise implicit.

The chapter by Justin O'Brien starts with the global investigation into the manipulation of key financial benchmarks. The misconduct has triggered an escalation of fines by regulatory and law enforcement agencies and has also prompted the exit of a number of financial institutions from the setting of bench-mark rates. Whilst primarily focused in the United Kingdom (UK) and the United States (US), the misconduct spans the globe. These events posed a range of practical and conceptual problems, which apply at national, regional and global levels. At a practical level, the credibility of the benchmarks, which are a public good, has been undermined, prompting an incremental but observable erosion of public confidence in market integrity. At the policy level, the investiga-tion of collusion brings competition regulators into the arcane world of financial regulation. Their focus on breaking up cartels changes the dynamics, prompting a rapid expansion of the regulatory perimeter. It also facilitates a fundamental rethinking of capital market purpose. This chapter evaluates how the conflu-ence of regulatory and criminal investigation offers a time-limited opportunity to transcend the incremental and flawed nature of technical reform. It assesses the conceptual coherence of attempts, driven by the UK, but with significant support from both the Financial Stability Board and the International Monetary Fund, to create 'fair and effective' markets by articulating a new vision of 'inclu-sive capitalism' and questions whether this addresses the observed institutional corruption.

Within the European Union (EU), the way forward for regulatory reform from 2016 onwards is encapsulated in the political slogan and legislative programme of the Capital Markets Union (CMU). The second chapter, by Dieter Pesendorfer, outlines and critically assesses this. Announced in 2014, consulted upon in 2015, to be legislated from 2016 onwards, CMU is a project for the entire EU, intended to complement and move on from the Eurozone's ill-starred Banking Union. Although the details of all the components of CMU will take several years to emerge – it is a relatively wide programme – the general approach adopted by the Commission in the conceptualisation and initial consultation phases of policy-making is revealed to be contentious, on the grounds that the basic policy design inadequately addresses neither the key lessons of the global financial crisis nor the inherent problems of a finance-led regime. Pesendorfer's chapter first introduces what capital markets are and discusses their evolution and challenges. Based on theoretical debates about financialisation, varieties of capitalism and integration, key questions and concerns are identified about the new strategies to redesign EU capital markets. Then the key features and priorities of the European Commission's approach are presented, analysed and discussed with regard to their tensions, conflicts and flaws. In particular, the key assumption of 'underdeveloped capital markets' and the claims about effects on the 'real economy' are challenged. On that basis, the chapter concludes that there are significant problems with the EU's approach and that an alternative approach is needed in order to assure a more resilient financing of the 'real economy' and to boost investment along a more sustainable pathway.

Brett Christophers's chapter on US and EU competition (anti-trust) policies vis-à-vis financial markets over the past three decades gives grounds for concern. Christophers first refers to the well known difference between the written law and the law as interpreted and applied in practice. In the case of the financial sector, many extra-legal considerations – political, economic, intellectual and more – have combined consistently to minimise levels of anti-trust intervention. The result, across Western Europe and the US, is the highly concentrated and only minimally competitive financial sector we have ended up with today. The author considers the prospects for such a vivified competition policy, concluding that the prospects thereof are in fact rather slim.

Thus, where O'Brien's primarily contemporary focus leads to a welcome for competition policy – as an active policy sibling of financial market regulation – Christophers's perspective leads to a less hopeful view on this aspect of command regulation. This suggests that, if we can speak of command, then it has often had the opposite effect of what 'the person in the street' might have been expecting. Pesendorfer's analysis of CMU arouses broadly similar concerns, by suggesting that revival of this integrationist vision within a neoliberal framework leads to undue convergence in terms of business models.

Generally, public regulation, whether at the international, regional or domestic level, remains something of a chameleon. Arguably, setting it up as something entirely distinct from market mentalities would be wrong, as then it could have little leverage. The question is, then, what is the relation? This is addressed in the two following parts of the book: first, in relation to specific issues of culture, context and interests that shape (and partially subvert) public policy reform intentions; and, secondly, in relation to aspects of private regulation beyond the state, which curve back upon the latter.

Culture

There will be readers for whom any state-versus-market narrative is intellectually, politically and practically *dépassé*. As the institutionalist literature posits, capital is not outside the state, nor vice versa: capitals' strategies and states' policy-making are mutually constitutive and their agents engage loosely with each other, through national, regional and international channels, networking and role-swapping. From that perspective, conceptualising public regulation as if it could ever be 'outside' such networking – and as if it could work upon markets as a subject works upon its object – would be as improbable as suggesting that market actors could get anything done if they stuck to economic matters, ignoring political, social and cultural.

Thus, a chairperson of the Economic and Monetary Committee of the European Parliament who on retirement takes up a senior role in the financial markets should not be categorised under the pejorative heading 'revolving chairs'; it is simply the way things work. The person who moves from an investment bank into a central bank, Treasury ministry or even prime ministership brings expertise to what would otherwise be a clueless public institution. Nor can it be wrong if these actors mix socially, drawing upon and revitalising a common culture. They may be potentially conflicted but what matters is that they behave with integrity in whichever role they find themselves at a particular time. The ethical standpoint is not the origins or trajectories of individuals, but their personal moral staunchness, bolstered by their common culture, the latter helping them to know right from wrong. That is the orientation that has been broadly favoured by parliamentary enquiries and regulators in the UK. Admittedly, that is somewhat in contrast with the rather more oppositionist atmosphere in the US where, despite close links behind closed doors, the public policy debate tends to set up public and private regulation as political alternatives (or so seemed the case at the time of writing in 2015).

The three chapters in Part II of the book address questions of culture, within the conceptually and politically complex middle ground between public and private regulation of financial markets. This middle ground has by no means been reduced by successive crises; indeed, it has expanded as an arena within which public actors cajole and chivvy market actors into a semblance of ethical respectability and social responsibility. The regulatory strategy is to respond to the moral morass revealed by crisis and misconduct, not simply by widening the grounds on which market participants can be found culpable, and not only further escalation of financial penalties against firms, but also through a reconstitution of the culture of financial markets generally. Finance has been diagnosed as having a cultural deficit, with market participants being too often confused between right and wrong and, when they can see the difference, not always caring too much. The UK's 'Fair and Effective Markets Review' (FEMR) (HM Treasury and others 2015; O'Brien: Chapter 1 in this volume) is intended by its sponsors to be an international flagship for remoralisation. It sets out a reform process: public actors provide a forum, within which market participants can clarify moral boundaries across all financial markets, thus allowing boards and senior managers not only to 'set the tone' in a general sense but also to generate clarity and discipline over specific issues. The specifics are not addressed here (see HM Treasury and others 2015); however, the general strategy of framing issues in terms of enculturation is directly and critically addressed.

What sense does it make to construe market conduct in terms of culture, and what conditions may be needed to make such an approach work? The chapters by Sally Wheeler, Jay Cullen, and Ron Kerr and Sarah Robinson address these questions in relation to organisational structure, stakeholders and the wider political economy.

First, Wheeler's chapter draws on sociological insights about organisational structures, occupational cultures and behaviour. She explores how – indeed whether – ethical cultures can be created within a financial market context. Given the scale and persistence of regulatory and legal actions, she suggests that a definition of ethical problems in terms of 'rogue traders' and 'bad apples' would be inadequate, since entire business areas have been resorting to collusive illegal behaviour. The concept of 'bad barrels' seems to capture the situation better: the culture of firms fails to discourage transgression and indeed induces it. Unpacking the links between regulatory objectives, the internal workings of firms and their relations with other firms, this chapter questions the chances of success of measures such as enhanced controls on individuals and restructured reward mechanisms. Financial firms typically have very flat, nodal structures, within which traders conceptualise themselves as an elite, in contrast to back office staff and also in contrast to managers. Traders' intra-firm functions and their occupational mobility mean that their linkages and attachments may be much stronger outside 'their' firm than within it. Performance, *camaraderie* and their linkages are important in all work situations, yet all the more so for traders in financial markets. Thus, whether regulators and senior management combine to send a clear and consistent message to traders – or whether the logic of the financial marketplace leads some firms to continue to send conflicting or ambivalent messages to them – misconduct is likely to continue to be a tough nut to crack.

Jay Cullen's contribution also acknowledges traders' internal/external orientations, whilst expanding the analysis to managers and investors, examining the bounded rationality and short-term orientations of all these actors. Clearly, excessive risk-taking and questionable individual *mores* characterised banker behaviour in the lead-up to the Global Financial Crisis. Amid claims of a systemic breakdown in banking culture, a principal aim of the resulting UK legislative and regulatory response has been to restore public trust in the industry. Reform to incentives, together with the introduction of extensive sanctions to deter egregious risk-taking, are vaunted as vital in upgrading flawed risk management and remedying a failure of cultural norms in the sector. In tandem, these new regulatory provisions are regarded as imperative in improving financial stability. Yet, Cullen points out, there are also significant limitations to the notion that altering individual incentives – at least in the form taken by recent regulatory reforms – may bring about reductions in risk-taking or long-term changes to banking culture. On this basis, his chapter suggests that the mechanisms formulated in the wake of the crisis pay insufficient attention to both practical and normative considerations: (i) inherent issues of credibility in criminalising individual conduct, and flaws in the design of overhauled compensation regulations; (ii) behavioural and institutional features of the financial market. The latter include cognitive limitations of market participants, shareholder preference, and bankers' motivations for risk-taking beyond compensation targets – in particular, pressures for career advancement. These institutional features may produce suboptimal capital structure choices in spite of reform to individual incentives.

The analyses of both Wheeler and Cullen give grounds for doubting the effectiveness of enculturation as a regulatory strategy, given the incentives provided by occupational structures within financial markets and by short termism of stakeholders. It would be a short step, the editor suggests, to consider whether constraints on remuneration could in some respects not only be ineffective, but also have unintended consequences. Perhaps the less audacious might feel constrained, but would-be 'movers and shakers' – risk takers seeking to move on to a higher position in another firm – might redoubly calculate that a stunning short-term performance plus a pledge to take greater care in future might add to their lustre. Be that as it may (reforms of cultural and remuneration will certainly be foci of research for years to come) the question arises as to the wider determinants of such mentalities.

Ron Kerr and Sarah Robinson's chapter asks how the ambition to change culture in finance – an ambition shared by public and private actors – can be reconciled with the wider context of a political economy that remains shaped by neoliberalism. Such an ambition goes hand in hand with calls in the popular press for a return to what Kerr and Robinson take to be a quasi-imaginary past, in which banking was a gentlemanly profession conducted, at senior levels at least, by and between honourable gentlemen. However, a historical recreation seems highly unlikely, even if it has the merit of indicating the scale and depth of transformation needed for real cultural change in the industry. Remaking banking as a gentlemanly pursuit would require an unthinkable social upheaval in social values and practices, going much wider than financial markets. It would require the recreation of an elite whose shared educational, socio-cultural and occupational trajectory would empower them to withstand and counter the norms of neoliberal competitive individualism. If this is absurd – history can never turn back and anyway widespread attachment to neoliberalism stands in the way – then what remains unsorted is the identification and creation of some alternative basis for culture and conduct in contemporary conditions.

To be fair to the official promulgators of cultural reconstruction, it is acknowledged that past approaches to blending public and private – variously called meta-regulation, co-regulation, partnership – failed to deliver the regulatory goods.

Worse, it has nurtured fraud, manipulation and scandal, as noted in the final report of the UK FEMR (HM Treasury and others 2015).

> The next few years offer a crucial opportunity for market participants to step forward and take responsibility for improving standards. However, we should not be naïve about the challenge that lies ahead. Bilateral market discipline played little or no part in helping to maintain standards in the pre-crisis period – and few people we spoke to felt confident that would change in the period ahead (HM Treasury and others 2015: 6).

The UK approach seeks to eschew both command regulation and private regulation as separate silos – preferring to try to (re)construct a deconflictualised perspective of regulatory partnership, culture and discipline. However, the chapters of Wheeler, Cullen, and Kerr and Robinson raise a number of reservations about this, taking into account the structures of firms, incentives of investors and the privileges of elites. Whilst one response to these difficulties would be to rely more on command in the narrow sense of deterrence, a quite different response would be to seek to relocate discipline within the market.

Concession

The book's four concluding chapters have been commissioned to cover important aspects of private regulation, which explicitly or implicitly have been conceded by public actors. Concession here refers to state actors' licensing of private regulation: either *implicitly*, by leaving certain areas unregulated; *explicitly*, by lending it post-hoc support and legitimation; *proactively*, by inviting it to act as lead partner in certain respects; *ambivalently*, by making it possible for certain regulatory resources to be 'borrowed' by private actors; or *inconsistently*, as when some form of co-regulation is adopted in some areas and not in others.

The analysis begins with Olha Cherednychenko's exploration of the persistence of co-regulation and meta-regulation in Europe, suggesting a cooperative relationship between public and private regulation. John Biggins and Colin Scott's analysis of financial market rule-making and enforcement vis-à-vis swaps and derivatives trading illustrates how the public authorities may turn to an international association in order to deal with regulatory gaps. Gerard Meijer and Richard Hansen, writing from the perspective of practising lawyers, advocate and describe developments in arbitration, which, although being a private method of dispute resolution, cannot completely escape the (laws of the) public domain. Finally, Nicholas Dorn looks at some hedge fund strategies involving the direction of claims – to targeted firms and sovereigns, to other market participants and, indeed, to public regulators and other officials – to the effect that hedge funds are acting in the public interest.

Illustrating that private regulation in financial markets is not new, Cherednychenko starts her chapter by underlining that, historically, the financial industry has played a major role in the regulation of financial services across the

EU. This reminds us of the return to public and private regulatory partnership that is invoked as 'cultural' approaches and the FEMR (see above). Cherednychenko sees an ebb and flow, with private regulation declining as public regulation grew in the decades before the financial crisis of 2007–2009, this being given further impetus in the immediate post-crisis years. The move away from principles-based public regulation and towards more prescriptive and centralised public regulation has resulted in the EU in 'European supervision private law': a body of rules made up of contract-related conduct of business clauses, cast as supervision standards, enforced by financial regulators.

Cherednychenko makes three main points. First, private regulation in the financial services field has not been entirely displaced by post-crisis public regulation. Secondly, more fundamentally, and contrary to the traditional dichotomy between purely private regulation and command and control public regulation, there is still room for exploration and interplay between public and private actors in governing financial services in a multi-level EU legal order. Thirdly, complementarity between public and private requires revisiting and recasting pre-crisis notions of co-regulation and meta-regulation. Under co-regulation, public regulators define mandatory open norms or minimum standards, which are then operationalised either by public regulators or private regulators. In meta-regulation, public regulation only provides an explicit framework for systems, procedures or controls that must be introduced within financial institutions. Both tendencies have been reputationally damaged by the crisis but are being tweaked. Cherednychenko mentions some strengths, weaknesses and challenges facing such approaches, including conflicts of interest, failures on both sides (insufficient compliance, sloppy supervision) and an uneasy relationship when public regulators are sometimes partners and sometimes discipliners.

However, Cherednychenko concludes that, in a multi-level system of governance such as that of the EU, and in light of the complexity of financial products and services, 'interplay between private regulation and public regulation under the auspices of the latter' will continue to be needed.

Moving to the transnational level, Biggins and Scott's chapter on the International Swaps and Derivatives Association (ISDA) points to its 'continuing centrality' in post-financial-crisis regulatory frameworks affecting the over-the-counter (OTC) derivatives markets. Despite ISDA's status as a private trade association, maligned in certain quarters in the immediate aftermath of the financial crisis, it clearly remains a pivotal actor by virtue of its embedded standard-setting role and associated activities. Interestingly, many of ISDA's post-crisis initiatives have been pursued at the behest (or at least with the tacit support) of public regulatory actors. This is illustrated by the issuance of the 2014 ISDA Resolution Stay Protocol. The key purpose of this Protocol, a contractual mechanism, is to address gaps in the jurisdictional application of national (e.g. US) and regional (e.g. EU) public regulatory reforms relating to the resolution of distressed banks. Such instruments can play a crucial role in underwriting the integrity of otherwise public regulatory frameworks. They form 'private soft law', which benefits from authority that is 'loaned' by public actors, thus illustrating the complementarity of public and private actions in contemporary governance of financial markets. The authors argue ISDA's broader symbiotic relationship with public actors has deepened in the wake of the financial crisis.

Concerning dispute resolution, Meijer and Hansen's chapter starts by noting that, in respect of disputes, the financial world has yet to embrace arbitration, instead steadily opting for litigation in front of the English or New York courts. However, arbitration of financial services disputes enjoys a number of advantages over court litigation of these matters, including widespread international enforceability under the New York Arbitration Convention. In order to enjoy such benefits, however, parties to financial services contracts must introduce a valid arbitration clause into their agreements. This 'how to' contribution focuses on this first step in the process of assuring that disputes that arise under financial services contracts can be settled through arbitration. The writers cover the most important aspects of drafting an effective arbitration clause, including specific issues that may arise with regard to arbitration in the financial services sector. Topics discussed include general notions regarding drafting arbitration clauses, model arbitration clauses of reputable arbitration institutes, the European Market Infrastructure Regulation (EMIR), parties to arbitration clauses, the place of arbitration, choice of law, the number and appointment of arbitrators, decision standards applied by the arbitral tribunal, the language of the proceedings, confidentiality and waivers.

Most writing on hedge funds and regulation poses the former as the target of the latter. Indeed, now that hedge funds have found their way into most institutional investment portfolios and some private individual ones – and also hedge fund-*like* strategies are becoming mainstreamed within capital markets – such regulation seems unexceptional (even if the industry at first and rather stupidly fought against it). Dorn's chapter looks, however, at the other side of the coin: hedge fund strategies that incorporate claims to be acting as market regulators. This coverage is by no means meant to be ironical; rather, it raises the question of whether this sector of the industry is in the early stages of construction of new elements of *lex mercatoria*, making moral, fairness and efficiency claims and drawing in public regulatory resources where they can. Three hedge fund strategies are examined: the 'activist' strategy of intervening in target companies in order to push up the share price; 'short and shout', seeking to drive down the share price; and legal and political strategies vis-à-vis distressed debt, notably that of sovereigns, where cases in US courts concerning Argentinean debt and investor 'holdouts' have upturned previous understandings of debt restructuring. All three strategies involve noisy claims-making, which in activist strategies is economic in tone and focuses on return on investment; in shorting strategies it is moral in tone, focusing on alleged misrepresentation and misconduct; and in distressed debt strategies it is legal, constructing a right not to be bound by a settlement arrived at by the majority of creditors. These three hedge fund strategies respectively mimic regulatory concerns with market efficiency (activists), conduct (shorts) and fairness (distressed debt). A concluding discussion raises some questions about mainstreaming of hedge fund strategies, about the purposes of financial markets and about the future of the public/private nexus of regulation.

Regulatory theory: pyramids, two-level games and hybrid spaces

The contributors to this book are engaged in attempts to understand, advance, transform and/or criticise financial market regulation. Such efforts are certainly urgently needed. Regulatory theorising over the 1990s and up until the crash of 2007–2009 could be characterised as something of a crowded trade, with too many participants running in the same direction. When financial markets crashed systemically, collateral damage included regulatory shame and academic revision.

Pre-crash regulatory theory revolved around two primary and complementary ideas. The first idea was famously advanced by John Braithwaite, himself a regulator and a criminologist, who together with colleagues and followers gave the field the idea of the 'regulatory pyramid' (Ayres and Braithwaite 1992). According to this, first there occur (corresponding to the base of the pyramid) conversations between the regulator and the industry, in order to clarify principles. Secondly, in response to any misunderstanding, implementation failure, or wilful lack of compliance by a minority of market participants, quiet conversations take place, shortfalls are pointed out and there is increasing regulatory pressure, aimed at getting market participants to put things right. Thirdly, as an exceptional response to the remaining presumably few transgressions that are repeated and/or flagrant, actual enforcement actions occur (corresponding in frequency and intensity to the top of the pyramid).

Another generally accepted pre-crisis idea was regulatory 'independence', meaning not so much independence vis-à-vis the markets – a degree of closeness being seen as necessary in order for the above-mentioned market-regulatory conversations to be fruitful – but rather independence of the regulator from the government of the day (or any other 'political', meaning non-market, pressures). Such a notion of independence ties in with the notion that if industry is to be responsive to the regulator, and vice versa, then a space needs to cordoned off within which this process can occur (for a critique of which, see Dorn 2014a).

Both these general ideas bit the dust after 2007–2009. The regulatory pyramid came to be seen as having harboured delaying tactics, game-playing, non-compliance and extreme risk-taking. Independence of the regulator was considered to have provided conditions for, at best, the neutralisation of the regulator by the market and, at worst, cognitive and institutional capture. It became apparent that the formal depoliticisation of the shared regulator–market space had been an illusion, since informal back channels were active in pleading special interests and in creating conditions in which the middle level of the regulatory pyramid became not only dysfunctional but also derisory. Better, then, to use the political power to remake the regulatory model.

Enter command regulation, squeezing out the definitely compromised and seemingly corrupt middle level of the regulatory pyramid. What is left then of the thinking behind the pyramid? One possible answer seems to be that the erstwhile middle of the pyramid is being dispersed both downwards and upwards: the new model of the 2010s has only two levels, both of which involve both public and private actors. At the lower, initial level, the actors jointly formulate the rules of the game. So far, this is broadly similar to the first lower level of the pyramid. However, the engagement is intended to be taken more seriously by both the regulator and the market, with the aim of constructing mutually acceptable principles, codes and rules.

Why should market participants engage any more sincerely and robustly with the rules than they did before? For the following reason. If market participants fail to comply with the rules for which they have become co-responsible, then the action moves directly and decisively into the enforcement phase – the upper level of the new model. Enforcement actions may be publicly- or privately-led or both (for example, heavy fines imposed by competition authorities, plus suspension or loss of market access). There is henceforth to be no middle ground, consisting of years of side-stepping the issue, during which the regulator plays the role of an indulgent and indefatigable parent, whilst the regulatee plays at being confused and promises to try harder, whilst at best making cosmetic changes and fine-tuning the gaming of the system.

The new two-level model posits that a deeper mutual emergence of rule-formulation *merits the conclusion* that any subsequent transgression is punishable. This time really is different: those who make the rules, 'own' them and may die by them. That is the new (mainstream) regulatory theory.

One immediately evident snag is that, if market participants are to be held accountable (at level two), then they may become so greatly interested in the rules of the game (formulated at level one) that their increased engagement reduces regulation to an industry wish-list. Any public interest in regulation may be absorbed into and reformulated within the parameters of the balance of power between private interests. Indeed, critics of the process of implementations of post-crisis regulation – for example of US Dodd-Frank regulation, UK Vickers, EU Liikanen, Capital Markets Union (CMU) – point to such processes (see for example Williams 2015). Lobbying seems to have blunted much of the intentions between such measures and also to have reintroduced pre-crisis arguments for deregulation. The enormous fuss raised around market misconduct in competition cases – notably Libor and forex – may be obscuring more fundamental, structural issues, as the industry partially fends off and rolls back 'post crisis' command regulation. From such a perspective, some large fines and public raps over the knuckles, in return for the industry's enhanced *entrée* into policy-making, might seem a questionable bargain.

There are alternative ways to view the emergent public–private space. For example, as Biggins and Scott (Chapter 8 in this volume) suggest, public–private dialogues – sometimes resulting from an initiative from the former to the latter – have the capacity to produce 'a species of "soft private law", a particular form of public-private complementarity in governance, which we are liable to see more of in the future'. In this vision, the emphasis is on practical problem-solving: public regulators perceive that they do not have the capacities necessary to command, but they do have the power to invite. We may indeed see more such hybrids in future. It remains to be seen how differently they function from past variants.

Inclusive capitalism?

Readers may wish to contextualise the issues covered in the chapters within a longer term historical trajectory, within which public regulation is a relatively recent arrival and has a precarious place. After a crisis-induced blip of public regulation, regulation may revert to its historical norm: several if not all the chapters of this book can be read as giving support to such a possibility.

Up to and including the 19th century, financial markets largely disciplined themselves (which is not to imply that such a state of affairs is optimal). Feudal guild systems of town-based market self-organisation persisted into modern times, maintaining internal order through the threat of exclusion of transgressors. In finance, these arrangements eventually received public recognition – as central banks standing at the apex of banking regulation, and as broader financial market regulatory agencies that built upon, formalised and bureaucratised guild traditions. In the second half of the 20th century, sectoral regulation coalesced into national regimes, formally constituted as public institutions (Moran 1988; Dorn 2014b).

Concerning the long period of private governance, one epic myth is that the mere twitching of the eyebrows of the governor of the Bank of England was enough to signal the boundaries of respectability, in the then (relatively) refined culture of London banking. Coming to the period following the Second World War, twitchy eyebrows and fireside chats had been thought to have been replaced by rule-books and routinised investigations and enforcement. However, it turns out that these historical vestiges survived and indeed thrived within the regulatory world, up until – and after – the financial market crisis of 2007–2009. Thus, even in 2015 the deputy governor of the Bank of England felt a need to declare that:

> The days when 'constructive ambiguity' was seen as a helpful foil for central bankers are behind us. Governors' eyebrows and fireside chats are no match for a clearly communicated framework in which information will be gathered and decisions made.
>
> (Shafik 2015: 2)

In historical perspective, it is decidedly odd that such a statement should have been made in 2015, given that financial market regulation had supposedly already become bureaucratised and rule-based – at least twice – once in the 1980s and again after the financial market crisis. The historical *tenacity* of cosy chats and constructive ambiguity reminds us that command has been the exception, concession the rule and culture shaped accordingly. It might be going too far to suggest that financial market regulation has never been hitherto and cannot become a truly public activity – an activity that is 'for the good of the people' (Carney 2015). However, at the very least, the market remains important in regulation in key respects: as the primary interlocutor with policy-makers (market influence was rolled back as a result of the crisis but both sides then re-engaged); as a shaper of the cognate and cultural space inhabited by both regulators and regulatees; and through rulebook-making and enforcement, which always depends first and foremost on firms, the market and its associations.

What then may be made of the claim that a corner has now been turned and that a new vista is opening up, drawing not only public regulators but potentially also the market into a new, *inclusive* future?

> Central banks' greatest contribution to inclusive capitalism may be driving financial reforms that are helping to rebuild the necessary social capital. In doing so, we need to recognise the tension between pure free market capitalism, which reinforces the primacy of the individual at the expense of the system, and social capital which requires from individuals a broader sense of responsibility for the system. A sense of self must be accompanied by a sense of the systemic (Carney 2014: 5).

In this discourse, central banks widen, socialise and moralise the hitherto primarily economic term 'systemic', so as to refer not only to the stability of markets but also to a version of the wider public good. Financial markets should make capitalism more inclusive, and dialogue between the markets and regulators can be the means of achieving this.

However, as Carney acknowledged in the same speech, such claims face difficulties in that regulatory policies hitherto seem more concerned with financial systems and entities than with wider public good. The distributional aspects of regulatory policies during the 2007–2009 financial market crisis and the Eurozone crisis are indeed politically ugly. Central banks strongly advised policy-makers to switch bank bondholders' losses onto public budgets (Taylor 2014), which has been a significant factor driving austerity policies in many Eurozone countries. Central banks also invented a new strategic resource – quantitative easing – the benefits of which are widely acknowledged as falling on financial asset holders (Draghi 2015). All in all, those emergency actions have not enhanced social inclusion, nor indeed was that the intention, although post-hoc attempts have been made to justify them in distributional terms (Draghi 2015).

As for subsequent reforms of aspects of finance, regulators have indeed been extraordinarily active at national, regional and international levels. However, market participants quickly re-engaged with their policy interlocutors and, by 2015, the tide had turned. For example, in the US and continental Europe, bank separation policies have been variously gutted or pre-empted (Hardie and

Macartney 2015). In the UK, the head of the Financial Conduct Authority (FCA), Martin Wheatley, was eased out. One commentary suggests the timing is significant, as it was 'just as the FCA is deciding what commercial interchanges may be permitted between universal banking groups and the tethered goats that are their ringfenced retail banks' (Ford 2015: 16). Whether that coincidence of timing indicates cause is a matter for future enquiry.

An equally or possibly more telling reference point for the defenestration of the conduct regulator may be the FEMR (HM Treasury and others 2015), a core proposition of which was that the construction of conduct should be more market-based (see also O'Brien: Chapter 1 in this volume and Cherednychenko: Chapter 7 in this volume). For this to work, both the industry and the Treasury believed that different leadership was required (Fortado and others 2015). The industry supported the FEMR's recommendation for a Market Standards Board – sitting between the industry and the regulator – in order to 'create a more constructive dialogue between regulators and the market' (Myles 2015). This would allow 'reengaging with FCA otherwise than in an enforcement context', which would bring 'greater regulatory certainty around conduct risk' (ibid, citing Linklaters' legal adviser on the Market Practitioner Panel supporting the Review). Conceivably, the shift in style and structure would imply changes not only in senior personnel but also institutional demotion for the conduct regulation authority, which had not been in the lead of the FEMR. As of 2015, the UK authorities were uploading the FEMR's main messages to the EU level (thus engaging with regulatory recalibration in the context of CMU) and to international partners as represented in the Financial Stability Board (chaired by the governor of the Bank of England).

Evidently, as of the mid-2010s, policy-makers in governments and in regulatory agencies were sending, at best, rather mixed and ambiguous signals, raising questions of interpretability. When looking back on this from future years, it may become easier to discern which specific messages would best be understood in terms of corporate communications policies (appropriate messages for specific audiences); which in terms of genuine uncertainty of direction, inviting engagement; and which in terms of a post-command inflection point. We have seen a period of command, which for a period of time appeared to subordinate private regulation, yet private regulation is resilient and adept at seizing opportunities.

Moreover, as history shows us, the relationship between public and private cannot be viewed as a zero sum game – rather it is a complex field, not static but often undergoing reconfiguration. During the mid-2010s, reconfiguration became represented through motifs such as market culture, fairness and discipline, to be broadly framed by public regulators, then to be filled in and 'owned' by market participants; failing which there remains the threat of further regulatory rule-making and heavier enforcement (HM Treasury and others 2015).

Whether the enlargement and political highlighting of this public–private space will in time be seen to represent a real paradigm change – or whether it may curve back to be revealed as the pre-crisis beast dressed in new clothing – remains to be seen (see Binham and Jenkins 2015 and video embedded in that report).

Given the issues discussed by contributors in Part II of the book, we may be for-given for remaining wary: firm-level, industry-wide and societal factors work pow-erfully against attempts to inculcate ethics in many sectors of finance. Admittedly, if one takes one's bearings from about 2015, then it is possible to see in this, and in the concomitant rise of competition activism, the potential for or even the promise of radical transformation. The counter-argument is that, unless competi-tion policy changes its spots – something that would require transformation of its political, legal and/or institutional features – then market concentration, with its concomitant social inequalities, may rise further, constraining financial market regulation. Considering all the above in European perspective, there is a possibil-ity that any benefits of CMU would flow more strongly to large finance firms (be they banks or non-banks) and to hedge funds (see Chapter 10 in this volume) than to small and medium size enterprises and their employees. Leaving aside intermi-nable debates over whether insufficient investment or demand lie at the core of Eurozone malaise, inserting more complexity and more intermediaries into the investment chain must imply value extraction, unless markets make magic. One would have to forget all of the above in order to be sure of a new beginning, as distinct from a historical reprise.

Finally, on the ascendancy of private regulation, whilst it can hardly be said that 'there is no alterative' – the immediate responses to crisis by public regula-tors proves otherwise – still it remains true that private regulation is both deeply entrenched and making strides in many directions. The diverse areas analysed by the contributors to Part III of the book illustrate how private regulators sometimes are tasked by public regulators (with mixed success, as in co- and meta-regulation); sometimes are invited to act by public regulators (swaps and derivatives); some-times work autonomously, pushing to extend their boundaries (arbitration); and sometimes constitute regulatory quandaries (hedge fund activists, shorters and holdouts). Given the political dynamics following the crises in financial markets and the Eurozone, it is not impossible that after a brief period of command regu-lation of financial markets, the converse is arising, with private actors once more coming to the fore, whilst activists in the public sphere step back. So, then, on to the chapters.

References

Ayres, I and Braithwaite, J, 1992, *Responsive Regulation: Transcending the Deregulation Debate*, New York: Oxford University Press.
Binham, C and Jenkins, P, 2015, 'UK bank rule reformers call end to age of big stick', *Financial Times* (11 June 2015) http://www.ft.com/intl/cms/s/0/184ec010-1063-11e5-b4dc-00144feabdc0.html (last accessed 12 September 2015).
Binham, C, 2015, 'Bank of England embroiled in money-market fraud probe', *Financial Times* (4 March 2015) http://www.ft.com/intl/cms/s/0/9b0fe180-c26d-11e4-bd9f-00144feab7de.html (last accessed 12 September 2015).
Carney, M, 2014, 'Inclusive capitalism: creating a sense of the systemic', Speech given at the Conference on Inclusive Capitalism, London: Bank of England (27 May 2014)

http://www.bankofengland.co.uk/publications/Documents/speeches/2014/speech731.pdf (last accessed 12 September 2015).

Carney, M, 2015, 'Building real markets for the good of the people', Speech given at the Lord Mayor's Banquet for Bankers and Merchants of the City of London at the Mansion House, London: Bank of England (10 June 2015) http://www.bankofengland.co.uk/publications/Documents/speeches/2015/speech821.pdf (last accessed 12 September 2015).

Dorn, N, 2014a, 'Financial markets and regulatory accountability: between technocratic autonomy and democratic direction', in Bianculli, A, Fernández-Marín, X and Jordana, J (eds), *Accountability and Regulatory Governance*, Basingstoke: Palgrave Macmillan.

Dorn, N, 2014b, *Democracy and Diversity in Financial Market Regulation*, Abingdon: Routledge.

Draghi, M, 2015, 'ECB: structural reforms, inflation and monetary policy', Speech, ECB Forum on Central Banking, Sintra, Frankfurt am Main: European Central Bank (22 May 2015) https://www.ecb.europa.eu/press/key/date/2015/html/sp150522.en.html (last accessed 12 September 2015).

Economist, 2012, 'First-mover disadvantage: Bob Diamond, Barclays and regulators are all battling to save their reputations', *The Economist* (7 July 2012) http://www.economist.com/node/21558300 (last accessed 12 September 2015).

Ford, J, 2015, 'More relief for banks as Osborne reins in watchdog', *Financial Times* (20 July 2015) http://www.ft.com/intl/cms/s/0/33d45960-2df7-11e5-8873-775ba7c2ea3d.html (last accessed 12 September 2015).

Fortado, L, Parker, G, Arnold, M and Binham, C, 2015, 'Martin Wheatley resigns as chief of Financial Conduct Authority', *Financial Times* (17 July 2015) http://www.ft.com/intl/cms/s/0/61f867fa-2c76-11e5-8613-e7aedbb7bdb7.html (last accessed 12 September 2015).

Grabiner, L, 2014, *Bank of England Foreign Exchange Market Investigation: A Report by Lord Grabiner QC*, London: Bank of England (12 November 2014) http://www.bankofengland.co.uk/publications/Documents/news/2014/grabiner.pdf (last accessed 12 September 2015).

Hardie, I and Macartney, H, 2015, 'Too big to separate? A French and German defence of their biggest banks', blog post, Brussels: Finance Watch (26 March 2015) http://www.finance-watch.org/hot-topics/blog/1067 (last accessed 12 September 2015).

HM Treasury, Bank of England and Financial Conduct Authority, 2015, 'Fair and Effective Markets Review. Final Report', London: Bank of England (10 June 2015) http://www.bankofengland.co.uk/markets/Documents/femrjun15.pdf (last accessed 12 September 2015).

House of Commons Treasury Select Committee, 2015, 'Lord Grabiner questioned on foreign exchange fixing scandal', House of Commons video (27th February 2015) https://www.youtube.com/watch?feature=player_embedded&v=es_jlj3I_XU (last accessed 12 September 2015).

Moran, M, 1988, 'Thatcherism and financial regulation', *The Political Quarterly*, 59(1), 20–27.

Myles, D, 2015, 'FEMR recommendations: the market responds', *International Financial Law Review*, (12 June 2015), http://www.iflr.com/Article/3461960/FEMR-recommendations-the-market-responds.html (last accessed 11 December 2015).

Shafik, M, 2015, 'Goodbye ambiguity, hello clarity: the Bank of England's relationship with financial markets', Speech on 26 February at the University of Warwick by the Deputy Governor for Markets and Banking, Bank of England http://www.bankofengland.co.uk/publications/Documents/speeches/2015/speech801.pdf (last accessed 12 September 2015).

Taylor, C, 2014, 'Trichet letter revealed: ECB threatened to stop emergency funding unless Ireland took bailout', *Irish Times* (6 November 2014) http://www.irishtimes.com/news/ireland/irish-news/trichet-letter-revealed-ecb-threatened-to-stop-emergency-funding-unless-ireland-took-bailout-1.1989869 (last accessed 12 September 2015).

Williams, J, 2015, 'Dodging Dodd-Frank: excessive speculation, commodities markets, and the burden of proof', *Law & Policy*, 37(1–2), 119–52.

Wolf, M, 2015, 'Why Finance is too much of a good thing', *Financial Times*, 26 May, http://www.ft.com/intl/cms/0/64c2f03a-03a0-11e5-a70f-00144feabdc0.html (last accessed 11 December 2015).

Command regulation: revitalised or mythological?

Chapter 1

On culture, ethics and the extending perimeter of financial regulation

Justin O'Brien

Introduction

Every June the financial denizens of the City of London gather at the Mansion House to receive a statement of intention from the Chancellor of the Exchequer. For the sixth consecutive time, the Chancellor George Osborne returned in 2015. Electorally triumphant, the governing Conservative Party nonetheless faces a multiplicity of tactical and strategic questions on the future of capital market governance. These focus less on technicalities but the more complex, contested and perennial issue of the role and function of finance in society (O'Brien 2014). No longer dependent on the Liberal Democrats, who had done much to anchor finance more securely to a renewed social contract, the chancellor, together with his party, wants to use the power of the City of London to drive an innovation agenda. Both he and it remain cognisant, however, that any lessening of regulatory oversight without evidence of meaningful change, risks breaking already fragile bonds of trust.

The increasingly shrill debate on the role of the City in British society is made manifest, for example, by the machinations over the future domicile of HSBC (Donnellan 2015a). The bank remains mired in scandal. It is reviewing not only its federated structure, which it accepts is no longer fit for purpose, but also whether to abandon the United Kingdom (UK), in part because of increased regulatory costs and in part because of the uncertainty associated with a promised referendum on European Union membership. It is a fear shared by many in the City. A British exit would have profound implications for the dominance of the City in European finance (Donnellan 2015b). George Osborne (2015) thus sought to untie the Gordian knot with the release of the 'Fair and Effective Markets Review' (FEMR) (HM Treasures and Others 2014).

As a reformulation of a 'social contract', it is designed to reposition the City as a global marketplace informed by the institutionalisation and internalisation of restraint. It is both a laudable and long-standing goal (Kennedy 1934). The unresolved question is whether it will work or whether it is simply an exercise in political symbolism, designed to mask rather than comprehensively deal with deeply embedded structural problems.

Announced the previous year at the Mansion House (Osborne 2014), the final findings of the FEMR offer, if implemented in full and, crucially, if its underpinning normative purpose is accepted by industry, an opportunity to shift a deeply corrosive narrative. There are, to be sure, reasons for scepticism. For a country that has had more intensive examination than most of the causes and consequences of malfeasance and misfeasance in the capital markets, the decision to constitute the FEMR was in itself, on one level, perplexing.

The UK had already diagnosed incompetence and hubris in the management of major financial services institutions (Financial Services Authority 2011); the limitations associated with short-termism (Kay 2012); the problems of regulatory capture (Treasury Select Committee 2012); and the institutionalisation of malign cultures (Parliamentary Committee on Banking Standards (PCBS) 2013). Why was it necessary to convene yet another inquiry? What would its purpose be? The answer lies in the wave of benchmark scandals that have engulfed the City of London, in the process fracturing belief in the efficacy of market ordering without credible oversight.

These scandals include the corruption of the London Interbank Offered Rate (Libor), a daily calculation of what a panel of banks determines to be the hypothetical cost of borrowing in a range of currencies and timeframes. It is the most important number in finance (Talley and Strimling 2013). To date billions of dollars of fines have been collected, the majority of which have been levied by the United States (US) with an increasing component booked by UK regulators (Financial Services Authority 2013; Financial Conduct Authority 2013, 2014a and 2014b).

The malfeasance uncovered also includes systemic manipulation of the multi-trillion dollar foreign exchange (forex) markets. The most important benchmark in this domain is the WM 4PM Fix, a calculation of paired currency rates administered by a subsidiary of State Street in conjunction with Thomson Reuters. Ever more stringent settlements related to Libor and forex manipulation have induced institutions that operate offshore subsidiary operations to plead guilty to corporate criminal misconduct (Department of Justice 2014; 2013). Individuals also have begun to enter guilty pleas (Binham 2014), as have holding companies (Baer 2015).

In many cases, reductions in financial penalties are brokered in exchange for ongoing cooperation with regulatory and law enforcement agencies. Increasingly, sophisticated investigatory methods are being deployed. Very deliberately, the Department of Justice in the US, for example, has signalled the ongoing deployment of undercover operatives inside financial institutions (Holder 2014). The policy problem is that fine escalation and, as yet, haphazard application of criminal and civil sanctions, have proven insufficient to change conduct in demonstrable, warranted ways.

From the implicated banks' perspective, the financial penalties have been written off as part of the (albeit increasingly expensive) cost of doing business (the arrival of anti-trust regulators into financial markets, may, however, cause a re-evaluation of that particular cost-benefit analysis: see Baer 2015). Notwithstanding the apparent insouciance of market sentiment, the result of institutionalised collusion has had profound practical and theoretical implications. It undermines, if not decisively then certainly damagingly, vaunted theoretical and practical reliance on the restraining power of market forces. This supposed more effective remedy than direct regulatory intervention has been largely missing-in-action. Understandably, the public remains angry and deeply sceptical.

For a trade-off that withdraws overt and invasive external regulation in favour of agonistic dialogue with the industry over the future trajectory of reform to be acceptable, there needs to be demonstrable change on the part of industry and the incentive to achieve this was precisely what George Osborne offered at the Mansion House in June 2015. Government, he argued, was ready and willing to exit ownership of the woefully-run Royal Bank of Scotland (RBS). Moreover, bank baiting was to end in favour of a dialogue designed to make London the destination of choice for global banking. The 'ratcheting up ever-larger fines' was neither sustainable nor, in policy terms, a 'long-term answer' (Osborne 2015), the chancellor told a receptive audience. In return, he asked for, indeed demanded, change. In order to effect that change, the Governor of the Bank of England set out the key performance indicators at the same dinner (Carney 2015).

The forced departure of the combative head of the Financial Conduct Authority (FCA), Martin Wheatley, announced later in the northern summer, does little to change this existential battle, notwithstanding orchestrated media claims to the contrary (see Binham and Guthrie 2015). Seeking an accommodation with the City does not necessarily pre-ordain capitulation. Indeed, the political risk of failing to address identified problems in the wholesale market has been magnified by Martin Wheatley's early departure, occasioned, it must be said, as much by pique as by design. From a design perspective the work is completed. The challenge now is implementation.

For banking, it is an exquisite but dangerous moment. As the banking editor of the *Financial Times* put it: 'a new era of finance feels within reach' (Jenkins 2015). The devil, however, will be in the detail. This chapter explores how the combination of regulatory and criminal investigation and a genuine offer of partnership offer a time-limited but potentially transformative opportunity. It assesses the conceptual coherence of attempts, driven by the UK Government, but with significant support from both the Financial Stability Board (FSB) and the International Monetary Fund (IMF), to create 'fair and effective' markets informed by the commitment of the sector to the changed demands of 'inclusive capitalism' (Carney 2014). The policy innovation leaves it to the market to negotiate the practical parameters and deliver tangible progress in improving market conduct. Crucially, this reframing of regulatory policy transcends narrow economic efficiency. It suggests that violation of the letter or spirit of the new proposed compact could have profound implications (although there is a worrying lack of detail on what sanctions are considered).

The chapter thus evaluates the theoretical justifications and how practical nudging could further advance policy objectives through, for example, enhanced contractual terms in the use of deferred prosecutions. First, it sets out the rationale for importing into finance the logic of responsibility. This derives primarily from the stated but as yet untested commitment of the finance sector to a professionalisation agenda, which is predicated on an obligation by it to uphold an underpinning social contract. Secondly, it evaluates specifically how the fair and effective markets rubric addresses the corruption of market integrity. Thirdly, and relatedly, it highlights the systemic nature of the problem, as evidenced by the admission of wholesale banks that, by default, they allowed cartels to operate with impunity. Fourthly, it excavates the philosophical foundations of the proposed solution. Fifthly, and finally, it notes a deep suspicion of associational governance and suggests that the expansion of the regulatory agenda shows no sign of abating. It concludes that what is on offer is not a return to the freedom to set standards once offered but squandered by the associational governance model but an invitation to verify stated commitment.

The rationale for professionalising finance

The moral failings of the market have been a defining feature of myriad official inquiries into the Global Financial Crisis. The British Parliamentary Commission on Banking Standards (PCBS) has carried out the most detailed evaluation of ethical deficits and whether these could be addressed by systematically importing norms and mores into the finance profession. From the beginning, the Commission identified a major problem. The professionalisation project presupposed that there existed within the capital markets a distinct kind of activity that could be characterised as having the attributes of professional life (e.g. specific tertiary educational requirements that act as a barrier to entry, ongoing continuous professional development, meaningful codes of conduct that are effectively monitored and enforced, effective and demonstrable commitment to the development and enhancement of professional standards and, crucially, mechanisms to suspend or withdraw a professional licence to operate in the event of misconduct). Notwithstanding the stated commitment of the British Banking Association of the need for a professional body with requisite regulatory power, the final report of the Parliamentary Commission demonstrates an acute wariness. Banking, it concludes, 'is a long way from being an industry where professional duties to customers, and to the integrity of the profession as a whole, trump an individual's own behavourial incentives' (PCBS vol 2: para 597). This was based on five inter-linked failings. First, the Commission noted a sharp decline in the membership of existing banking associations. Secondly, it questioned these associations' actual commitment to upholding their stated values, noting that the industry to date had proved unwilling or unable to use existing sanctions (PCBS vol 2: para 586). Thirdly, the lack of 'a large common core of skills and values inculcated in the course of pre-qualification education or training [means that] banking is not a profession in the same way [as law, medicine and accountancy]' and cannot become so by the stroke of a pen' (PCBS vol 2: para 606).

Fourthly, it discounted the credibility of proposed remedial strategies, noting that a 'set of expected qualifications which forces bank clerks to night school for years to come, but gives a free pass to those working in wholesale banking or at more senior levels – the groups which most conspicuously failed in recent years – would ignore the lessons of the crisis' (PCBS, vol 2: para 607). Fifthly, and most damningly, it detected in the push for the fast-tracked establishment of a professional standards board an inappropriate attempt to garner regulatory power: 'On the basis of our assessment of the nature of the banking industry, we believe that the creation of a professional body is a long way off and may take at least a generation' (PCBS vol 2: para 601).

Notwithstanding these concerns, the Commission did leave open the possibility for the industry to demonstrate commitment to upholding professional values by setting out a series of milestones that could provide evidence of change. These milestones are further developed in the FEMR. They include the need for comprehensive coverage, the integration of wholesale and retail components, and the development of credible sanctions, with applicability across industry. Crucially, progress towards these objectives does not necessarily mean commitment on the part of regulatory or political authorities to a scaling back of the regulatory perimeter. In fact the opposite is the case. In the search for accountable governance, policy remains regulative rather than constitutive and is likely to remain so. There is an invitation to industry to buy in and thereby avail of a seat at the regulatory table. What is most definitely not on offer is a blank cheque or return to unverifiable principles-based regulation. The need for such a sceptical approach has been magnified by the extent to which market integrity has been compromised by the corruption of core financial benchmarks.

Benchmarks and the corruption of integrity

The manipulation of financial benchmarks can be unpacked at three distinct levels. Each provides deleterious feedback loops to the others. First, at the level of the firm, the capacity to monitor conduct was and remains low. The extraordinary testimony provided by senior bankers at RBS to the PCBS (2013) is talismanic in this regard. It demonstrated the weakness of risk management systems. It also left little doubt of the pernicious effects on market integrity of the tacit toleration of moral rule-breaking within discrete organisational cultures. Following a standard script, the RBS executives said that they were, in turn, shocked at the crookedness involved in the manipulation of Libor, dismayed at the lack of moral restraint and keen to differentiate between ethical bankers and amoral traders. If the bankers, ostensibly in control, were guilty of anything it was, according to the then head of investment banking, John Hourican, 'excessive trust' (Ebrahimi and Wilson 2013). As the RBS executives conceived the issue, benchmark manipulation was not a core concern, given the fact that: 'we [presumably meaning the board and senior executives] had to deal with an existential threat to the bank'. Instead of dealing with misaligned incentives, the bank (by inference including Hourican) had exhibited 'blind faith' in the actions of its traders. It was a message repeated by the then chief executive, Stephen Hester. The scale of the abuse was, Hester intoned, 'too readily redolent of a selfish and self-serving culture in banking which I think needs to be addressed and is exactly the reason for this commission's existence'. Such lofty rhetoric is hard to reconcile with the involvement of RBS traders in forex manipulation *after* the Libor settlement! Remedial action to bring activity inside the regulatory perimeter through technical measures alone does little to address such an ethical (and potentially criminally negligent) deficit.

At the second level, that of the market as a whole, the manipulation of financial benchmarks threatens a narrative that focuses on the problem of 'bad apples' rather than a manifestation of a corrupted culture. The discovery that capital markets have been rigged, with none of the restraining forces of a Nevada casino, raises profound legitimacy questions. The Nevada Gaming Control Board (2012: 5), for example, can find a casino liable for 'failure to conduct gaming operations in accordance with proper standards of custom, decorum and decency, or permit any type of conduct in the gaming establishment which reflects or tends to reflect on the repute of the State of Nevada and act as a detriment to the gaming industry'. Such commitment to probity, by both regulators and regulated alike, has been sadly missing in financial regulation.

This brings us to the third level, i.e. the interaction between the regulatory and political domains. The failure of either presents ongoing legitimacy problems. It is particularly telling, for example, that the 'approved person' regime did not and does not bear up to scrutiny. The regime was, for example, dismissed by the PCBS (2013 vol 2: para 584) as a Potemkin façade, providing 'a largely illusory impression of regulatory control over individuals, while meaningful responsibilities were not in practice attributed to anyone'. In an exceptionally critical assessment of prior regulatory design, compliance was dismissed as a key architectural innovation that gives 'the appearance of effective control and oversight without the reality' (ibid: para 566). The fact that 'prolonged and blatant misconduct' as evidenced in the Libor and associated scandals occurred without comment, suggested to the Commission systemic institutional corruption. It was institutional in that the benchmark serves a public good by providing a reference rate on which to price derivatives. The remarkable thing is that this appears not to have entered the heads of either regulator or regulated, notwithstanding the corruption risk.

The 'dismal' and 'striking limitation on the sense of personal responsibility and accountability' of banking leaders, the Parliamentary Commission concluded in its final summary report (PCBS 2013 vol 1: 11), meant that incremental change 'will no longer suffice'. Changing banking for good, a deeply sardonic title for a report that repays careful reading, however, requires not only regulatory recalibration. It also necessitates the corporate and political will to transcend the bifurcation between state and market that informs and shapes discourse in profound ways. Changing this will not be easy. It is a deeply ingrained worldview informed by the considerations and interests of *haute finance* (Polyani 1944: 10). The fact that

RBS traders could continue to engage in misconduct in relation to Libor long after being bailed out by the British state is symptomatic of a malaise in which responsibility evaporates in the face of transaction opportunities. This is not to say the culture of the finance sector is impermeable to change and it is the articulation of the justification for change that gives both the Parliamentary Commission and its successor, the FEMR, such potential paradigmatic power.

The sustainability of *haute finance* depends on the strength of the eco-system that underpins it and on the conditions of practice within it. Whilst economic activity is buoyant, it is difficult if not impossible to dislodge ingrained world-views. Substantive change in the standard of what is considered permissible or acceptable requires an existential crisis, which is precisely what the benchmark manipulation has occasioned. What we have witnessed is the vindication of Susan Strange's caustic analysis that 'casino capitalism' (Strange 1986) had degenerated into psychosis (Strange 1998).

The need for a fundamental reconceptualisation of regulatory and political purpose now informs international discourse. Characterising the power of major financial institutions as malign, 'this kind of capitalism was more extractive than inclusive', warned Christine Lagarde (2014), the managing director of the IMF in a landmark speech delivered in London, the epicentre of global finance. 'The size and complexity of the megabanks meant that, in some ways, they could hold policy-makers to ransom', she added before concluding 'thankfully, the crisis has prompted a major course correction – with the understanding that the true role of the financial sector is to serve, not to rule, the economy'. The reason for such international concern is clear. If, through accident or design, the system has become corrupted, then the underpinning belief system that facilitates it must be challenged on core normative as well as practical grounds.

Ongoing contestation over what caused the crisis, degree of responsibility and over what constitutes or should constitute the balance between rights and duties in the creation and maintenance of market integrity, reflects changing power relations within the bounded community of practice or 'structured action field' constituting financial regulation (Fligstein and Dauter 2007). This field deline-ates the range of 'rational' and, therefore, acceptable responses. It is informed by embedded norms.

In summary, to understand the dynamics of global finance, one has to look at the underlying basis of belief. This is informed by what the influential French sociologist Pierre Bourdieu (1990: 28) has termed the 'logic of practice', prac-tice that accepted past ethical myopia. The benchmark scandals offer the most contingent opportunity faced by regulators in a generation to challenge this. Precisely because the misconduct has been endemic and systemic, occurred after state intervention to protect misguided executives and destroyed corporate, political and regulatory reputations alike, it has profoundly destabilising implica-tions. The unresolved question is whether each or all have the ambition, drive and skill to use the *contingent moment* to deliver truly transformative outcomes. The critical move, and one explicitly mentioned by the FEMR final report (HM

Treasury and others 2015), is the entry of anti-trust regulators, with the capacity to impose financial penalties that dwarf those inflated sums that worry George Osborne.

Cartels: the changed rationale for intervention

The core innovation adopted by national and international regulators is to use competition priorities to reconnect financial institutions to the societies in which they function. Unanchored since the rise of *haute finance*, the strategy represents a potentially fundamental shift in power within financial regulation at both national and international level. It is indicative, for example, that the final report of the FEMR (HM Treasury and others 2015) explicitly draws the attention of financial institutions, as well as their traders, to the scale of anti-competitive penalties and the problems of defection if a single institution avails itself of leniency programmes. Market rigging, which is inherently anti-competitive, it infers, will not be tolerated precisely because of the political risks.

Three immediate paradoxes come to mind. The agenda for change focuses on the City of London itself. The driving force is the Bank of England, which is led by Mark Carney, a former Goldman Sachs banker. His agenda has the active support of the FSB, which he chairs, and the IMF, the managing director of which is a former Baker & McKenzie partner, Christine Lagarde. Also, in the United Kingdom, the fulcrum of misconduct and an important site for the framing of an alternative conception of purpose, a Conservative Party Government is sanctioning what can only be described as a more invasive (if delayed) corporate governance agenda. In his Mansion House speech in June 2014, for example, Osborne gave approval to the Bank of England, the Treasury and the FCA to scope out an agenda for change. Although designed to be consistent with international reform imperatives, the symbiosis is obvious. Given the critical role played by both Carney and the head of the FCA, Martin Wheatley, in facilitating, and through leadership positions shaping, international discourse, the imperatives of both fuse seamlessly. A year later, in conceptual terms at least, the job is complete. Although, as noted above, Wheatley has been removed from office, he retains an advisory role monitoring implementation of the FEMR. Therefore, he retains significant residual power if political compromise weakens the reform agenda to the point of ineffectiveness. The terms of reference, as envisaged by both Carney and Wheatley and allies within the IMF and the FSB, combine three elements. Structural reform is accompanied by a broadening of the regulatory perimeter. This is achieved through legislative reform, including substantially increased civil and criminal penalties. Critically, the purposive dimension of structural and legislative change is rendered explicit, with a normative repositioning of the purpose of capital markets and their role in society, issues which had been comprehensively signalled in the consultation phase (Shafik 2014; Carney 2015). Finally, the stated ambition of the G20 to use capital markets as a force for driving growth in the real economy potentially has locked in political support. Admittedly, all this could result, yet again, in the elevation of the symbolic over the substantive, a dismal reality all too familiar to students of regulatory politics (O'Brien 2003; 2007; 2009; 2014). The cost of inaction, or of the privileging of the symbolic over the substantive, has, however, never been higher, as politicians and regulators alike have acknowledged.

The simplicity of the financial benchmark scandals, and the pivotal role that the institutional doyens of the City of London played in facilitating them by not addressing conduct risk, have created a litigation tsunami on both sides of the Atlantic and beyond. It has spawned multiple investigations and brought competition regulators, with their focus on breaking up cartels, into an increasingly crowded litigation marketplace. The deeper the investigation goes into questionable practices, the more problematic the situation becomes, not least because the Competition Directorate of the European Commission has extracted an admission from implicated banks in a €1.7 billion settlement that they permitted a cartel to operate, through their failures of risk management. The outgoing European Competition Commissioner, Joaquin Almunia (2014) highlighted that proceedings continue against those banks that had refused to settle. The European Commission probe has been augmented by one in New Zealand, where the Trade Commission has formally launched an investigation into financial benchmark manipulation following receipt of a leniency application. The belief that Libor and associated benchmark corruption derives from the existence of a cartel, albeit through default, also informs the International Organisation of Securities Commissions (IOSCO) agenda. The drip feed of revelations that traders in the multi-trillion dollar forex markets were routinely exchanging information in chat rooms given monikers such as 'the pirates' and 'the cartel' is exceptionally problematic in this regard (Baer 2015). It calls into question the efficacy of a reform agenda based solely on technical measures, a point underscored by the FSB, of which IOSCO is a core component. In a report released in 2014 on identified problems in the forex market, the FSB noted:

> at a minimum, this market structure creates optics of dealers 'trading ahead' of the fix even where the activity is essentially under instruction from clients. Worse, it can create an opportunity and an incentive for dealers to try to influence the exchange rate – allegedly including by collusion or otherwise inappropriate sharing of information – to try to ensure that the market price at the fix generates a rate which ensures a profit from the fix trading. That is, it is the incentive and opportunity for improper trading behaviour of market participants around the fix, more than the methodology for computing the fix (although the two interact), which could lead to potential adverse outcomes for clients.
>
> (FSB 2014: 2)

The Federal Reserve Bank of New York, led by former Goldman Sachs partner William Dudley, expressed considerable unease at the failure of industry to shift its cultural norms. In a speech at New York University, Dudley (2014) bemoaned what was uncovered in the initial Libor investigations (and which could equally apply to the broader forex probe):

> The questionable behavioral norms in the industry—along with the weak control environments and compliance processes—that were uncovered during the investigations, exacerbated and facilitated the misalignment of incentives that are specific to LIBOR. It is a sad state of affairs if unethical behavior is socialized among new traders with the explanation that this is business as usual, and, if compliance and risk management are inadequate as a counterweight to prevent or identify wrongdoing. It is untenable if people working in compliance and risk are treated as second-class citizens relative to the firms' revenue generators.

In describing these practices as untenable, the New York Fed president consciously, if obliquely, references the concerns expressed by Christine Lagarde (2014), who noted that the scandals 'violate the most basic ethical norms . . . To restore trust, we need a shift toward greater integrity and accountability. We need a stronger and systematic ethical dimension'. It would be easy, but erroneous, to dismiss these concerns as mere hand-wringing or window-dressing.

Whilst the US can provide the enforcement muscle, and the IMF gravitas, it is in the UK where the most concentrated work has been conducted, in part because of its reputational damage. In his address to the Mansion House, George Osborne (2014) noted the alignment of corporate, regulatory and political interests:

> Britain was the undisputed centre of the global financial system. But all this can so easily be put at risk. By badly conceived EU rules that only reinforce the case for reform in Europe. By populist proposals for self-defeating bonus taxes and punitive income tax rates . . . We should be candid tonight about another risk. The risk that scandals on our trading floors calls into question the integrity of our financial markets. People should know that when they trade in London, whether in commodities or currencies or fixed income instruments, that they are trading in markets that are fair and effective.

The reasons for resolute action (and the curtailment of options) were spelled out even before the extent of the malaise became apparent. In a cutting warning, the PCBS (2013: para 273) noted that:

> if the arguments for complacency and inaction are heeded now, when the crisis in banking standards has been laid bare, they are yet more certain to be heeded when memories have faded. If politicians allow the necessary reforms to fall at one of the first hurdles, then the next crisis in banking standards and culture may come sooner, and be more severe.

The unresolved question is to what extent the underpinning regulatory philosophy proposed is both *coherent* and *cohesive*. The following section outlines the rationale, coherence and implications of this repositioning in a domestic and international context and evaluates whether it can, in fact, facilitate the restraining of *haute finance*.

The conceptual foundations of inclusive capitalism

Even before Carney's elevation to the governorship of the Bank of England, he had set out the need for the finance sector to determine value beyond narrow definitions of economic efficiency. A realist, Carney (2013) accepted that 'virtue cannot be regulated. Even the strongest supervision cannot guarantee good conduct. Essential will be the re-discovery of core values, and ultimately this is a question of individual responsibility'. It was an exhortation that has long informed regulatory policy in the capital markets. In fact it goes back to the very first public address by the first chairman of the Securities and Exchange Commission (SEC) in the United States, Joseph Kennedy (1934):

> [The SEC's aim is to] recreate, rebuild, restore confidence. Confidence is an outgrowth of character. We believe that character exists strongly in the financial world, so we do not have to compel virtue; we seek to prevent vice. Our whole formula is to bar wrongdoers from operating under the aegis of those who feel a sense of ethical responsibility. We are eager to see finance as self-contained as it deserves to be when ruled by Honor and Responsibility . . . But you best can help yourselves. You can make the investing of money honest. Then you will truly become your brother's keeper. And to me that is to acquire merit.

The problem faced by Kennedy in the 1930s is similar to that facing his successors. Industry has consistently engaged in bad faith. Stated intention has not been matched by warranted action. An egregious example of this mismatch can be found at the Mansion House in 2010 when, just prior to a major conference on values and trust, leaders of British-domiciled financial institutions made a remarkable pledge. Organised by the then chairman of Barclays, Marcus Agius, the pledge was designed to demonstrate commitment to change. Given the wave of scandals that subsequently crashed ashore, including most notably Barclays' own ensnarement in the Libor manipulation, that pledge and the commitments given by Marcus Agius and his counterparts (Agius and others 2010) are worth recalling in detail:

> In the run-up to the recent crisis it must have seemed to the public at large that for many financial institutions the only arbiters of economic action were law and profit. If these were indeed the only arbiters of action, then there can be no lasting or effective response to what went before without the development

and inculcation of a different and more enlightened culture; regulatory and fiscal actions alone will not suffice . . . There is, of course, a necessary distinction between the duties owed by traders to their counterparties and the duties owed by investment advisers to their clients. But in the end both should not be bound only by the requirements of law to engage in profitable business in the service of their shareholders, but also be motivated by, and subject to, a larger social and moral purpose which governs and limits how they behave . . . Law and regulation are there to protect people. But of themselves they cannot create or sustain the imperatives that motivate financial institutions and those who work in them. That can only come from the culture of organizations, and what they see themselves as existing to do, and how they ensure this culture is promoted and strengthened. In all this, it is essential to restate and affirm the social purpose of financial institutions as well as affirming the personal vocation of those who work in the industry . . . Ultimately, it is the responsibility of the leaders of financial institutions – not their regulators, shareholders or other stakeholders – to create, oversee and imbue their organizations with an enlightened culture based on professionalism and integrity. As leaders of financial institutions we recognise and accept this personal responsibility.

The public commitment to change advanced in the Mansion House in 2010 was broadly welcomed, not least by the then regulator, the Financial Services Authority. Its then chief executive, Hector Sants (2010), argued that: 'it is crucial that we improve behaviours and judgments. To do this we must address the role that culture and ethics play in shaping these. I believe that until this issue is addressed we will not be able to prevent another crisis of this magnitude from occurring again, and will never fully restore the trust of society in the financial system'. Sants then made clear, however, that unless this was done voluntarily, regulators had a duty to intervene. What is equally apparent in recent history is that stated improvements by industry, whilst laudable, are in themselves insufficient drivers for change. They run the risk of privileging cliché over substance, not least because of a failure to warrant change across potentially incommensurate risk management programmes.

The contours of the changed approach were sketched out in a pivotal speech in 2014 on 'inclusive capitalism', given again, not surprisingly, at the Mansion House. Mark Carney set out an ambitious, if still vague agenda for renegotiation of the social contract linking the finance industry to broader society. Using 'fair and effective' as an organising framework, he argued that the industry faced an existential choice. What gave particular theoretical strength to the speech was its emphasis on how the economic rationale was itself a political construct, a throwback to a canon of political economy jettisoned in favour of ideological posturing:

> All ideologies are prone to extremes. Capitalism loses its sense of moderation when the belief in the power of the market enters the realm of faith. In the

decades prior to the crisis, such radicalism came to dominate economic ideas and became a pattern of social behaviour . . . Market fundamentalism – in the form of light-touch regulation, the belief that bubbles cannot be identified and that markets always clear – contributed directly to the financial crisis and the associated erosion of social capital.

(Carney 2014)

Critically, Carney suggested that the inculcation and the living through practice of broader sets of values must accompany stated commitment. These, he argued, must subjugate individual rights to the needs of the collective, if only to ensure that societal needs are protected. (This was a belief system that, it will be recalled, informed the unsubstantiated commitments given in 2010 by industry itself.) For Carney, as an institution, the Bank of England had a pivotal role to play in this reordering. As the primary regulator, it could no longer stand aside, wedded to falsified theoretical assumptions that were informed by ideational rather than rational belief. In a clear throwback to the exhortation by Kennedy (1934) to the business community in Boston, he declared that the function of the market is to develop the economy through the internalisation of professional obligation. Similar philosophical reasoning informed Christine Lagarde's new-found prioritisation of normative issues: 'By making capitalism more inclusive, we make capitalism more effective, and possibly more sustainable. But if inclusive capitalism is not an oxymoron, it is not intuitive either, and it is more of a constant quest than a definitive destination' (Lagarde 2014).

The agenda, as articulated in the Mansion House in June 2015, is the basis for such a renegotiation of the social contract. Implementation requires some delegation of authority. Ironically, given the decision of the chancellor to dispense with his services, the navigational pilot for this journey remains Martin Wheatley, the combative (and now former) chief of the FCA. From the initial investigation into the corruption of Libor, to the management of a still burgeoning review of problems within the forex markets, Wheatley has become one of the most influential market conduct regulators globally. For Wheatley, the malaise reflects both a lack of regulatory jurisdictional power and a failure of the banks to self-regulate. In recent speeches and interviews (e.g. Wheatley 2014), he has reflected growing frustration with an industry that appears not to see that its own self-interest lies in demonstrating commitment to its stated intentions. For Wheatley, progress demands more activist strategies, not mere nudging. There has, therefore, been a discernible hardening of his position. In a speech just before the announcement of his elevation to the FEMR panel, for example, he set out his stall. Both industry and regulators, he argued, were 'navigating make or break debates around the social utility of some of our biggest firms, as well as witnessing sweeping changes in technology, demographics, public attitudes, and so on and so forth. So, in a very real sense, the decisions and directions we take today are likely to reverberate for many years to come' (Wheatley 2014).

This is now, as a consequence of George Osborne's Mansion House address in June 2015, settled government policy. As such, the opportunity for change has been linked directly to the political cycle. As with the articulation of the securities model of oversight first championed in the New Deal, there is a thorough grounding in ethical reasoning; namely it cannot reasonably be objected to; it is both optimum, and universally willable. In essence, the policy is fusing the philosophical and practical imperatives identified by Derek Parfit (2007) – Kant's categorical imperative and Bentham's utilitarian ethics – in the context of an audacious experiment to transform *haute finance*. There is, of course, a degree of narrow British national self-interest in this regard but, as that most astute of political advisers once noted, the end justifies the means only in pursuit of a noble objective (Machiavelli 2003). Self-interest can, after all, deliver optimum outcomes if tied to societal commitment. Neither industry nor the chancellor is rid of Wheatley, the quintessential troublesome courtier. Indeed, a negative determination by Wheatley of progress could be disastrous for Osborne's ambition to succeed David Cameron as leader of the Conservative Party and hence as prime minister within this parliamentary term. Wheatley and his colleagues have positioned themselves carefully, referencing back to domestic political commitments to uphold market integrity. The consultation documents for the review, for example noted that 'credibility . . . can be undermined if the benchmark can be distorted, either by accidental errors in its compilation or calculation, through the exposure of participants to conflicts of interest or incentives to manipulate the benchmark, or through abuse of a dominant competitive position in the compilation of a benchmark' (Bank of England 2014: 4).

Those conclusions base the case for intervention on three main criteria: scale, jurisdictional power and transactions not covered comprehensively by existing market abuse regulation. They reflect a changed worldview in which trust in reputational capital is unquestionably and, understandably, operating at a steep discount. It has the added advantage of changing the cost-benefit calculus, precisely because fairness and effectiveness now displace an emphasis on economic efficiency. It is equally clever to link progress on implementation to international oversight.

Whilst the framework is sound, operational questions remain on the efficacy of external oversight of managerial imperatives, not least because of a lack of research capability in IOSCO itself. The IOSCO review into the WM 4PM Fix for foreign exchange, for example, was at best cursory. The veracity of WM's responses was not checked, other than against the policy and working documents that WM itself supplied voluntarily and at the review team's request. The review team did not observe directly the practices that WM asserted that it followed. Moreover, IOSCO acknowledges 'a key part of this report is the description of the status of any plans for WM to fully implement (or to ensure a greater degree of implementation of) the Principles. The report does not assess these plans; it simply describes them' (IOSCO 2014: 7). This, in turn, suggests that reform will require a carefully considered approach as to what constitutes responsibility for upholding the public good of benchmarks.

The expanding regulatory perimeter

In summary, three distinct agendas are being followed in relation to regulatory enforcement in both the UK and the US, by far the most important actors in this space. The first focuses on ex post enforcement. The second focuses on ex ante structural change to the nature of specific benchmarks, with particular emphasis on governance, data quality and benchmark construction methodology, as well as internal controls and accountability. Thirdly, there is a renewed focus on the broader question of culture and normative change. These three agendas are integrative rather than distinct. Critically, they reflect a growing sophistication in both litigation and settlement negotiations.

This framing suggests that it is insufficient to rely on stated commitments to change, such as those outlined in the failed industry pledge articulated at the Mansion House in 2010. It appears that mandating corporate governance reform and ensuring evaluation through verifiable performance indicators, as part of settlement negotiations, offers the most sustainable approach to benchmark integrity. It does so because industry has failed to demonstrate its good faith.

Faced with existential questions, it is futile to remain wedded to falsified assumptions. The efficacy of the deferred prosecution mechanism depends crucially on the strength of the contractual terms. If drawn too weakly, they risk privileging what has been termed the 'façade of enforcement'. The ongoing nature of the investigations offers a contingent moment to lever public outrage in order to achieve the overdue falsification of a deeply embedded worldview. Nowhere has this changed state of affairs been more comprehensively signalled than in London and New York. As William Dudley (2014) has acidly pointed out, 'it is time to get on with it'.

In line with its consultation document, the UK's FEMR seeks to develop a global code (or codes) of conduct for Fixed Income Commodity and Currency markets (FICC), which are 'written by the market in terms that market participants understand' (HM Treasury and others 2014: 4). The headlines are: 'bringing trading in certain FICC markets more fully into the scope of regulation; further steps to strengthen the translation of firm-level standards into more effective control and incentive structures; stronger tools for ensuring that firms' hiring and promotion decisions take due account of conduct; greater use of electronic surveillance tools by firms; and stronger penalties for staff breaching internal guidelines' (ibid). Taken together, these moves could add up to the biggest change in financial regulation since the emergence of the disclosure paradigm in the United States in the 1930s. This time, industry's stated commitment to upholding market integrity is not taken at face value. Failure to deliver would allow for prosecution for deceptive conduct.

None of this is to suggest that the most appropriate response is coercion. Self-regulation is the most effective restraint but only if it is internalised and warranted. Indeed, the FEMR is explicit on this point, offering to provide guidance in the event that it feels that industry commitments have sufficient granularity to be effective and to be deserving of public trust. The collective action problem is minimised if there are sufficient moves by industry itself to police itself, precisely because it has the capacity to have global application.

Moreover, the establishment of registers, the creation of early-warning systems within the industry and effective communication channels to regulators, could stave off problems and disseminate best-practice models, thus generating the dynamic for an upward trajectory in risk management and corporate governance rather than a race to the bottom. At the same time, given the failure of deferred prosecutions to effect the kind of behavioural change expected, it is incumbent on prosecutors and regulatory authorities to strengthen the contractual terms significantly. Failure to do so would result in an incremental but decisive loss of authority, precisely because it would privilege the erection of a symbolic façade. In such circumstances the triumphant return of Osborne to the Mansion House will be a pyrrhic one.

Conclusion

Any successful proposal to extend responsibility and accountability – rather than clarifying the enabling conditions – constitutes a major shift in the structure of the financial services industry. The integration of more interventionist normative objectives with enabling ones may also significantly change the ethical boundaries of global finance. It is this possibility that informs the 'inclusive capitalism' agenda. Rebuilding and restoring trust animates the entire 'fair and efficient' markets thesis. The emphasis on 'fair and effective' markets represents a significant advance precisely because it implies the dynamic integration of rules, principles and social norms within an interlocking responsive framework without, at this stage, ceding regulatory authority. As John Kay (2012: 9) has persuasively argued, sustainable reform must be predicated on capability to 'restore relationships of trust and confidence in the investment chain, underpinned by the application of fiduciary standards of care by all those who manage or advise on the investments of others'. This is particularly the case in the Libor and forex domains, precisely because price setting on verifiable and uncorrupted benchmarks is an undoubted public good, which, to be protected, requires honest cultures. As we have seen, within the capital markets context, efficiency has been predominantly privileged. Ostensible improvements, measured largely through short-term financial performance, provided a proxy for societal progress and, as a consequence, political legitimacy. This was, however, a flawed prospectus, informed as much by ideational as rational grounds.

Ineffective or inefficient markets do not necessarily result in a crisis of legitimacy. Past inefficiencies can be – and often are – redressed by the passage of further ostensibly more stringent rules, expansion of regulatory perimeters or more granular articulation of overarching principles. This dynamic is particularly apparent in corporate governance and financial regulation reform, where these initiatives are often presented as evidence of increased accountability. More often than not, however, these same initiatives tend to privilege the politics of symbolism. This is no longer sustainable, as Mark Carney and Martin Wheatley, Christine Lagarde and William Dudley have ably demonstrated. Whether they have the capacity to translate theory into practice is another matter entirely.

Change requires industry to commit to solving its own collective action problem by creating verifiable enforcement protocols. If the response of banking is restricted to it viewing financial penalties as the price of doing business, then demands for regime change are unlikely to gain traction. Notwithstanding the declamations of senior banking executives that the misconduct could not, and should not be condoned, reform is unsustainable without a reconceptualisation by them (under regulatory guidance) of market or regulatory purpose. Necessarily, this must link duties and responsibilities with the rights associated with the licensing regime. Critically, international coordination is essential to prevent arbitrage and a reduction in regulatory effectiveness at national level, given the reality of global capital and national regulation, ongoing threats of capital flight and variable capacities of regulatory agencies to influence political outcomes.

It also necessitates much more invasive oversight, time-limited through the application of a deferred prosecution mechanism which, if violated, triggers at least partial licence revocation. Unless this occurs, the problem of too big to fail, too big to jail and too big to regulate once more moves centre stage. The coming years offer an unprecedented opportunity to reshape discourse and practice, rather than remaining wedded to outmoded assumptions that have been falsified. The critical innovation associated with the 'inclusive capitalism' agenda is the invitation by regulators to industry to verify its stated commitment. It is not designed to be coercive but failure will, necessarily and justifiably, have coercive implications.

References

Agius, M and others, 2010, 'Financial leaders pledge excellence and integrity', Letter to the Editor, *Financial Times* (29 September 2010) http://www.ft.com/intl/cms/s/0/eb26484e-cb2d-11df-95c0-00144feab49a.html?siteedition=intl#axzz3F5O2mZt9 (last accessed 13 September 2015).

Almunia, J, 2014, 'Some highlights from EU competition enforcement', Speech delivered at the IBA Conference, Florence (19 September 2014).

Baer, B, 2015, 'Assistant Attorney General Bill Baer delivers remarks at a press conference on foreign exchange spot market manipulation', Speech delivered at Department of Justice, Washington DC (20 May 2015) http://www.justice.gov/opa/speech/assistant-attorney-general-bill-baer-delivers-remarks-press-conference-foreign-exchange (last accessed 13 September 2015).

Bank of England 2014, Recommendations on additional financial benchmarks to be brought into UK regulatory scope. FEMR Report to HM Treasury (August) http://www.bankofengland.co.uk/markets/Documents/femraug2014.pdf

Binham, C, 2014, 'SFO secures first UK guilty Libor plea', *Financial Times* (7 October 2014) http://www.ft.com/intl/cms/s/0/cbf41b2a-4b1e-11e4-b1be-00144feab7de.html#axzz3FZ1rdWBc (last accessed 13 September 2015).

Binham, C and Guthrie J, 2015, 'FCA: on the wrong side of the argument', *Financial Times* (3 July 2015) http://www.ft.com/cms/s/0/d3001740-1b3c-11e5-8201-cbdb03d71480. html#axzz3haVJ6nil (last accessed 13 September 2015).

Bourdieu, P, 1990, *The Logic of Practice*, London: Polity Press.

Carney, M, 2013, 'Rebuilding trust in global banking', Speech delivered at the Western University, London, Ontario (25 February 2013).

Carney, M, 2014, 'Inclusive capitalism: creating a sense of the systemic', Speech delivered at the Inclusive Capitalism Conference, London (27 May 2014) http://www.bankof england.co.uk/publications/Documents/speeches/2014/speech731.pdf (last accessed 13 September 2015).

Carney, M, 2015, 'Building real markets for the good of the people', Speech delivered at the Mansion House, City of London (10 June 2015) http://www.bankofengland.co.uk/ publications/Pages/speeches/2015/821.aspx (last accessed 13 September 2015).

Department of Justice, 2013, 'UBS Securities Japan Co. Ltd sentenced for long-running manipulation of Libor', Press release, Washington DC (18 September 2013).

Department of Justice 2014, RBS Securities Japan Ltd Sentenced for Manipulation of Yen Libor, press release (January 6), Washington, DC, http://www.justice.gov/opa/pr/ rbs-securities-japan-ltd-sentenced-manipulation-yen-libor (last accessed 11 December 2015)

Donnellan, A, 2015a, 'Please don't go . . .', *Sunday Times* (14 June 2015) B5.

Donnellan, A, 2015b, 'Fund giants lay plans to quit city over Brexit', *Sunday Times* (14 June 2015) B1.

Dudley, W, 2014, 'Restoring confidence in reference rates', Speech delivered at the Stern Business School, New York University (2 October 2014) http://www.ny.frb.org/ newsevents/speeches/2014/dud141002.html (last accessed 13 September 2015).

Ebrahimi, H and Wilson, H, 2013, 'RBS executive John Hourican tells colleagues "not to waste my death"', *Daily Telegraph* (11 February 2013) http://www.telegraph.co.uk/ finance/newsbysector/banksandfinance/9863797/RBS-executive-John-Hourican-tells-colleagues-not-to-waste-my-death.html (last accessed 13 September 2015).

Financial Conduct Authority, 2013, 'ICAP Europe Limited fined £14 million for signifi-cant failings in relation to LIBOR', Press release (25 September 2013) https://www.fca. org.uk/news/icap-europe-limited-fined (last accessed 11 December 2015).

Financial Conduct Authority, 2014a, 'Lloyds Banking Group fined £105m for serious LIBOR and other benchmark failings', Press release, London (28 July 2014) https:// www.fca.org.uk/news/lloyds-banking-group-fined-105m-libor-benchmark-failings (last accessed 11 December 2015).

Financial Conduct Authority, 2014b, *Enforcement Annual Performance Account 2013–2014*, FCA: London http://www.fca.org.uk/static/documents/corporate/enforcement-annual-per formance-account-13-14.pdf (last accessed 13 September 2015).

Financial Services Authority, 2011, *The Failure of the Royal Bank of Scotland* FSA: London (December 2011) http://www.fsa.gov.uk/pubs/other/rbs.pdf (last accessed 13 September 2015).

Financial Services Authority, 2013, Final Notice 2013: Royal Bank of Scotland, FSA: London (6 February 2013) https://www.fca.org.uk/static/fca/documents/final-notices/ rbs.pdf (last accessed 11 December 2015).

Financial Stability Board, 2014, *Foreign Exchange Benchmarks*, Final Report (30 September 2014) http://www.financialstabilityboard.org/publications/r_140930.pdf (last accessed 13 September 2015).

Fligstein, N and Dauter, L, 2007, 'The sociology of markets', *Annual Review of Sociology*, 33: 21.

HM Treasury, Bank of England and Financial Conduct Authority, 2014, *How Fair and Effective are the Fixed Income, Foreign Exchange and Commodities Markets?* Consultation Document, Bank of England, http://www.bankofengland.co.uk/markets/Documents/femr/consultation271014.pdf (last accessed 11 December 2015).

HM Treasury, Bank of England and Financial Conduct Authority, 2015, *Fair and Effective Markets: Final Report*, Bank of England, http://www.bankofengland.co.uk/markets/Documents/femrjun15.pdf (last accessed 13 September 2015).

Holder, E, 2014, 'Remarks on financial fraud prosecutions', Speech delivered at New York University (17 September 2014).

IOSCO, 2014, *Review of the Implementation of IOSCO's Principles for Financial Benchmarks by WM in respect of the WM/Reuters 4 p.m. Closing Spot Rate* (30 September 2014) http://www.iosco.org/library/pubdocs/pdf/IOSCOPD451.pdf (last accessed 13 September 2015).

Jenkins, P, 2015, 'The financial world can look beyond the crisis', *Financial Times* (13 June 2014) 11.

Kay, J, 2012, *The Kay Review of UK Equity Markets and Long Term Decision-Making*, London: HM Stationery Office (July 2012)https://www.gov.uk/government/uploads/system/uploads/attachment_data/file/253454/bis-12-917-kay-review-of-equity-markets-final-report.pdf (last accessed 13 September 2015).

Kennedy, J, 1934, 'Securities and Exchange Commission', *The Certified Public Accountant* (December 1934) 722–36.

Lagarde, C, 2014, 'Economic inclusion and financial integrity', Speech delivered to the Inclusive Capitalism Conference, London (24 May 2014) https://www.imf.org/external/np/speeches/2014/052714.htm (last accessed 11 December 2015).

Machiavelli, N, 2003 (edn), *The Prince*, London: Penguin.

Nevada Gaming Control Board, 2012, *Regulation 5 Operation of Gaming Establishments*, (November 2012) http://gaming.nv.gov/modules/showdocument.aspx?documentid=256 (last accessed 13 September 2015).

O'Brien, J, 2003, *Wall Street on Trial*, Chichester: John Wiley & Sons.

O'Brien, J, 2007, *Redesigning Financial Regulation: The Politics of Enforcement*, Chichester: John Wiley & Sons.

O'Brien, J, 2009, *Engineering a Financial Bloodbath*, London: Imperial College Press.

O'Brien, J, 2014, *The Triumph, Tragedy and Lost Legacy of James M Landis*, Oxford: Bloomsbury.

Osborne, G, 2014, 'Annual Mansion House Speech by Chancellor of the Exchequer', Speech delivered at the Mansion House, London (12 June 2014) https://www.gov.uk/government/speeches/mansion-house-2014-speech-by-the-chancellor-of-the-exchequer (last accessed 13 September 2015).

Osborne, G, 2015, 'Annual Mansion House Speech by Chancellor of the Exchequer', Speech delivered at the Mansion House, London (10 June 2015) https://www.gov.uk/government/speeches/mansion-house-2015-speech-by-the-chancellor-of-the-exchequer (last accessed 13 September 2015).

Parfit, D, 2007, *On What Matters*, Oxford: Oxford University Press.

PCBS [Parliamentary Commission on Banking Standards], 2013, *Changing Banking For Good*, London: HM Stationery Office (June 2013) http://www.parliament.uk/documents/banking-commission/Banking-final-report-vol-ii.pdf (last accessed 13 September 2015).

Polanyi, K, 1944, *The Great Transformation: The Political and Economic Origins of Our Time*, New York: Farrar & Reinhart.

Sants, H, 2010, 'Can culture be regulated', Speech delivered at the Mansion House, London (4 October 2010) http://www.fsa.gov.uk/pages/Library/Communication/Speeches/2010/1004_hs.shtml (last accessed 8 October 2015).

Shafik, M, 2014, 'Fairer markets that will serve us all', *Financial Times* (25 September 2014) http://www.ft.com/intl/cms/s/0/0c166078-449e-11e4-ab0c-00144feabdc0.html?siteedition=intl#axzz3EnRQhvD8 (last accessed 13 September 2015).

Strange, S, 1986, *Casino Capitalism*, Chichester: Wiley-Blackwell.

Strange, S, 1998, *Mad Money*, Manchester: Manchester University Press.

Talley, E and Strimling, S, 2013, 'The world's most important number: how a web of skewed incentives, broken hierarchies, and compliance cultures conspired to undermine Libor', in J O'Brien and G Gilligan (eds), *Integrity, Risk and Accountability in Capital Markets: Regulating Culture*, Oxford: Hart Publishing, 131–42.

Treasury Select Committee, 2012, *Fixing Libor: Some Preliminary Findings*, London: HM Stationery Office (July 2012) http://www.publications.parliament.uk/pa/cm201213/cmselect/cmtreasy/481/481.pdf (last accessed 13 September 2015).

Wheatley, M, 2014, 'Good conduct and market integrity', Speech delivered at General Insurance Conference, London (2 June 2014) http://www.fca.org.uk/news/good-conduct-and-market-integrity (last accessed 8 October 2015).

Chapter 2

EU Capital Markets Union: tensions, conflicts, flaws

Dieter Pesendorfer

In early 2015, the European Commission (EC) launched consultations to shape the future Capital Markets Union (CMU), intended to complement the Eurozone's Banking Union. Both broad programmes are conventionally thought of as contributing to more resilient financial markets and deeper integration. The European Union (EU) first presented the idea of a CMU in 2014 as part of the incoming Commission's focus on growth, jobs and investment. Based on an action plan in 2015, the Commission (EC 2015a: 28) plans 'to put in place by 2019 the building blocks for an integrated, well regulated, transparent and liquid Capital Markets Union for all 28 Member States'.

Capital markets are a particular part of financial markets, underpinning the medium and long-term financing needs of governments, businesses and individuals. Their role and design has a significant impact on particular forms of growth and innovation and how investments are pooled and risks distributed throughout a financial system. Since the global financial crisis started, investor trust in markets suffered enormously and many features of capital markets and developments over the past decades have become highly criticised.

This chapter focuses on the EU's approach to redesign its capital markets in order to increase its growth potential and overall competitiveness, whilst also aiming at increased financial stability. It first introduces what capital markets are and discusses evolution and challenges. Based on theoretical debates about financialisation, varieties of capitalism and integration, I identify key questions and concerns about the new strategies to redesign capital markets. Then the Commission's approach is presented and analysed with regard to tensions, conflicts and flaws. The chapter concludes by stating that there are significant problems with the Commission's approach and an alternative approach would be necessary for more resilient financing of the 'real economy'.

Capital markets: a critical view on evolution and challenges

Capital markets play a crucial and increasing role in contemporary capitalism. Bringing together users of capital and investors in primary markets such as for stocks and bonds, and traders and investors in secondary markets where previously issued securities are traded, capital markets can very broadly be defined as markets for buying and selling equity and debt instruments. In a narrower sense, capital markets are distinguished from money markets, which are used for short-term finance.

On the actors' side, capital markets include various suppliers of capital such as retail or institutional investors, and a variety of users of capital such as businesses, central and local governments, and individuals. The latter group uses capital markets for its medium and long-term financing needs, with the aim of securing its financial needs at minimum cost. Suppliers of capital aim naturally for a maximum return with a minimum risk. Borrowers and lenders are often identified and connected by financial intermediaries, who play a key role in price-making and the overall efficiency of resource allocation. Financial intermediaries can maximise their profits when transparency is limited and when they control large, concentrated markets. Balancing and checking the different interests and goals is the role of regulators, who also have an interest in the contribution of capital markets to growth and financial market stability.

The size and complexity of capital markets has increased enormously over the past decades, with the United States (US) having the largest capital markets. In Europe their importance is still much lower, despite rapid growth over the past two decades, with some Member States such as the United Kingdom (UK) already having well developed capital markets, whilst other Member States do not (Anderson and others 2015; EC 2015a; EC 2015b). Regulators and market participants in the EU are now trying to emulate the US market in order to increase their markets' competitiveness and to attract more international investment.

The general assumption amongst supporters of an increased reliance on capital markets is that financing through traditional banking is more expensive and that capital markets can provide medium and long-term financing more cheaply and efficiently. Moreover, capital markets would increase private sector risk sharing and financial stability (Anderson and others 2015: 9). The diversification of funding sources is not seen as a binary choice between more reliance on banks or on capital markets, nor as a strategy to decrease the importance of banks. It is presented as a positive sum game of maximising investment opportunities in the most efficient way, although this might include absorbing financial resources from other, non-EU countries in the global economy.

Banks remain important in that situation; indeed, they have been drivers of deeper capital markets. Although they are sometimes described as powerful institutions that are hostile to the idea of deepening and expanding capital markets, and although they are sometimes presented as having an '[intense] dislike [of] the prospect of competition from alternative financing channels' and 'warn[ing] against the perils of "shadow banking" and regulatory arbitrage' (Véron 2014), the reality is that banks, especially those with strong investment banking arms, are highly involved in capital markets. The Commission (EC 2015b: 5) acknowledged this, stating that the 'traditional distinction' between bank-based models and capital markets-based models 'is less valid now as banks have become increasingly active in capital market intermediation'.

At the centre of the debate is a hypothesis about significant welfare losses in systems with 'underdeveloped capital markets'. So far, there has been a rather limited debate about the advantages of bank-based versus capital markets-based systems with regard to economic growth (Levine 2002) and recovery (Allard and Blavy 2011). A more nuanced debate about the risk–risk trade-off between a system more based on banking and one based more on capital markets has only started, whilst various actors already focus on strategies to boost supply of credit with quantitatively larger capital markets with some qualitative reforms such as sound securitisation and increased transparency. It remains controversial how each of those systems affects finance-driven growth strategies and financial (in) stability and how best to organise, limit or expand capital markets. A much more nuanced understanding of the qualitative transformations that have characterised the development of capital markets seems necessary, given the importance of the system redesign decision.

Serious questions have to be asked about the role of capital markets prior to and during the financial crisis. It is well known that investors lost trust in banks because of the interconnectivity in the market, including banks' links to the shadow banking system, the lack of transparency and the enormous risks related to modern financial products, with many of them turning toxic. Much has been learned about capital markets in recent years and about their role in building up risks in the areas of shadow banking, derivatives and securitisation; however, some key lessons are still insufficiently reflected in current regulatory debates.

The crisis taught us that the pre-crisis assumptions about capital markets' positive contributions to stability, long-term sustainable growth, democratisation of finance, liquidity and market efficiency have been flawed. Studies showed that there is an optimum level of financial development and that, above that threshold, instability increases, undermining long-term growth (cf. Cecchetti and Kharroubi 2015). Also, not all areas of capital markets contribute positively and some are socially harmful. Badly designed, poorly regulated and opaque capital markets increase the overall liquidity and risk appetite, leading to extreme leverage and increasing the costs of crises. Wealth generated in capital markets increases inequality and undermines social peace and democracy (cf. Cournède and others 2015). Derivative markets, namely over-the-counter (OTC) derivatives and securitisation, were at the centre of the financial meltdown – shadow banks can also be in need of bail-outs.

Post-crisis reforms did not resolve these problems. The recent introduction of central clearing houses and trade repositories for OTC derivatives, for example, shifted the risk of bail-outs to these new institutions. Frameworks for recovery and orderly resolution are now in preparation. Regulators have criticised the lack of transparency in this redesigned market, characterised by competing private firms with little interest in sharing data: the overall risks would appear to be as high as before the crisis (*EurActiv* 2015a). The Joint Committee of the European

Supervisory Authorities (ESAs 2015) concluded that financial system risks in the EU have intensified, yet hopes that implementation of recent capital markets reforms and the introduction of a CMU will reverse the trends.

Particular institutions have also been in the centre of critique. The demand to regulate shadow banks just like banks because of their similar function in funding or their systemic relevance (Krugman 2008) was largely ignored, especially with regard to required capital buffers. Only the managers of alternative investment funds have become regulated (Title IV of the Dodd-Frank Wall Street Reform and Consumer Protection Act made numerous changes to the registration and reporting and record-keeping requirement of 'investment advisers'; the EU adopted the Alternative Investment Fund Managers Directive). Hedge funds have been criticised for under-performing, whilst charging overpriced fees from investors. Investment banks trade against the interests of clients instead of serving them. Goldman Sachs, for example, frequently came under attack after 2009 for 'betting against clients'. These and other experiences have significantly undermined the trust of investors. The short lesson is that capital markets need much more transparency and supervision if not a significant downsizing in certain areas.

Large institutional and retail investors also lost trust in capital markets because of high frequency trading (HFT) and law-makers have done little to react to this development. High frequency traders deflected critical debates successfully by emphasising that they would increase liquidity and efficiency and that every small investor profits from HFT activities. However, many investors regard HFT as similar to insider trading, increasing transaction costs for others. Large institutional investors shifted a substantial amount of trading to 'dark pools' for transactions in an unregulated, opaque and secret environment.

In Europe the Markets in Financial Instruments Directive insufficiently regulates these venues. If poorly regulated or unregulated, dark pools are 'vulnerable to conflicts of interest, predatory trading practices and market abuse' (Deutsche Börse 2015: 25). Indeed, this has already happened: in the US, banks sold investors the opportunity to hide their activities from HFT but betrayed their customers by selling access to the dark pool to high frequency trading firms. The Justice Department and the FBI started investigations into HFT for possible insider trading and other wrongdoing (McCrank 2014).

These examples should be sufficient to demonstrate that there are serious problems with the current design and regulation of capital markets and a simple quantitative expansion of these markets will only increase financial instability and other problematic trends.

Financialisation, varieties of capitalism, integration and CMU

Three theoretical debates are of key importance in analysing CMU and its possible effects. First, the concept of financialisation plays a key role in understanding and criticising problematic long-term trends in finance. Secondly, the varieties of capitalism approach raises important questions about how deepening capital markets in Europe would affect national models of capitalism and how this might affect their overall competitiveness in the global economy. It also provides explanations for various tensions and conflicts. Thirdly, questions about integration have to be asked, as there are serious issues to be debated about whether economic growth and innovation are best driven by competition between different national and regional systems or by harmonisation.

The concept of financialisation has been developed in an attempt to criticise developments in financial markets and their relationship to states and to the 'real economy' of non-financial firms. It means 'the increasing role of financial motives, financial markets, financial players and financial institutions in the operation of the domestic and international economies' (Epstein 2005). Krippner (2005: 174) defined the term 'as a pattern of accumulation in which profits accrue primarily through financial channels rather than through trade and commodity production'. The result is an increasing importance of speculation over productive investments also for non-financial firms.

The concept has been used to demand radical changes, ranging from an introduction of capital controls and strict mechanisms to deal with economic imbalances, to downsizing finance through various measures such as structural reforms or a financial transaction tax (FTT). The concept, however, has also become popular in a less radical sense, as a pillar of hopes that stronger and better capital markets might have a potential for democratising finance requiring financial education and more transparency in markets. Both interpretations are of relevance for redesigning capital markets.

According to the EC's approach, European economies should become more similar to the US market. Different models of capitalism – with different degrees of financialisation – have long been explanatory factors for economic success or failure and growth or stagnation. Many debates in recent years have centred on the variety of capitalism (VoC) approach (cf. Hancké 2009), which was developed by Hall and Soskice (2001) as a contribution to the globalisation debate, challenging the then popular assumption that economic pressures would force countries to become more similar and to converge towards the Anglo-American model of capitalism, with its dominant features shareholder value and markets-based funding.

Building on historical institutionalism, their approach argues that there are comparative advantages of different models of capitalism. The ideal versions of liberal market economies (LMEs) and coordinated market economies (CMEs) would generate especially high comparative advantages. Actors would be reluctant to push reforms too far in any single direction because that could undermine their model; rather, they would prefer to protect institutional complementarities that generate and reinforce advantages.

Firms secure competitive advantages and states comparative advantages. The institutional complementarities reproducing these advantages are complex and their interplay explains why, for example, LMEs are more successful in securing patents in areas where quick access to risk capital and an environment that allows quick hiring and firing is necessary, whilst CMEs are more successful in areas of 'incremental innovation' where more long-term commitment in investments is required. 'In LMEs', Hall and Soskice (2001: 27f) emphasise, 'firms rely more heavily on market relations to resolve the coordination problems that firms in CMEs address more often via forms of non-market coordination that entails collaboration and strategic interaction'. In LMEs, firms are encouraged 'to be attentive to current earnings and the price of their shares on equity markets' and the regulatory regimes are more 'tolerant of mergers and acquisitions, including hostile takeovers'.

If the EU is to be developed from a mostly (transformed) bank-based to a highly capital markets-based system, then one can assume knock-on effects on other features of CMEs, which might undermine competitive advantages and therefore result in opposition and conflicts. In this regard it is interesting to point to an International Monetary Fund (IMF) study showing that, although capital markets-based economies seem to have some comparative advantages over bank-based systems in economic recoveries, these advantages becomes less significant if employment and product market flexibility are taken into account (Allard and Blavy 2011: 3). In short, the VoC approach not only explains different policy preferences of EU Member States, but it also draws attention to the potential conflicts harmonisation through CMU might have: some actors might overlook long-term unintended consequences for specific forms of European capitalism, whilst others might even push for intended consequences to transform Europe into a more shareholder value driven economy.

The third theoretical debate of relevance for the future CMU is about its possible (un)intended effects on European integration. Despite efforts to integrate financial and capital markets, especially since the introduction of monetary union, they have remained fragmented, not least because of the competition between different national systems. Moreover, financial market integration suffered a significant backlash during the ongoing financial and economic crises, leading to further fragmentation and creating significant challenges for cross-border activities. The creation of banking union and CMU are now intended to drive deeper integration.

Majone (2014: 18) made an important intervention in the post-crisis reform debate by emphasising that:

> the European global dominance of the past was made possible not by centralization, but by fragmentation. The mistake of today's integrationist leaders has been to assume a unilinear development from the nation state to something fulfilling much the same functions, on a grander scale and allegedly more effectively. History suggests that there is something unnatural in this approach ... European unity has never been the unity of empire or even of a large transnational federation, but a much subtler unity in diversity achieved through a unique mixture of competition, cooperation, and imitation.

Whilst capital markets as a core area of the single market clearly require some degree of coordination, the question remains whether a fragmented system would not be more shock resilient (Dorn 2014). Majone's point finds a wider echo in recent debates about evaluating regional integration and new trade agreements. The highly controversial Transatlantic Trade and Investment Partnership (TTIP) being negotiated between the US and EU has led to the question of what the results of this agreement would be. The main proponents of TTIP, including the EC, expect advantages to stem from further harmonisation and integration at a pan-Atlantic level. Financial regulation is part of TTIP negotiations and, as such, is highly relevant for a CMU. It is one of the areas where many critics expect lowering standards as a result of increased regulatory competition. In short, the integration debates suggest the need for a more nuanced debate about harmonisation and regulatory competition in combination.

The emerging CMU

In 2014, the new EC, led by its President Jean-Claude Juncker, launched new initiatives to revive investment in the 'real economy', promoted by the slogan 'unlocking funding for Europe's growth', and with specific emphasis on the advantages this would have for small and medium-sized enterprises (SMEs). SMEs are defined as a group of micro, small and medium-sized enterprises that historically make the biggest contribution to growth and employment.

The Commission's approach to a CMU

Major elements of the Commission's strategy to boost economic recovery are an Investment Plan (EC 2014) and a CMU. Juncker (2014) announced the idea of a CMU as a key element of 'a deeper and fairer internal market with a strengthened industrial base' and as a strategy to 'further develop and integrate capital markets', increasing Europe's competitiveness for (foreign) investment. To signal the significance of a CMU symbolically, it was incorporated into the title for Jonathan Hill, new Commissioner for Financial Stability, Financial Services and Capital Markets Union. Both selecting a British candidate for this area and announcing a CMU were strong signals, after the creation of the banking union, taking into account not only the interests of the Eurozone members but the interests of all 28 Member States, especially of the UK with its financial centre in London (thereby speaking to some of the British EU reform demands). The banking union had been designed in a way that it can be joined by all Member States; however, clearly Britain will not join, and it remains concerned about the possibility of losing influence over future EU financial regulation and supervision. The plan to create a CMU was therefore explicitly welcome at the political level in the UK (House of Lords 2015).

The idea of a CMU was not entirely new (Segré 1966) and it gained renewed attention under the previous Commission launching various regulatory initiatives for capital markets. However, at the time of President Juncker's announcement to include CMU within one of the 10 priorities of his Commission (priority 4: a deeper and fairer internal market) it was little more than an empty signifier for what came to be advocated as 'the creation of a true single market for capital'. Véron (2014) described it as 'a largely undefined policy object'. Despite the lack of a common understanding at that point, expectations for the project were extremely high (Mersch 2014).

In February 2015, the Commission published the Green Paper entitled 'Building a Capital Markets Union' (EC 2015a) for public consultation, with separate consultations on sound securitisation (EC 2015c) and on the Prospectus Directive (EC 2015d). The CMU Green Paper consultation resulted in 425 responses (see ec.europa.eu/finance/consultations/2015/capital-markets-union/index_en.htm). The consultation on a new framework for simple, transparent and standardised securitisation received 124 responses and the one on the Prospectus Directive 181 responses. At the time of writing this chapter the Commission had not published the responses, but some were already available online elsewhere. (On 30 September 2015 the European Commission published its own synopsis of responses, alongside the Action Plan on CMU and other material: see EC 2015e and EC 2015f.) The following analysis is therefore reflecting on a limited number of actors' views, focusing foremost on the Commission Green Paper itself (EC 2015a), a staff working paper (EC 2015b) and some earlier research.

The Commission presented the CMU as a logical and rational next step in internal market integration, after the agreement on the banking union, and basically as a continuation of previous policies aiming at creating a fully integrated financial market. The Commission's fundamental rationale is the belief that 'underdeveloped capital markets' and a bank-based funding system have to be overcome, in order to develop the full potential of European economies. Commissioner Hill has presented CMU 'as an instrument of sustainable growth' (Hill 2015) and as a policy that would lead to 'finance serving the economy' (Hill 2014) and contribute to the new Commission's priorities of creating jobs and growth.

The policy announcement also clearly indicated a deregulatory approach, based on the assumption that post-crisis reforms would have led to negative cumulative effects, and that the huge number of regulatory initiatives and proposals over recent years had created uncertainty for businesses and especially the financial industry. In this vein, Hill (2014) asked 'have we always struck the right balance between reducing risk and encouraging growth?', whilst also promising that '(t)here can be no going back to the old, pre-crisis, ways' and that there will definitely be no 'big bonfire of existing regulations in the name of growth'.

Despite these assurances, various interests behind CMU drive a strong deregulatory agenda, which undermines stricter reforms adopted in the aftermath of the financial meltdown and ambitious proposals that still await adaptation. As with any regulatory change nowadays, the development of a CMU is subject to processes of better regulation that have emerged within the EU over recent decades. This includes a general assumption that regulation should only be adopted when there are no better alternatives and, whenever regulation is designed, stakeholder consultations and regulatory impact assessment (RIA) are necessary. The Juncker Commission started with a strong commitment to reforming the 'better regulation' agenda, in order to support its main goal of creating more jobs and growth (Juncker 2014). The Green Paper clearly reflects this new approach, with a strong commitment to leaving several areas to market developments, and to think about measures supporting these through means other than legislation, alongside a strong emphasis on deregulation.

Better regulation, deregulation, financialisation and CMU

This approach is anything but surprising, given the trends that can be seen in the history of financial regulation: deregulation and the lowering of regulatory standards are typical, following on from and to some extent rolling back the stricter regulation that is adopted immediately after a crisis (Persaud 2008). Deregulation can be predicted by the financialisation literature, which in part is concerned with the power of finance and with the privileges of specific business interests (Pesendorfer 2014). The British Bankers' Association (BBA 2014) started to demand the use of RIA, not only for Commission proposals but also for inter-institutional compromises – on the grounds that proposals can undergo significant change as they go through the complex European law-making processes, resulting in consequences that have not been subject to rigid RIA, giving rise to the possibility of over regulation. The Commission somehow responds to that demand, by raising the issue of cumulated effects of recently adopted regulations.

The Green Paper acknowledges worries about 'gold plating' (EC 2015a: 22). Industry argues that, in areas of minimum harmonisation, some Member States go beyond minimum requirements (ironically, this is sometimes true of the UK). This 'gold plating' is interpreted by industry as creating entirely unjustified, unnecessary bureaucratic hurdles, which the Commission should end (cf. Deutsche Kreditwirtschaft 2015). The new approach towards an ever more business-friendly regulatory environment, including the creation of powerful veto-positions within the Commission to stop over-regulation early, has been welcomed by the British Government as a step in the right direction, responding to that country's critique of European over-regulation (*EurActiv* 2015b).

In fairness to the Commission, it has to be said that it demands stricter harmonisation in some areas and stricter oversight by the various European regulators, in order to avoid regulatory competition through diverse forms of implementation and enforcement at Member State level. This is an area where conflicts are predictable, as several Member States have concerns about harmonisation and prefer cooperation and competition. The issue of further harmonised oversight, for example by a single EU supervisor for financial market infrastructure, is a contested one (Anderson and others 2015: 21).

Whilst many actors strongly support the latest modifications of the Better

Regulation framework as a welcome contribution to boosting jobs and growth, others voiced reservations about deregulation and a too business-friendly approach, fearing an erosion of balance between private and public interests. More than 50 European non-governmental organisations reacted with the creation of a new 'watchdog to protect the rights of citizens, workers and consumers', called Better Regulation Watchdog (*EurActiv* 2015c).

The Green Paper can be read as inviting all kinds of technical responses from firms – whilst limiting the scope for critique of the general approach of the 'under-developed market' hypothesis, and limiting questions about what role finance and capital markets should have in the future. The Commission did not invite a discussion about the assumptions or problem analysis behind its preferred policy option but only sought 'views on the early policy priorities' (Section 3) and 'on the barriers' and 'obstacles' (Section 4). Although that did not stop actors from responding more broadly (e.g. Finance Watch 2015), this framing of discourse demonstrates the direction in which the Commission seeks support from stakeholders and shows unwillingness to modify its approach.

The language used in the Green Paper suggests that the goal is a fundamental transformation of European economies, but demonstrates at the same time the realisation of the original integrationist vision: 'The free flow of capital was one of the fundamental principles on which the EU was built. More than fifty years on from the Treaty of Rome, let us seize this opportunity to turn that vision into reality' (EC 2015a: 3).

However, the Commission did not provide an in-depth analysis why integration in the past had failed. Nor is there an engagement with the question if the significant shift in the importance of capital markets and securitisation that is now advocated is really nothing more than finally achieving a fully functioning single market for capital or whether this is an attempt to transform the European economy into a much more shareholder value driven system? Rather, the Commission points to a process of systematically identifying and knocking down barriers 'one by one', leading to a dynamic 'momentum', producing an action plan 'to put in place the building blocks for a fully functioning Capital Markets Union by 2019' (EC 2015a: 3).

In fact, the transformation envisaged by the Commission and key CMU supporters are much more far-reaching than the realisation of an early (1950s) idea of integrated capital markets. Rather, what is being advanced is a particular form of financialisation, aiming at dramatically extending the influence, scope and depth of finance. As such it is a continuation of a pre-crisis trend that was disrupted for a short period in the aftermath of the financial meltdown. It is in direct conflict with demands to downsize and transform finance, in order to re-embed finance into society. It is clearly *anything but* what has been advocated by groups such as Finance Watch (2015; Hache 2014) – a return to 'boring banking', with more traditional trust structures between banks as intermediaries and non-financial firms.

Interests, conflicts and tensions

The Commission's presentation of CMU as being not merely in the interest of finance but also in the interest of investors, SMEs and the general public has drawn criticism. Véron (2014) predicted that 'a capital-markets development agenda will run against deeply-seated ideological scepticism, particularly in parts of continental Europe where markets are viewed with inherent suspicion'. He emphasised that such strong beliefs – which I would interpret as being rooted in European varieties of capitalism and reflecting protection of institutional complementarities – will persist, since economists have so far failed 'to produce a convincing model for the financial sector that would provide a consensus basis to quantify the economic benefits of market-friendly reform' (ibid: 4). Véron also describes the UK as most likely to profit from this policy, by becoming Europe's only financial centre, with actors who then 'shy away from acknowledging that a logical implication must be to align its regulatory framework with the European public interest'.

The proposal for a CMU has indeed found broad support in the UK (Anderson and others 2015; House of Lords 2015). The House of Lords' European Union Committee described this initiative as an excellent opportunity for the UK that requires that British actors be 'at the forefront of the debates as the Capital Markets Union agenda takes shape' (House of Lords 2015: 33). However, with a Brexit looming, British advantages might not be realised. Compared with other issues in the domestic Eurosceptic referendum debate, CMU might turn out to be a relatively minor issue and – more importantly for the future design of CMU – other Member States have a strong interest in expanding their financial industries in competition with London. Some actors might even speculate about where the next European financial centre might emerge, once the UK leaves the Union.

Another debate about different national approaches emerged when France demanded that CMU should be used as an opportunity to support European champions, thus raising UK fears against old-style French 'dirigism' (*EurActiv* 2015c).

In short, several tensions and potential conflicts between Member States have emerged at an early stage of the debate, as expected from the VoC approach, and from the fact that financial integration in Europe was always a 'battle of the systems' (Story and Walter 1997). The final CMU design might reflect a mix of different national preferences, although there seems to be a strategy to use peer review and the European semester (the EU's annual cycle of economic policy guidance and surveillance) to push Member States into the desired direction (EC 2015a: 6).

Broad CMU support comes from business. Firms might hope for better and cheaper access to funding sources. SMEs might especially hope so, given the Commission's rhetoric and despite the evidence that capital markets are rather unsuitable for SMEs (see below). The financial industry in particular is expecting new opportunities. Given the variety of financial firms, expectations differ and are in parts even in conflict with each other. Banks, already highly involved in deepening capital markets, hope for reduced funding costs, resulting from a more integrated covered bond market that would also provide new opportunities for investors. Large banks expect an improved situation for cross-border activities and expansion: the trend towards ever-larger European banks might therefore be boosted.

Investors want trust in capital markets revived, more transparency and better investor protection. Institutions focusing on long-term investment, such as pension funds and insurance companies, want to review the results of recent regulatory change, with a view to increasing returns; some want improved conditions for long-term investments. Alternative investment fund managers, who are regulated under the fiercely fought AIFM Directive, are pushing for reduced costs for setting up funds and cross-border marketing and some other changes that improve their growth potential. Tensions between countries with a large number of alternative investment funds (highly concentrated in a small number of Member States) and the other states are predictable. Other tensions are foreseeable between financial institutions focusing on all sorts of profit-maximising investment strategies, and those limiting themselves to sustainable investment and corporate social responsibility (an area mentioned in the Green Paper but one which does not seem to be a priority).

The Commission does not identify any need for action and seems satisfied with the voluntary guidelines currently developed by market participants (EC 2015a: 15). One could easily summarise that the Commission is not serious about sustainability and environmental policy integration, although both are Treaty requirements. Not only are broad sustainability topics such as greening business, green growth or even de-growth ignored, so are subsidies that largely distort markets and investments.

Central bankers and legislators expect that integrated financial markets in the euro area would greatly facilitate the implementation of the European Central Bank's (ECB) monetary policy. Financial stability experts hope to link CMU to a better control of shadow banking, derivative markets and securitisation (Mersch 2014), areas that have been identified as key for any sound control of capital markets. However, current proposals for sound securitisation and controlling shadow banking do not reflect wider demands for downsizing these markets.

The huge variety of interests will be difficult to balance in the action plan. Anticipating this problem, the House of Lords' EU Committee Report (House of Lords 2015) warned there may be too much in the Commission's Green Paper and that the Commission risks losing focus on the most promising aspects.

Controversies can also be expected in areas that the Commission ignored, such as HFT and dark pools. The CMU Green Paper only once mentions HFT (in the context of new technology without any discussion), followed by a single general question about how the EU can 'best support' new technologies and business models (EC 2015: 26). The Commission staff working document (EC 2015b) does not discuss HFT. Stricter regulation or banning HFT or reducing it indirectly through an FTT is obviously outside of its scope, unless investors and Member

States push massively for incorporation into the action plan. Not even Finance Watch (2015) raised HFT or dark pools in its consultation contribution.

Although the Green Paper mentions differences in tax regimes very generally, the Commission does not consider any issues about how CMU might be affected – at least in certain areas – by an FTT. This is rather surprising given the aims with regard to certain capital markets activities that should be achieved by introducing an FTT. Concerns that an FTT undermines the goal of establishing a CMU or significantly reduces the benefits that do exist have been raised (Deutsche Börse 2015: 18; Elliott 2015). The strong commitment to investor protection and the linkage to international trade and investment agreements (EC 2015a: 21) will most likely be discussed critically, given the TTIP controversies.

Explaining the funding problems of the European real economy and how to curb investment

The contested nature of the claim that Europe would be better off with a capital markets-based, rather than with an already transformed or simpler bank-based system, has already been mentioned. The Commission has not provided sufficient evidence in support of its preferred policy option. This would be a far-reaching decision, affecting the future of European economies and societies. The Commission very much follows a presentation of capital markets as 'phoenixes' and banks as 'lame ducks', to use a metaphor by Allard and Blavy (2011), and it would be naïve to expect that this will be corrected once the action plan and further proposals will be presented with regulatory impact assessments.

According to the Bank for International Settlements (BIS 2015), real investment in Europe, including the large Eurozone economies, has not recovered to pre-recession levels. Despite cheap borrowing costs thanks to the particularly low interest rates, borrowing has remained low, although the ECB's quantitative easing showed some improvement in spring 2015. Explanations for the slow recoveries range from the frequent US critique that economic imbalances have to be resolved by reducing the German trade surplus, and that the ECB was too slow in flooding markets with money, to critics of austerity understanding the prolonged crisis as a result of reducing debt levels in the private and state sectors simultaneously, resulting in a lack of aggregate consumer demand.

In a rather narrow debate, advocates of a CMU have been arguing that it is Europe's bank-based funding, over-regulation and administrative barriers that slow down economic recovery and the transformation to more innovative European economies. The UK as a LME with more developed capital markets, however, has *not* been more successful in providing SMEs' funding. German SMEs, on the other hand, performed as amongst the most innovative ones in Europe. For the US, it has been argued that the recovery there has not been driven by SMEs, despite the more developed capital markets (Brookings Institution 2015a).

It seems more likely that, contrary to the Commission's evaluation, investment is not low in the EU because of financial and capital markets structures and insufficient diversification of funding sources, but as a result of austerity, debt reduction attempts in the state and private sectors, wage losses, reduced consumption, and political and economic uncertainties multiplied by the political failure to resolve the Eurozone crisis. These factors have reduced businesses' and investors' expectations about future economic conditions. The BIS (2015) also sees this as a more plausible explanation than the 'underdeveloped financial markets' hypothesis.

Little evidence has been presented as to how and why the CMU would improve SME access to credit. Compared with the Commission's presentation, the House of Lords' (2015) report emphasises that the onus of gaining access to capital markets would be with SMEs and not all SMEs are likely to be winners. Neither the Commission nor the House of Lords linked their analysis of lacking credit for SMEs with an analysis of austerity. In summary, it remains an unproven claim that deeper financial markets would have made a positive difference in the past years.

Conclusion

Financial markets will exhibit financial instability, with a probability of crisis, no matter how well they are designed and whatever the balance between bank and capital markets funding might be. Shifting medium and long-term borrowing and lending, from a (relatively) bank-based to a capital markets-based system, is a policy option that transforms where risks occur, how risks, profits and losses are shared, and how risks build up over time before culminating in a crisis.

The increasing reliance on capital markets over the past decades is an illustration of a particular version of financialisation, which led to significant problems and contributed to the global financial crisis. Evaluations of the past, as well as models for the future, show that the probability and the depth of crises depend on system design: a shift to a more capital markets-based funding system does not automatically lead to higher financial stability. The contrary is quite possible and financial instability might increase. There is 'evidence indicating that capital market-based financing might increase pro-cyclicality' (Dombret 2015). A Bank of England study concluded that a more capital market-based system might fail to deal with a large shock and financial instability would then easily spread to other countries (Anderson and others 2015: 16).

Also the assumptions that CMU would provide additional funding for the 'real economy' and especially for SMEs and assure growth are on shaky ground. The idea of a CMU goes into a wrong direction and entirely ignores demands to use the opportunity to downsize finance and to make finance truly serve the 'real economy'. In its envisaged design, its value for the 'real economy' and for SMEs is more than questionable.

Elliot (2015) warned about risks of overstating the advantages for SMEs, given the many measures with 'relatively little effect' on SMEs, and suggested that banks are much better suited for funding SMEs. Wider understanding of this could undermine political support for CMU. Commissioner Hill has already reduced expectations for SMEs, saying that CMU is more in the interest of medium-sized enterprises with the potential to become large firms (Brookings Institution 2015b). The SME rhetoric would only sell the idea, the Commissioner confessed. Hill also argued that the financial transaction tax was an idea of the immediate post-crisis situation and the 'different environment now' would require a focus on jobs and growth. An FTT would only work globally and Hill will assess 'any proposals' with 'potential downside effects on the Capital Markets Union' (Brookings Institution 2015b).

The CMU might have strong support; however, a closer look at it reveals serious tensions and conflicts between different interests – especially between different European capitalisms (the 'battle of the systems') and between different business actors and investors – throwing up a number of serious issues that might not be easily resolved. The overall approach is based on the belief that it is a good idea to revive complex financial market structures, the deregulatory agenda, and flawed empirical evidence about growth and wealth-generation in capital markets-based systems. An alternative way to obtain resilient financing of the 'real economy' based on more old-fashioned 'relationship' banking, downsizing finance and measures to boost investment for a more sustainable pathway is needed. At this stage it seems unlikely that the action plan and related measures will go in that direction.

References

Allard, J and Blavy, R, 2011, 'Market phoenixes and banking ducks: are recoveries faster in market-based financial systems?', *IMF Working Paper*, WP/11/213, Washington: IMF.

Anderson, N, Brooke, M, Hume, M and Kürstösiová, M, 2015, 'A European capital markets union: implications for growth and stability', Bank of England, *Financial Stability Paper*, No. 33, London: Bank of England.

Brookings Institution 2015a, 'Examining the role of capital markets in the economy', Washington, DC: Brookings Institution.

Brookings Institution 2015b, 'European financial regulation and transatlantic collaboration', Washington, DC: Brookings Institution.

BIS 2015, Quarterly Review March 2015: International Banking and Financial Market Developments, Bank for International Settlements, Basel.

BBA 2014, *Turning 'Capital Markets Union' to Deliver an Engine for European Growth*, British Bankers' Association (December 2014).

Cecchetti, S and Kharroubi, E, 2015, 'Why does financial sector growth crowd out real economic growth', *BIS Working Papers*, No. 490, Basel: Bank for International Settlements.

Cournède, B, Denk, O and Hoeller, P, 2015, 'Finance and inclusive growth', *OECD Economic Policy Paper*, No. 14, Paris: OECD.

Deutsche Börse Group, 2015, 'Principles for a European capital markets union: strengthening capital markets to foster growth', Policy Paper, Frankfurt/Main: Deutsche Börse AG.

Deutsche Kreditwirtschaft, 2015, 'Neue Agenda der EU zur besseren Rechtsetzung macht Hoffnung auf mehr Transparenz und weniger Bürokratie für die Wirtschaft', Press release (19 May 2015).

Dombret, A, 2015, 'What can capital markets deliver?', Speech at the ILF Conference on European Capital Markets Union, Frankfurt am Main (18 March 2015) http://www.bundesbank.de/Redaktion/DE/Reden/2015/2015_03_18_dombret.html (last accessed 8 October 2015).

Dorn, N, 2014, *Democracy and Diversity in Financial Market Regulation*, Abingdon: Routledge.

EC, 2014, Communication from the Commission to the European Parliament, the Council, the European Central Bank, the European Economic and Social Committee, the Committee of the Regions and the European Investment Bank: 'An investment plan for Europe', COM(2014) 903 final, Brussels (26 November 2014).

EC, 2015a, Green Paper 'Building a capital markets union', COM(2015) 63, Brussels (18 February 2015).

EC, 2015b, *Initial reflections on the obstacles to the development of deep and integrated EU capital markets*, accompanying the document Green Paper 'Building a capital markets union', Commission Staff Working Document SWD(2015) 13, Brussels.

EC' 2015c, Consultation Document: 'An EU framework for simple, transparent and standardised securitisation', Brussels (18 February 2015).

EC, 2015d, Consultation Document: 'Review of the Prospectus Directive', Brussels (18 February 2015).

EC, 2015e, *Feedback Statement on the Green Paper 'Building a Capital Markets Union'*, Brussels http://ec.europa.eu/finance/consultations/2015/capital-markets-union/docs/summary-of-responses_en.pdf (last accessed 8 October 2015).

EC, 2015f, *Action Plan on Building a Capital Markets Union*, Brussels http://ec.europa.eu/finance/capital-markets-union/docs/building-cmu-action-plan_en.pdf (last accessed 8 October 2015).

Elliot, D. J, 2015, 'Capital markets union in Europe: initial impressions', Brookings Institution Paper (23 February 2015) Washington, DC: Brookings Institution.

Epstein, G. A, 2005, 'Introduction', in Epstein, G. A. (ed), *Financialization and the World Economy*, 3–16, Cheltenham: Edward Elgar.

ESAs (Joint Committee of the European Supervisory Authorities) 2015, Joint Committee Report on Risks and Vulnerabilities in the EU Financial System (March 2015) ESMA, EBA, EIOPA.

EurActiv, 2015a, 'Regulators warn over-the-counter derivatives are out of control', EurActiv 14 April 2015, http://www.euractiv.com/sections/euro-finance/regulators-warn-over-counter-derivatives-are-out-control-313723 (last accessed 17 December 2015).

EurActiv, 2015b, 'France wants EU's Capital Markets Union to back 'European champions', EurActiv 21 May 2015, www.euractiv.com/sections/innovation-industry/france-wants-eus-capital-markets-union-back-european-champions-314754 (last accessed 17 December 2015).

EurActiv, 2015c, 'NGOs launch watchdog to keep an eye on the Commission's 'Better Regulation'', EurActiv 19 May 2015, http://www.euractiv.com/sections/health-consumers/ngos-launch-watchdog-keep-eye-commissions-better-regulation-314644 (last accessed 17 December 2015).

Finance Watch, 2015, 'Response to the European Commission green paper on Building a Capital Markets Union', consultation response, Brussels (13 May 2015).

Hache, F, 2014, 'A missed opportunity to revive "boring" finance? A Position Paper on the long term financing initiative, good securitisation and securities financing', Brussels: Finance Watch (December 2014).

Hall, P. A and Soskice, D (eds), 2001, *Varieties of Capitalism: The Institutional Foundations of Comparative Advantage*, Oxford: Oxford University Press.

Hancké, B (ed), 2009, *Debating Varieties of Capitalism: A Reader*, Oxford: Oxford University Press.

Hill, J, 2014, 'Capital markets union: finance serving the economy', Speech, Brussels (6 November 2014).

Hill, J, 2015, 'Finance at your service: capital markets union as an instrument of sustainable growth', Speech, Brussels (4 February 2015).

House of Lords, 2015, *Capital Markets Union: A Welcome Start*, Report by the House of Lords European Union Committee, London: The Stationery Office (20 March 2015).

Juncker, J.-C, 2014, 'A new start for Europe: my agenda for jobs, growth, fairness and democratic change', Political Guidelines for the next European Commission, Opening Statement in the European Parliament Plenary Session, Strasbourg (15 July 2014).

Krippner, G. R, 2005, 'The financialization of the American economy', *Socio-Economic Review*, 3(2), 173–208.

Krugman, P, 2008, *The Return of Depression Economics and the Crisis of 2008*, London: Penguin Books.

Levine, R, 2002, 'Bank-based or market-based financial systems: which is better?', *NBER Working Paper* http://www.nber.org/papers/w9138 (last accessed 16 September 2015).

Majone, G, 2014, *Rethinking the Union of Europe Post-Crisis: Has Integration Gone Too Far?*, Cambridge: Cambridge University Press.

McCrank, J, 2014, 'Dark markets may be more harmful than high-frequency trading', Reuters, 7 April 2014.

Mersch, Y, 2014, 'Capital markets union: the "why" and the "how"', Speech at the Joint EIB-IMF High Level Workshop, Brussels (22 October 2014) http://www.ecb.europa.eu/press/key/date/2014/html/sp141022_1.en.html (last accessed 16 September 2015).

Persaud, A, 2008, 'The inappropriateness of financial regulation', in Felton, A and Reinhart, C (eds), *The First Global Financial Crisis of the 21st Century*, London: CEPR.

Pesendorfer, D, 2014, 'Beyond financialisation? Transformative strategies for more sustainable financial markets in the European Union', *European Journal of Law Reform*, 16(4), 692–712.

Segré, C, 1966, *The Development of a European Capital Market: Report of a Group of Experts appointed by the EEC Commission* (November 1996), Brussels: European Economic Community. http://www.steuerrecht.jku.at/gwk/Dokumentation/Steuerpolitik/Gemeinschaftsdokumente/EN/Segre.pdf (last accessed 11 December 2015).

Story, J and Walter, I, 1997, *Political Economy of Financial Integration in Europe: The Battle of the Systems*, Cambridge, MA: The MIT Press.

Véron, N, 2014, *Defining Europe's Capital Markets Union*, Bruegel Policy Contribution 2014/12 (November), http://bruegel.org/wp-content/uploads/imported/publications/pc_2014_12_cmu.pdf

Chapter 3

Petals not thorns: competition policy and finance

Brett Christophers

One of the principal tools available to states and regulators to control financial capital and the financial markets in which financial institutions operate is competition policy (also commonly referred to, especially in the United States (US), as antitrust). Effectively born in its modern form with the US's Sherman Antitrust Act of 1890, albeit presaged in various ways by legacy legal formations such as common law of contracts in restraint of trade, competition law developed during the 20th century to become a more-or-less ubiquitous feature of the regulatory architectures of advanced capitalist states.

Although its specific, legislated objectives vary somewhat both geographically and temporally, antitrust's essential *raison d'être* is straightforward and is best conceived in terms not of what it is 'for' but what it is against: anti-competitive conduct. Such conduct ranges from price fixing to exclusive dealing and from product tying to economic rent extraction, and is widely seen to be facilitated by monopolistic or oligopolistic industry structures and the market power they potentially confer.

A healthy degree of competition has long been regarded as important to the financial sector and to the latter's role in the wider economy and society. As Claessens (2009: 83–84) notes, competition in finance matters for a number of reasons: 'the efficiency of the production of financial services, the quality of financial products', the 'degree of innovation', 'the access of firms and households to financial services', the 'cost of financial intermediation' and so on. As such, the financial sector has been a sphere of avowed interest for competition law and competition lawyers since such law's earliest days (Shull 1996).

Nevertheless, this chapter argues that such interest is, in significant measure, academic. Focusing geographically on the experience of the US and of Western Europe – often held, in accounts diverging from this one, to display amongst the world's more competitive financial sectors – and historically on the experience of recent decades, it submits that competition policy has actually done little to prevent or terminate anti-competitive conduct by financial institutions. Enforcement has typically been minimal; levels of competition are generally low and getting lower; and, notwithstanding high-profile post-financial crisis cases relating to financial benchmark (e.g. Libor) manipulation, the prospects for stricter broadly-based enforcement on an enduring basis are poor. In sum, the control over finance nominally wielded by competition law is, I conclude, largely illusory.

Financial sector competition

Recent decades have been remarkable for a lack of discernible, vigorous enforcement of competition policy in the financial sector in the US and in all major Western European markets. This dearth of activity has been apparent – and widely documented – in two pertinent regards. First, there has, until very recently (see the section '(Re)gaining control?', below), been very little intervention aimed at punishing and/or eradicating existing forms of anti-competitive conduct. Second, there has been equally little resistance to the single structural development deemed by most commentators to be that which is most likely to *engender* such conduct in the first place: that is, industry consolidation.

Carletti and Vives (2007: 18), for example, make this case explicitly for continental Europe, reporting a lax overall attitude towards competition issues in finance and observing that 'market power at the local level does not seem to be always perceived as a big problem by national authorities'. Numerous scholars (e.g. Krippner 2011) have documented a similarly hands-off bearing on the part of the US antitrust authorities. Such authorities had never been particularly active in a commercial banking milieu where decentralisation had been maintained by other regulatory frameworks (especially those restricting interstate banking), but they *remained* inactive even after the purchase of those other regulations began to fade in the 1980s.

Meanwhile, the same authorities have stayed well away from investment banking ever since their celebrated suit against Wall Street (*United States v Henry S. Morgan*) initiated in 1947 (and lost in 1953), leaving the Securities and Exchange Commission, at least in principle, to handle competition concerns through regulation. The United Kingdom (UK) presents a comparable history, with Kay (2012a: 11) recently concluding that, where finance is concerned, the authorities have historically given 'little attention to issues of market structure and the nature and effectiveness of competition'.

> Since 'Big Bang' removed obstacles to the consolidation of financial services businesses in 1986, regulation has not concerned itself with issues of market structure. Indeed, the application of competition policy, the main policy tool for influencing market structure, has been restricted in financial services. The approach has been to let market structure emerge as a result of market forces. If the results are unsatisfactory, the policy response has been to develop detailed prescriptive rules governing the conduct of financial services firms. (Kay 2012a: 43)

The most visible upshot of this generally non-interventionist stance has been massive and typically uncontested consolidation of the financial sector in all major

Western markets, beginning in earnest in the 1980s and continuing through to the present (e.g. Vives 2011: 482). In Europe, such consolidation has occurred both domestically and across borders; it has led to increasing levels of industry concentration, most notably in Austria, Belgium, Finland, the Netherlands, Portugal, Switzerland and the UK (Carletti and Vives 2007: 18); and it has been particularly rapid since the turn of the millennium (Casu and Girardone 2009).

In the US, consolidation and concentration trends have been similarly pronounced (e.g. Dymski 1999) and have seen substantial erosion of the important historic divide between commercial and investment banking (Wilmarth 2002), not only since the Gramm-Leach-Bliley Act of 1999 formally dissolved the mandatory separation of the two but also, in practice, from before that (Funk and Hirschman 2014).

All of this raises, of course, a crucial question: *why* has enforcement been so weak? The following section provides a series of answers. But first, in the rest of this section, I pause critically to address the specific explanation typically advanced – to the extent that it engages with the question at all – by the financial sector itself. Competition policy has been able to take a back-seat regulatory role, the industry and its supporters assert, because, quite simply, it is not needed. The financial sector has been – and, notwithstanding the aforementioned history of consolidation, remains – highly competitive. As such, interventionist antitrust has not been required. Non-intervention has, in short, been the *appropriate* response to an evolving industry formation in which the market itself has maintained competitive discipline.

The bulk of existing evidence suggests that this explanation is without merit, in the bulk of the geographic markets under consideration. Levels of sector competition, although varying widely, are generally low (see e.g. Bikker and Haaf 2002; Claessens and Laeven 2003). This is the case even in countries where levels of industry concentration, traditionally believed to be inversely correlated with levels of competition, are *also* relatively low. At the time of the Bikker and Haaf and Claessens and Laeven studies, the US was arguably still an example of such a country: in both of those studies, banking was found to be less competitive in the US than in any of Australia, Canada, the Netherlands or the UK.

It is for the last of these countries that we have perhaps the fullest evidence of a lack of competitive intensity, provided both by academic studies and by regulatory inquiries. Concerns about a lack of effective competition were officially highlighted as early as 2000 in an influential report compiled for the Chancellor of the Exchequer (Cruickshank 2000). More recently, two key announcements have indicated that the same concerns remain. First, in November 2014, the Competition and Markets Authority (CMA) launched a full investigation into the personal current account and small and medium-sized enterprise retail banking markets owing to persistent evidence of low levels of customer switching, limited transparency, high and stable levels of industry concentration (with the four largest banks providing over three-quarters of personal and business current accounts), and high barriers to entry. Then, in February 2015, the Financial Conduct Authority

(FCA) – which has gained new competition powers of its own – announced its plan to launch a full investigation into the investment and corporate banking markets, a preliminary review thereof having similarly found limited transparency, high barriers to entry and numerous potential conflicts of interest, thus concluding 'that competition is not working effectively' (Financial Conduct Authority 2015: 11).

More striking and significant than such evidence of low levels of financial sector competition in advanced capitalist markets are two further, related findings. The first is that low competition applies particularly on the one variable that, ultimately, matters most of all: price. Financial institutions often will gladly compete on other grounds, the evidence suggests, but the one non-negotiable – the one on which all 'competitors' tend to fall into line – is the one that most directly affects the industry's bottom line. It is also, pointedly, the one that competition authorities primarily use to substantiate anti-competitive conditions, market power usually being defined as the ability profitably to raise prices above a competitive level for a non-transitory period.

Tabacco (2015), for instance, in a study of national banking markets in the European Union (EU) from 2007 to 2012, finds, 'with very few exceptions' (namely, Estonia and the Netherlands), 'a lack of price competition intensity', with the four least competitive markets being in Germany, Luxembourg, the UK and Italy. Liu and Ritter (2011) argue that the underwriting industry represents a series of local oligopolies, where competition occurs on the basis of things such as analyst coverage and industry expertise but *not* price. Similarly, the above-mentioned study by Kay (2012a) found, in the UK fund management industry, a 'pattern of misdirected competition, focusing on marketing and product proliferation but', again, 'not price'. And here, lastly, making the same point more emphatically still, is the banker-turned-business writer William D Cohan:

> Although banks will argue that all fees are negotiable, every corporate issuer knows the rules: Initial public offerings are priced at a 7 percent fee; high-yield-debt underwriting is priced at 3 percent; loan syndications are priced at about 1 percent. M&A deals are still priced off the 'Lehman formula,' even though there is no more Lehman Brothers.
>
> (Cohan 2012)

The second striking finding is that, in addition to levels of sector competition being low, they have also over the past two decades been getting *lower* – not unexpectedly, perhaps, given the ongoing consolidation patterns visible in all major markets. In a recently published study of data for 148 countries for the period 1997 to 2010, Clerides, Delis and Kokas (2014) calculate changes in levels of competition using three different indices. Each index reveals a similar overall pattern over time and for most national markets: a gradual decline in the intensity of competition from 1997 through to 2006, a brief reversal of this trend over the next two years, followed by further weakening of competition from 2008 to 2010.

This progressive weakening of competition, furthermore, has manifestly been exacerbated during – indeed, *due to* – the global financial crisis. Lehman Brothers was allowed to fail, but it was the exception, of course, rather than the rule. Where other major financial institutions were perceived to be at risk of failure, both in the US and elsewhere, where they were not nationalised they were typically acquired by or merged with erstwhile competitors. Lloyds TSB merged with HBOS in the UK, whilst the US witnessed a series of major, crisis-induced pairings, including Bank of America with Merrill Lynch, JP Morgan with Bear Stearns and Wells Fargo with Wachovia. The result, needless to say, has been ever higher levels of industry concentration and, it is argued, of market power. 'The oligopoly has tightened', as Mark Zandi, chief economist at Moody's Analytics, observed of the US situation (cited in Cho 2009).

A pivotal concern in this regard has been that banks that were already in many cases deemed 'too big to fail' are now even bigger and benefit from this outsized status in ways that are themselves inherently anti-competitive. Specifically, it becomes progressively harder for smaller institutions to compete with behemoths that can borrow more cheaply because creditors assume they will not be allowed to fail – Federal Deposit Insurance Corporation data indeed showing that the spread between the borrowing rates of large US banks (with more than US$100 billion in assets) and the rest of the industry had widened from 0.08 percentage points in 2007 to 0.34 points by mid-2009 (ibid).

In sum, we evidently need to find other explanations for why competition law authorities have stood passively by on the margins of the financial sector in recent decades. The argument that such passivity represents purely a rational stance, reflective of healthy competition in the sector, does not hold water; and it holds less water as time goes by. Such an argument, as mentioned, is most closely associated with the dominant institutions within that sector, which is to say those that benefit most precisely from the lack of competition. Such institutions, just as one would expect, have fought stridently against both the CMA and FCA's intentions more fully to investigate competitive conditions in UK finance, with this hostility writ large in formal responses to the authorities' statements (e.g. Competition and Markets Authority 2015). However, it is not only financial institutions that have made the case for the existence of robust competition, and this fact should be recognised in concluding this section.

For example, Bell and Hindmoor (2015) place the question of competition front-and-centre as explanatory cause for the financial crisis; yet surely they have their argument back to front. They argue that the reason that the crisis developed in the financial sectors of the US and UK, rather than for instance those of Australia and Canada, is that the former were intensely competitive and the latter were not. To maintain or grow returns, US and UK banks were compelled, *by competition*, to take excessive risks. However, this argument flies in the face of most existing evidence (which indicates, as we have seen, that competition levels in US and UK banking were and are not just low, but low*er* than elsewhere). Moreover the new evidence brought to bear to substantiate the argument is decidedly tenuous, consisting almost entirely of post-crisis, post hoc rationalisations of risk-taking by shamed bank executives – to the effect that competition forced their hands. To take such rationalisations at face value is, in reality, to display an extraordinary degree of credulity. After all, what, as the Dick Fulds (Lehman) and Chuck Princes (Citigroup) of the world explained themselves to furious politicians and publics, would one *expect* them to say?

Accounting for non-intervention

If not by reference to actually-existing competitive conditions, how then *can* we explain historically minimal levels of antitrust enforcement in the financial sector? Inevitably, some of the most important explanations are 'local' ones, in the sense that they pertain either to specific territories, or to specific subsectors, or to both. I have examined two such specifically local explanations in previous work.

One of these I have referred to as the 'investment banking exception' (Christophers 2013: 568–69). Even in territories where the competition authorities have sought to exert a modicum of influence over developments in commercial banking, they have tended to 'except' investment banking, giving companies in that business largely free rein. Why is that? The US Government's historic failure in the landmark *Morgan* case (see above) may have supplied an additional guard-edness in that particular territory, but the more general reason for investment banking's exception was expressed thus by a British antitrust lawyer (McGrath 2010): historically, 'the unspoken policy assumption seemed to be that investment banking customers were big enough to look after themselves and that competition in investment banking was vigorous enough to prevent problems emerging. As a result, intervention was limited to retail financial markets'. In other words, *unlike* vulnerable retail customers, the customers of investment banks – mainly large corporations – did not need looking out for.

The second local explanation worth noting concerns US commercial banking (Christophers 2014a). There, one of the most significant determinants of antitrust's non-interventionism, specifically when it comes to mergers involving banks with different geographical footprints, has been a particular technicality of US antitrust market analysis. That is, it has conventionally been assumed that commercial banks compete with one another primarily locally; and hence when US banks, as thousands have done in recent decades, announce plans to merge, it is the potential effects on *local* levels of competition that the antitrust authorities have taken into consideration. Competitive conditions at the national level have been downplayed, or even ignored because, in theory, banks do not compete at that scale. The result is that, whilst mergers threatening high levels of concentration in particular local markets have (sometimes) been challenged, those removing sources of competition at the national scale have not. Or, where mergers threaten to do both, it is the local effects that are required to be remedied:

> What I have seen since 1994 is that the number one bank in the country will merge with the number five bank in the country and create a multi-state

institution, with billions of dollars in assets, and if it is found to violate the antitrust laws, the solution is to knock off half a dozen branches in the Peoria area or something like that, which makes me wonder: Do we really have an effective law of antitrust for banks?

(Felsenfeld 2008: 512)

Notwithstanding these significant territory- or subsector-specific explanations, however, there are more general explanations for competition law's long-standing passivity, and we shall focus on these in the remainder of this section. Such explanations pertain across most of the territories under consideration in this chapter and for most of the period we have been looking at. Three are of special and enduring significance.

The first and most important such explanation relates to the allegedly 'special' nature of the financial sector. It is, regulatory authorities have long believed and declared, not quite like other sectors of the economy. In particular, society places a much higher premium on financial sector stability. If, by way of counter-example, conditions in say the automotive industry were to become substantially unstable, this would certainly be problematic for companies and employees in that sector, for customers relying on its products and for the sector's main suppliers. However, conventional economic wisdom, based on historic observation, suggests that the negative consequences of such instability would probably not spread further afield and that they would certainly not be rapidly generalised across the economy and society at large. The financial sector is believed to be different in the sense that if the financial sector is beset by instability it potentially affects everyone and everything, from borrowers to lenders and from governments to non-financial corporations, households and individuals. Hence the panicked scramble at the peak of the recent crisis to prevent 'contagion', ring-fence 'toxic' assets and rescue at-risk institutions.

The connection to competition issues is that 'excess' competition has long been regarded as a potential catalyst of instability. Expose banks to severe competitive pressures, the argument runs, and the risk grows of them taking undue risks and fomenting instability in the process – the same argument that, as we saw earlier, Bell and Hindmoor (2015) apply to the question of the causes of the financial crisis.

As a result, there has always been a critical caveat to states' and regulators' determination – where it exists – to have a competitive financial sector. Yes, competition is beneficial and should be encouraged, but not at the expense of stability. Competition has therefore always been a relative rather than absolute ambition, and generally it has been seen as *less* important. Where competition and stability are in opposition, in other words, the latter should take precedence: 'While competition may be desirable up to a point in deposit banking' Berle (1949: 592) influentially submitted, 'there is a clear bottom limit to its desirability'. He went on: 'a high degree of cooperation among banks is essential'.

Accordingly, the history of competition policy in relation to the financial sector is a history of equivocation, underwritten by exactly such concerns. We have our first general explanation for generally weak enforcement. In many countries, in many periods, states and regulators, concerned first and foremost with stability, have been 'complacent about collusion agreements among banks and preferred to deal with a concentrated sector with soft rivalry' (Vives 2011: 479). In the US, on just such grounds, the financial sector enjoyed what was essentially complete immunity from competition regulators and laws until as late as the 1940s. Kay (2012b), meanwhile, extends this argument where the UK is concerned, claiming that: 'throughout the 20th century, we maintained stability in British banking through oligopoly, with minimal competition, no new entry and no banking failure of any significance'.

The second generalised explanation for weak competition law enforcement in relation to financial institutions has nothing to do with the alleged specificity of finance but instead concerns changes in the interpretation and practice of such law per se. From the early 1980s onwards competition authorities around the world became *generally* less interventionist (Christophers 2016: ch 6), and this impacted conditions in the financial sector, just as it did conditions in other sectors of the economy.

This shift in practice occurred first, and arguably most markedly, in the US, and the changes that have occurred elsewhere have in many cases – including in the EU – been influenced directly by those US-centred developments. Declining levels of intervention from the early 1980s were tied in the US to the rise of the so-called Chicago School of law and economics. Associated closely with legal scholars such as Robert Bork and Richard Posner, both of whom also served as judges, the Chicago School thoroughly rewrote conventional readings of antitrust and what it was 'for'. Competition, it was now argued, was at best a subsidiary objective.

The most important objective of economic regulation was consumer economic welfare and this was delivered not – or at least not primarily – by competition but rather by productive efficiency. Moreover, there was no guarantee that competitive industrial configurations were more efficient than monopolistic ones. In a stroke, the age-old symbiosis of competition policy with competition had been severed, and an intellectual rationale for the authorities to step back from regulation of competition issues – even in sectors, such as US finance, that either already were or were rapidly becoming demonstrably *un*competitive – was made available.

By the mid-1980s, the Chicago School was dominant in the US; however, competition authorities elsewhere typically took longer to embrace the new orthodoxy. This was very much the case in Europe. Until the mid-1990s the European Commission (EC), which had the main responsibility for developing and applying EU competition laws, clung to 'traditional' competition policy – with its prioritisation of competition rather than efficiency – despite periodic calls to head Chicagowards, and thus it remained more interventionist across the board.

Since then, however, 'overall EC competition law has been moving much closer toward U.S. antitrust' (Niels and Ten Kate 2004: 17), and thus to a less interventionist stance. The pace of such movement quickened, furthermore, from 2004, when EU competition law explicitly adopted a so-called 'more economic approach' – which was and is an approach more definitively keyed to efficiency concerns. All the while, the relative influence of such EU law versus the respective competition laws of the individual Member States has been growing, increasingly negating the materiality of any traditionalist redoubts. Since 2004, the European Union has required Member States to apply EU rather than national law in most significant competition cases.

Our second general explanation for meek antitrust enforcement in the financial sector, therefore, is the more generalised defanging of competition policy, courtesy of proliferating Chicago School hegemony.

This leaves a third and final general explanation, which we find in the realms of politics, as opposed to legal interpretation (although it would be wrong to suggest that the Chicago School was somehow apolitical: it most definitely was not). This third, political explanation turns on the critical distinction between competition and competitiveness. The key to understanding this particular factor lies in the recognition that financial markets and the provision of financial services have both become increasingly international in recent decades. As a result, financial institutions headquartered in one territory often compete not only with domestic rivals but with foreign companies, on their own home 'turf' and/or overseas. What this means, in turn, is that competition law almost inevitably becomes politically fraught.

Imagine, by way of illustration, how a US bank dominant domestically and seeking to establish itself overseas, might react to having its wings clipped by the US antitrust authorities, and especially to the implications of such clipping for its competitive positioning vis-à-vis foreign rivals – again, both in domestic and in foreign markets. It might well say that it expected more support from 'its' government, not least a government perennially struggling – as in the US case – with persistent trade deficits and not able to call on many more successful export sectors than financial services itself.

This, it turns out, is exactly what has happened in the past three decades. Governments – including, but not only, the US Government – have increasingly sacrificed finance sector *competition* at the altar of international *competitiveness*. They have refrained from stamping down on anti-competitive conduct amongst their leading domestic financial corporations, out of fear that in doing so they would make (or would be seen to make) such corporations less competitive against ambitious foreign rivals. In this regard, Nguyen and Watkins (2000) and Wilmarth (2009) have discussed long-standing US Government support for bigger and stronger national banking 'champions'.

Other commentators have identified similar dynamics at work in Europe: 'In general', write Carletti and Vives (2007: 18–19, emphasis added), 'national regulatory authorities in [continental] Europe *with the acquiescence of competition authorities* have worried more about protecting and enlarging their national [banking] champions than about the possible consequences of consolidation for customers'. Competitiveness trumps competition. Although the same authors claim that the UK (as well as the EC) has 'taken a tougher stance', this is not true. An influential *Economist* editorial on limp UK competition policy in the 1990s lamented that the government had 'more interest in nurturing national industrial champions than championing the interests of the nation's consumers' (*Economist* 1994).

All three such general factors – the prioritisation of financial stability, the rise of the Chicago School approach to antitrust and the concern with international competitiveness – have been tremendously important, over the past three decades, in limiting the extent of enforcement of competition policy in the financial sector.

To conclude this section, therefore, it remains only to re-emphasise that this hands-off stance persisted during the recent financial crisis. Not only were the crisis-period mega-mergers between banks in the UK and in the US – and indeed elsewhere – swiftly sanctioned by states and regulators; in many cases they were, to one degree or another, *orchestrated by* them. Furthermore, in many cases the swift approval of mergers involved states making exceptions, typically on financial stability grounds, to long-standing local competition policy – specifically, exceptions to antitrust authorities' market share guidelines in the US case (Cho 2009) and to merger referral guidelines in the UK (Nicholls and O'Brien 2014: 180).

(Re)gaining control?

We have seen that recent decades have been characterised by a highly passive stance vis-à-vis the financial sector on the part of US and European competition authorities. We have also seen, however, that such a stance is not explainable by reference to actual competitive conditions in the markets in question. On the contrary: the financial sector displays for the most part low levels of competitive intensity, and these levels have generally been getting lower. On the face of things, therefore, there would certainly appear to be a pressing market need for precisely the kind of interventionist antitrust that has been so conspicuously lacking.

In this final section of the chapter, I ask how likely a substantive future vivification of banking-focused antitrust might be. This is not an idle question. Three related sets of recent developments make it a highly pertinent and timely one. First, the post-crisis years have seen a series of high-profile antitrust suits against banks and bankers in both the US and Europe, with large fines being levied on multiple multi-national financial institutions, for example in relation to alleged collusive manipulation of interest rate benchmarks such as the London Interbank Offered Rate (Libor). The antitrust authorities, in other words, suddenly became active in regard to finance – arguably more active than at any time in recent history. Secondly, the authorities have not only been unusually active in *prosecuting* alleged competition infractions, they have also shown signs of greater determination to *identify and substantiate* anti-competitive dynamics – witness the recent above-mentioned announcements of market investigations by the UK's CMA and FCA.

Thirdly, scholarly commentators, observing these two sets of developments, are increasingly predicting an era of sustained antitrust interventionism in the financial sector. Franchoo, Baeten and Salem (2014: 581, 568) comment on the EC's 'vigorous approach to antitrust enforcement' in the financial sector since 2013 and anticipate that this approach 'will no doubt continue'. Nicholls and O'Brien (2014) and O'Brien (Chapter 1 in this volume) submit that such dynamism and determination might even see competition law eclipsing financial regulation per se. In short, there are suggestions that the recent animation of antitrust in the financial sector could become a deep-seated and enduring phenomenon.

In what follows, I take a contrarian view. Of course, all such crystal ball-gazing is inherently speculative. Yet, the idea that in the medium- or longer term we will see a materially different approach to competition policy application in the financial sector than we have become accustomed to – i.e. that we will see vigorous, broadly-based and sustained enforcement – goes against the grain, I argue, of historic and contemporary legal, political and political-economic realities. My view rests on six separate observations.

First, it is crucial to recognise that the recent financial sector antitrust prosecutions relating to Libor and foreign exchange benchmark manipulation are of a very particular type. They are prosecutions of egregious, universally-condemned and arguably *criminal* behaviour. Such behaviour, once exposed, could not *not* be prosecuted, and the outcome (guilty) was never really in doubt, even if the size of fines was. What such cases are not are more stock-in-trade competition policy actions such as interventions to block or remedy mergers or to force disposals where excess market power has been structurally accumulated (interventions where the outcome is always contested and frequently difficult to predict).

It is entirely conceivable that the financial sector could be rid of egregious, collusive market manipulation, yet remain deeply non-competitive in its core inter-firm dynamics. Antitrust 'enforcement' in the shape of findings of market manipulation and the imposition of fines is *not* the same as 'enforcement' in the shape of robust administrative application of policy designed to mitigate the monopolistic or oligopolistic conditions in which anti-competitive conduct thrives. If the recent antitrust actions had taken aim at the 'too big to fail' nature of the financial sector and the fundamental tilting of the competitive playing field that it is widely seen to effect, then a more positive prognosis for competition law's general efficacy and impact would perhaps be warranted. However, the actions taken are demonstrably not of such a type. To interpret actions specifically against rate benchmark-fixing as bespeaking a fundamental shift in the underlying antitrust stance vis-à-vis an entire industry would be to make a categorical error.

Secondly, we should not overlook the significance of how these recent prosecutions have been handled, and especially of the primary objectives revealed thereby. In prosecuting those implicated in the manipulation of Libor and other benchmarks, has a restoration of competitive market conditions been to the fore-front? No. What the prosecutions – including those explicitly involving competition law authorities – show instead is a concern primarily for the market-making 'value' of the benchmarks themselves.

As Ashton and Christophers (2015: 205) write in relation specifically to Libor and specifically to the role of the UK bank Barclays, 'the enforcement actions focus in large measure on the potential effects of different forms of Libor arbitrage on the integrity of the index'; and hence 'the primary legal norm mobilized against Barclays' actions is presented as a loss of trust in the neutrality and arbitration qualities of Libor itself, *not* harm done to other creditors or counterparties' – or, still less perhaps, to competitors. To be sure, harm was hard to establish and impossible to quantify, and it was not denied. But for all the involvement of antitrust authorities, *competition*, and thus the market conditions facing the aforementioned 'creditors and counterparties', was typically not the key issue.

Thirdly, it is difficult to imagine that what we have shown to be perhaps *the* primary obstacle to active antitrust enforcement in the financial sector historically – the political privileging of financial stability – has somehow now become less of a concern, least of all in the immediate wake of a global crisis that demonstrated just how *un*stable the financial sector can easily be. It has not.

In fact, stability is more of a watchword than ever. The conversion of the international Financial Stability Forum into the Financial Stability Board in 2009 saw a broadening, not weakening, of its mandate. Europe (or at least, the euro area Member States) now has the European Stability Mechanism, its 'permanent crisis resolution' vehicle. One of the key components of post-crisis reform of the UK's financial regulatory framework has been the creation, within the Bank of England, of the Financial Policy Committee, with the maintenance of financial stability as its primary objective. One of the key components of the parallel programme of reform in the US was the establishment of the Financial Stability Oversight Council. And so on. The implications of stability's prioritisation for the possibility of robust competition policy enforcement, needless to say, have not changed: in a climate where stability is sacrosanct, competition concerns are perforce subordinate.

Fourthly, prevailing interpretations of competition law have not changed, either; or, it would perhaps be better to say that they have not changed *much*. Many scholars of antitrust argue that the dominance of orthodox Chicago School thinking began to wane from the mid-1990s and that the subsequent period is properly viewed as a 'post-Chicago' era. However, although the period in question has certainly seen modifications in antitrust thinking and practice, these pale beside the changes that the rise of the Chicago School itself ushered in. As Niels and Ten Kate (2004: 10–11) observed, 'the rise of post-Chicago has not affected the prevalence of the Chicago ground rules for antitrust'. They continued: 'When post-Chicago theories are used it is to assess the economic effects of the specific business practices or mergers concerned – but still largely within the competition-efficiency framework laid out by Chicago'. Even in a nominally post-Chicago world, antitrust remains largely non-interventionist.

Fifthly, faced with the prospect of a generalised strengthening of competition law enforcement, financial sector opposition – and especially the opposition of those dominant firms that benefit most, by definition, from the sector's weakly-competitive nature – would be strident. The 'too big to fail' financial institutions that preside over global finance not only enjoy and actively safeguard their market power and the competitive advantages it confers, but they enjoy *being* (seen to be) too big to fail.

And why would they not? Of course, the views of such institutions and their top executives would be neither here nor there, were they unable to exert influence over policy-making in areas such as antitrust. However, as numerous accounts have shown (e.g. Johnson and Kwak 2010; Suárez and Kolodny 2011), no analysis of either the pre-crisis consolidation and deregulation of the US financial sector or the stymying of post-crisis reform efforts is complete without attention to the political muscle of the financial sector; and the story in Europe is similar (Christophers 2014a). Indeed, when Claessens (2009: 85) submits that 'certain odious relationships' between the financial and political sectors 'can make achieving effective competition [in the financial sector] a complex task', he is putting it mildly.

Finally, but by no means least, the geography of the contemporary financial industry also renders effective competition law enforcement challenging to a degree that was never quite the case in the past. As discussed earlier in relation to the competition-versus-competitiveness question, the provision of financial services has become increasingly international in recent decades. That is to say, companies compete with one another transnationally and, equally important, they engage in anti-competitive conduct transnationally. This would not be a problem for antitrust enforcement if there existed, beyond the EU, meaningful international or global competition laws and competition authorities. But there do not: 'In general', observes Gerber (2012: 3), 'the laws that are applied to global markets are not themselves global – or even transnational! Instead, the *laws of individual states* govern *global markets*'.

Also, in industries where antitrust has historically been more vigorously enforced than it has been in the financial sector, those individual states and their individual competition authorities, lacking effective collaboration with their foreign counterparts, have repeatedly been shown to be impotent to stamp out transnational infractions. To suppose that cross-border enforcement in the financial sector – which, after all, is one of, if not the most globalised industry sectors of all – would somehow be more successful, is to make a considerable leap of faith. Not for nothing does the UK's FCA, noting in a preliminary report on competition issues in investment and corporate banking that 'many of these services are global in nature', worry out loud about its 'ability to intervene effectively at a UK level' (Financial Conduct Authority 2015: 9).

In sum, therefore, taking into consideration all six of these issues, it is difficult to imagine that the last few years represent some kind of watershed moment in the history of competition law enforcement in the financial sector in Western Europe and the US. The history of large-scale *non*-enforcement is too long and too entrenched; and the obstacles to realisation of a new paradigm appear too material.

Conclusion

Popular imagery of the financial sector often portrays it as the very apotheosis of no-holds-barred, take-no-prisoner competitive capitalism. Such imagery is propagated by people and institutions within the sector itself but also in newspapers, in film and in literature. The reality, however, is rather different. When Schumpeter, in the 1940s, famously described mid-century Western capitalism as politely 'corespective' (Schumpeter 1942: 90), he might just as well have been describing late 20th or early-21st century *financial* capitalism. This is not to say that companies in the financial sector never meaningfully compete with one another. Of course, they do. However, the intensity of that competition is considerably weaker than is commonly supposed and the particular form of competition that is most dangerous to incumbents in the sense of most threatening to their profitable reproduction – that is, price competition – is assiduously avoided.

The fact that this is so demonstrates that the control that the state's nominal guardians of competition – its competition authorities, with their competition laws – exert over actors in the financial sector is, in significant measure, illusory. To be sure, those financial actors can frequently be heard to protest that they are forced to navigate a thicket of intrusive legislation and regulation that circumscribes their operational freedom and prevents them from fully realising their market potential. This may be true, but the thicket in question does not include, on any reasonable reading, competition policy; or, if it does, such policy, in practice, generally confronts those needing to navigate it with petals rather than thorns.

This chapter has attempted to explain why this is the case. It has shown that even if the necessary laws exist on paper, in the statute books, to enforce and maintain competitive conditions in the financial sector (and, arguably, they do), there is a world of difference between the written law and the law as interpreted and applied in practice. The latter is always and everywhere shaped by all manner of 'extra-legal' considerations – political, economic, intellectual and more – and in the case of the financial sector in recent decades, these factors have combined consistently to minimise levels of antitrust intervention. The result, across Western Europe and the US, is the highly concentrated and only minimally competitive financial sector we have ended up with today.

References

Ashton, P and Christophers, B, 2015, 'On arbitration, arbitrage and arbitrariness in financial markets and their governance: unpacking LIBOR and the LIBOR scandal', *Economy and Society*, 44, 188–217.

Bell, S and Hindmoor, A, 2015, *Masters of the Universe, Slaves of the Market*, Cambridge, MA: Harvard University Press.

Berle, A, 1949, 'Banking under the anti-trust laws', *Columbia Law Review*, 49, 589–606.

Bikker, J and Haaf, K, 2002, 'Competition, concentration and their relationship: an empirical analysis of the banking industry', *Journal of Money, Credit and Banking*, 35, 2191–214.

Carletti, E and Vives, X, 2007, *Regulation and competition policy in the banking sector*, prepared for the IESE Business School Conference 'Fifty years of the treaty: assessment and perspectives of competition policy in Europe' https://www.cesifo-group.de/portal/pls/portal/!PORTAL.wwpob_page.show?_docname=1005863.PDF (last accessed 16 September 2015).

Casu, B and Girardone, C, 2009, 'Competition issues in European banking', *Journal of Financial Regulation and Compliance*, 17(2), 119–33.

Cho, D, 2009, 'Banks 'Too big to fail' have grown even bigger', *The Washington Post* (28 August 2009).

Christophers, B, 2013, 'Banking and competition in exceptional times', *Seattle University Law Review*, 36, 563–76.

Christophers, B, 2014a, 'Competition, law, and the power of (imagined) geography: market definition and the emergence of too-big-to-fail banking in the United States', *Economic Geography*, 90, 429–50.

Christophers, B, 2014b, 'Geographies of finance III: regulation and 'after-crisis' financial futures', *Progress in Human Geography*, doi: 10.1177/0309132514564046.

Christophers, B, 2016, *The Great Leveler: Capitalism and Competition in the Court of Law*, Cambridge, MA: Harvard University Press.

Claessens, S, 2009, 'Competition in the financial sector: overview of competition policies', *The World Bank Research Observer*, 24, 83–118.

Claessens, S and Laeven, L, 2003, *What Drives Bank Competition? Some International Evidence*, World Bank Policy Research Working Paper No. 3113 http://ssrn.com/abstract=509605 (last accessed 16 September 2015).

Clerides, S, Delis, M and Kokas, S, 2014, 'A new data set on competition in national banking markets', SSRN http://ssrn.com/abstract=2448938 (last accessed 16 September 2015).

Cohan, W, 2012, 'Wall Street turned crisis into a cartel', *Bloomberg News* (23 January 2012) http://www.bloombergview.com/articles/2012-01-09/cohan-how-wall-street-turned-a-crisis-into-a-cartel.html (last accessed 8 October 2015).

Competition and Markets Authority, 2015, 'Retail banking market investigation: responses to the updated issues statement' https://www.gov.uk/cma-cases/review-of-banking-for-small-and-medium-sized-businesses-smes-in-the-uk#responses-to-the-updated-issues-statement (last accessed 16 September 2015).

Cruickshank, D, 2000, *Competition in UK Banking: A Report to the Chancellor of the Exchequer*, London: HMSO.

Dymski, G, 1999, *The Bank Merger Wave: The Economic Causes and Social Consequences of Financial Consolidation*, Armonk, NY: M. E. Sharpe.

Economist, 1994, 'Screaming at the umpire' (21 May 1994).

Felsenfeld, C, 2008, 'Contribution to Symposium: The antitrust aspects of bank mergers (Panel discussion I: development of bank merger law)', *Fordham Journal of Corporate and Financial Law*, 13, 511–547.

Financial Conduct Authority, 2015, *Wholesale sector competition review 2014–15: Feedback statement* https://www.fca.org.uk/static/documents/feedback-statements/fs15-02.pdf (last accessed 16 September 2015).

Franchoo, T, Baeten, N and Salem, O, 2014, 'The application of European competition law in the financial services sector', *Journal of European Competition Law & Practice*, 5, 568–91.

Funk, R and Hirschman, D, 2014, 'Derivatives and deregulation: financial innovation and the demise of Glass–Steagall', *Administrative Science Quarterly*, 59, 669–704.

Gerber, D, 2012, *Global Competition: Law, Markets, and Globalization*, Oxford: Oxford University Press.

Johnson, S and Kwak, J, 2010, *13 Bankers: The Wall Street Takeover and the Next Financial Meltdown*, New York: Pantheon.

Kay, J, 2012a, *The Kay Review of UK Equity Markets and Long-Term Decision-making* http://www.ft.com/cms/s/0/da96880a-98f8-11e1-948a-00144feabdc0.html (last accessed 11 December 2015).

Kay, J, 2012b, 'It is time to end the oligopoly in banking', *Financial Times* (8 May 2012).

Krippner, G, 2011, *Capitalizing on Crisis: The Political Origins of the Rise of Finance*, Cambridge, MA: Harvard University Press.

Liu, X and Ritter, J, 2011, 'Local underwriter oligopolies and IPO underpricing', *Journal of Financial Economics*, 102, 579–601.

McGrath, B, 2010, *Banking in the Antitrust Crosshairs: The EU Situation* (16 April); London: Lexology (LockeLord LLP) http://www.lexology.com/library/detail.aspx?g=506c4fb7-ed3f-4a1a-a1b3-feee837bb206 (last accessed 16 September 2015).

Nguyen, A and Watkins, M, 2000, 'Recent legislation: financial services reform', *Harvard Journal on Legislation*, 37, 579–92.

Nicholls, R and O'Brien, J, 2014, 'Hanging together or hanging separately: is competition law in the process of eclipsing financial regulation?', *Law and Financial Markets Review*, 8(2), 178–84.

Niels, G and Ten Kate, A, 2004, 'Introduction: antitrust in the US and the EU–converging or diverging paths', *Antitrust Bulletin*, 49, 1–28.

Schumpeter, J, 1942, *Capitalism, Socialism and Democracy*, New York: Harper & Row.

Shull, B, 1996, 'The origins of antitrust in banking: an historical perspective', *Antitrust Bulletin*, 41, 255–88.

Suárez, S and Kolodny, R, 2011, 'Paving the road to "too big to fail": business interests and the politics of financial deregulation in the United States', *Politics & Society*, 39, 74–102.

Tabacco, G, 2015, 'Market structure and intensity of price competition in EU banking', *Journal of Competition Law & Economics*, 11(2): 353–363.

Vives, X, 2011, 'Competition policy in banking', *Oxford Review of Economic Policy*, 27, 479–97.

Wilmarth, A, 2002, 'Transformation of the US financial services industry, 1975–2000: competition, consolidation, and increased risks', *University of Illinois Law Review*, 2002, 215–476.

Wilmarth, A, 2009, 'The dark side of universal banking: financial conglomerates and the origins of the subprime financial crisis', *Connecticut Law Review*, 41, 963–1050.

Part II

Culture: organisations, stakeholders and politics

Chapter 4

Reconstruction of ethical conduct within financial firms

Sally Wheeler

In a telephone conversation, Trader A explained to Broker A of Broker Firm A: 'if you keep 6s [i.e. the six-month Japanese Libor rate] unchanged today . . . I will fucking do one humongous deal with you . . . Like a 50,000 buck deal, whatever. I need you to keep it as low as possible . . . if you do that . . . I'll pay you, you know, 50,000 dollars, 100,000 dollars . . . whatever you want . . . I'm a man of my word'.

Trader A was an employee of UBS and this conversation apparently occurred on 18 September 2008. It was contained in the Final Notice from the Financial Services Authority (FSA) to UBS of 19 December 2012, which fined UBS £160 million for manipulation of Libor (FSA 2012: 4).

'We all know these events are not representative of our culture', said Bob Diamond in a memo to Barclays staff on 2 July 2012, the day before he resigned as chief executive of Barclays as the Libor scandal unfolded (*The Economist* 2012).

Bob Diamond's view of the 'culture' prevailing not just within Barclays but also across the financial sector has turned out to be, at best, unduly optimistic and, at worst, simply wrong. In very simple terms we might say that, whilst *technical* explanations (Engelen and others 2012) have differed, three relatively straightforward *narrative* themes, running broadly consecutively with some temporal overlap (Brown 2005; Whittle and Mueller 2011; Schifferes and Roberts 2015), have captured the popular imagination (Bennett and Kottasz 2012). These emerge from governmental, regulatory and sectoral inquiries (Walker 2009; Parliamentary Banking Standards Commission 2013; Financial Stability Board 2013; Kay 2012) into the global financial crisis (GFC) and the events that have followed in its wake, such as the Libor, forex and gold-fixing scandals. These themes have run their course in all the jurisdictions that have experienced the GFC. Those national financial systems such as Australia that have not experienced the shock of the GFC, but where areas of malpractice have been uncovered (O'Brien 2013), have nevertheless examined their financial sectors for signs of the presence of these three themes (Financial System Inquiry 2014).

First, there was the revelation that some business models (Northern Rock for example – see Keasey and Veronesi 2008; Marshall and others 2012) and some products and practices (sub-prime mortgages and securitisation, payment protection insurance for example – see Aalbers 2008; Sassen 2012) were flawed. Secondly, there was the unmasking of individuals, such as Bernie Madoff, about whose business practices the regulators seemed not to have heeded warnings (Langevoort 2009); and revelations that senior executive leaders of banks that had been the recipients of government or federal reserve support or fire sales were continuing to enjoy pre-crash levels of compensation and bonuses (de Goede 2009; Matthews and Matthews 2010). Thirdly, there was the gradual revelation – not surprising to academics working in the fields of regulation and business ethics – that it was not only those at the pinnacle of the financial services industry whose behaviour was in question: there were issues about the prevailing culture in firms throughout the financial sector. These were not stories about rogue traders as 'bad apples' (Gilligan 2011) but rather stories about entire business areas within firms operating in open contravention of, if not the rules themselves, then certainly the spirit of the rules – and then resorting to illegal collusive behaviour to maximise their gains.

The ease and openness with which this collusive behaviour occurred suggests that there had been a collective breakdown of appropriate cultural *mores* within financial sector business firms. In other words, drawing on the metaphors used by theorists of organisational structures and behaviours, what we appear to have ended up with is a prevalence of 'bad barrels' rather than 'bad apples'. In this chapter, 'unethical' is given a wide definition, which includes both illegal acts and behaviour by individuals that would be unacceptable to the wider community. Thus, the violation of professional standards and ethical norms, whether they are enshrined in law or not, are considered to be unethical (Jones 1991). Classically, unethical behaviour is explained by the presence within an organisation of individuals who are morally flawed, and whose personal characters predispose them to poor behaviour. A reference to bad barrels moves from an individual to a broader social basis of explanation, indicating that the culture of an organisation is such that it operates as an influence over individuals, inducing them to transgress or perhaps failing to discourage them from transgressing. Later in this chapter we look at how an organisation can send conflicting or ambivalent messages to its members about its preferences in relation to unethical practices, through its use of rewards and prohibitions (Ashforth and Anand 2003). Current empirical work on ethical transgression within organisations would suggest that bad barrels and bad apples are not an either/or option. Rather, they are likely to co-exist (Treviño and Youngblood 1990; Treviño, Weaver and Reynolds 2006).

Definitions or descriptions of what is meant by organisational, or as I prefer in this context, firm, culture vary hugely from study to study, depending on the underpinning theoretical assumptions made (Alvesson and Sveningsson 2008: 36). For example, culture may be seen as one variable amongst others or as a dynamic concept that is fundamental to the nature of the organisation (Smirich 1983). Nevertheless, most studies share some thematic coherence (Hofstede and others 1990). The model of culture that is adopted in this chapter is derived from the work of Schein (Schein 1985), often referred to as a pyramid or onion model. For

Schein, culture can be seen as the 'rules' of the organisation that a new member has to learn and absorb in order to progress. These rules have been constructed by existing members of the organisation as the best way of coping with external pressures and internal integration. Usefully, Schein is the cultural organisation theorist drawn upon in the Salz Review of Barclays, information drawn from which informs the latter part of this chapter (Salz 2013).

At the centre of Schein's onion, and forming the cornerstone of the organisational edifice, are shared assumptions and beliefs. These shared assumptions and beliefs are likely to be unexpressed and tacit and form the beating heart of the firm. They are the governing assumptions of those who work at the firm and, as such, structure their actions as individuals and the actions of the firm itself. Issues such as the business of the firm, how that business relates to other organisational actors such as other firms and bureaucracies, including government and regulators, as well as social relations between employees, are all cornerstone assumptions. Radiating outwards from the onion, there are the values and norms that the firm holds out both publicly and internally to its employees as being significant to it. These are generally explicitly expressed; their significance might, for example, be underlined by the existences of codes, the endorsement of externally produced codes or expressed statements of values. These values and norms can evolve and change over time and, if they change, so will the behaviours of individuals. Then there are what Schein terms 'artefacts'. These are surface level, easily observable instances around issues such as the 'water cooler' rules about dress and employee birthday celebration rituals in the office, for example. The significance of Schein's model is its inference that, the deeper a practice or value is embedded into the firm, then the harder it is to effect change around it.

This chapter establishes the link between the internal workings of the firm and regulatory traction. It then looks at the relationship between the ethical values of individuals and their workplace behaviour. It examines the nature of culture in financial sector firms from a top-down and bottom-up perspective, by drawing on various ethnographic accounts of 'firm life' and on more inquisitorial and corporately generated sources, such as the Salz Review of Barclays and Goldman Sachs' *Business Standards Committee Report*, in the way that Schein, who was heavily influenced by anthropology, suggests is necessary to decipher and assess the reality of what is occurring in terms of organisational culture (Schein 1996). Barclays commissioned the Salz Review as an independent review of its business practices. Barclays and Goldman Sachs represent opposite poles of the financial sector – different business locus and genus for example. Additionally, Barclays survived the GFC without receiving a bail-out, whilst Goldman Sachs did receive financial assistance. Taking these firms together, their experiences can be broadly seen as representative of the sector.

Building on proposals for rebuilding of in-firm culture, using the characteristics of individuals and organisational leadership suggested by the Treviño and others co-existence model referred to above, the chapter asks whether regulators' and governments' demands for achieving cultural change, and assurances to do this

emanating from firms, are realistic. Can banks and their senior managers inculcate a 'culture which tells people that there are things they shouldn't do, even
if they are legal, even if they are profitable and even if it is highly likely that the
supervisor will never spot them' (Turner 2012)?

The link between firm culture and regulation

Much attention has been paid in the post GFC era to 'new governance' regulatory
models: styles of regulation that go beyond traditional models of command and
control and instances of regulatory failure, with the aim of diagnosing whether
these models are at least partly to blame for the crisis and how regulation might be
remodelled, providing control strategies for the future. Complexity of the financial
marketplace and of its products are identified as stumbling blocks for regulation,
as is regulatory capture and generalised corporate governance failure. The purpose here is not to look at the successes and failures of different regulatory models
and the role of other intervening causes in the GFC. This has been well mined
elsewhere (Davies 2010). Rather, we point out that all new governance regulatory
styles have a considerable dependence upon the attitudinal settings (also known as
cultural disposition) of the regulated population (firms and/or employees).

Attitudinal setting in the context of the firm is part of the core of firm culture
that Schein identifies. It refers to the place accorded to regulatory intervention,
regulatory adoption and regulatory compliance within the governing assumptions
that form the cornerstone of firm culture. A firm might be disposed towards adopting and complying with regulation in a meaningful way, refining and developing
its response over time – or it may see regulatory intervention and subsequent
compliance as a cost of doing business that is to be kept as minimal as possible
(Laufer 1999). The attitudinal setting of a firm, in its broadest sense, provides the
scaffolding for regulatory traction.

Black reviews the performance of principles-based regulation, meta-regulation
and risk-based regulation in the financial crisis as a foreground for suggesting
that if regulatory governance is to be used successfully in different contexts, there
is a need to understand the impact of its 'organizational, technical/functional
and cognitive dimensions' (Black 2012). In relation to principles-based regulation, she cites the observation of Hector Sants (Finch 2009), which states that it
is doomed to failure if those charged with its maintaining its integrity have no
principles. Whilst that may be a rather rhetorically charged sentiment, reflecting
the zeal of the convert (Tomasic 2010: 113–114), as Black points out it remains
the case that a key building block of such a regulatory style is that it relies on the
internal structures and ultimately the attitudinal setting of the regulated firm to
address the requirements of the broad and general rules offered by the regulatory
actor. If these 'back office' systems are not in place, then the principles have no
traction.

Meta-regulation is even more dependent on the operating culture within
the targeted or regulated firm, requiring less intervention from regulators than

principles-based regulation. The culture of the firm has to be open to the goals of the regulation and the cultural disposition set to embrace positively the necessary compliance systems and then monitor those systems. Regulators have to be able to rely on the culture of a regulated entity being such that its reports of compliance are an accurate representation of firm life rather than an idealised or falsified picture. Risk-based regulation is attractive in a neo-liberal era, and in times of state austerity, in that it allows the cost of regulation to be reduced, whilst at the same time also allowing the state to argue that the resources available for regulation are being targeted upon real and identified risks to a chosen regulatory strategy. This attractiveness is evidenced by the popularity that risk-based regulation currently enjoys across the world, in sectors as diverse as environmental protection, financial services and food safety. To offer protection from the identified risks, the regulator needs to know not only that reporting against risks by the regulated population is accurate, but also that the system adopted is sufficiently flexible to pick up emerging risks. Resource prioritisation of risks requires the regulated population to have the internal design capacity for information collection, and for onward transmission, in a format that reflects the regulator's understanding of the risks.

In Baldwin and Black's detailed discussion of the opportunity that risk-based regulation gives a regulator to be 'really responsive' (Baldwin and Black 2008), the 'behaviour, attitudes, and cultures' of those regulated (Black and Baldwin 2010: 186) are key considerations in the identification of risks and in the assessment of the likelihood of them occurring, on both an industry wide and firm specific platform. What is encompassed in this is the firm's commitment to the regulatory endeavour and the permeability of its management structures to the requirements of regulation. There is a danger that the firms enlisted into this endeavour are those that are already culturally disposed towards compliance (Gunningham 2009). For regulators relying on the internal systems of their regulated populations to respond to regulation and generate compliance, there is the obvious difficulty that each firm may operate to different standards of risk control, adopting of the spirit of principles in different ways and so reporting in different ways. This makes risk identification and assessment very difficult.

Within each regulated firm, there are likely to be internal structures, such as divisions, separate cost centres and different business models, based upon jurisdiction perhaps. As this chapter explains, this is particularly true of firms in the financial sector, where groups of employees such as traders may be employed on the basis of a very different business model from others such as investment bankers, although they are part of the same firm. These employees have widely differing perspectives on many aspects of firm life, including responding to regulation. Different parts of the same firm will be required to respond to different regulators and the relationships they construct with these regulators might be quite different. This is an aspect of firm life which receives rather scant attention in the regulation literature (cf. Heimer 2013); however, it goes to the heart of questions about the role of firm culture in regulation and to the challenges that need to be addressed in trying to change or reorientate culture.

If firm culture and intra-firm relationships and structures are important in the design and development of regulation, then they are crucial in the context of regulatory compliance. We know a comparatively large amount about compliance behaviour from the perspective of the regulated: how compliance is seen as a flexible concept, how it is negotiated between regulators and the regulated population and why a regulated population might be prepared to exceed regulatory requirements for example (Gunningham, Kagan and Thornton 2004; Gray and Shadbegian 2005; Edelman and Talesh 2011). These insights do not, for the most part, come from studying actors or practices where compliance is a separate and ring-fenced activity from the commercial activities of the firm, as it is in the financial sector. There are studies of compliance officers and the compliance function in the financial sector but they are few and far between (Weait 1994; Bamberger and Mulligan 2011). This chapter is not intended to add to these studies but rather makes the point that the ambivalent relationship between (i) the very separated and segregated compliance function (Lenglet 2012: 61–66) within financial service firms and, (ii) other employees, who are literally making markets at the very edge of innovative practice (Lerner 2006), makes embedding new cultural practices a very nuanced and complex task.

Any demand by government or by an arm's length regulator that a firm alter its internal structure to satisfy a regulatory requirement has the potential to effect a change in its operating. For example, the Cadbury Report of 1992 (Spira and Slinn 2013), now largely contained in the UK Corporate Governance Code 2014 (Financial Reporting Council 2014), imposed inter alia the requirements that there be a remuneration committee within a PLC, and that the roles of chairman of the board and chief executive be held by different individuals, and that firms should either operate these structures or explain why not, on pain of losing their stock exchange listing. This required a recontextualisation of relationships within firms – and outwith firms – in respect of their shareholders and auditors. The choice of how to implement and manage these changes remains with the regulated firm. The extent to which change was embraced, and operating culture altered and subsequently modified and moulded to achieve the best governance outcomes for shareholders, depends upon the attitudinal setting of the firm at the deepest of Schein's levels, and on the values and norms that exist at his second intermediate level.

A form of regulatory intervention that is driven further into the firm by outside forces, excluding firm choice around design and implementation, is the compliance and ethics requirement imposed as a result of non-prosecution and deferred prosecution agreements (DPAs), beloved of United States (US) regulators over the last 15 years and now much more recently part of the United Kingdom (UK) regulatory enforcement armoury. As O'Brien and Dixon point out, there are significant differences between the UK and US approaches to deferred prosecution (O'Brien and Dixon 2014); however, both offer – as a possible condition for not prosecuting – the appointment of a corporate monitor, to oversee the installation of enhanced ethics and compliance programmes. The potential of this appointment lies in the fact that it is neither made by nor subsequently controlled in its operation by the corporation. In some instances, the monitor might be required to oversee changes in the firm's approach to compliance that it would have introduced itself at some point. In other instances, what is mandated goes much further and amounts to a re-engineering of its position (Garrett 2007).

The high water mark for the appointment of corporate monitors as part of settlements brokered by the US authorities has probably passed, with numbers dropping from around 15 to less than 5 in recent years (according to Barrett's database at http://lib.law.virginia.edu/Garrett/prosecution_agreements (last accessed on 26 September 2015)); however, there is no available data on the UK yet. In the US, numerous detailed accounts of monitorships suggest that the rate of recidivism is high (Garrett 2014) and express concerns about the lack of regulation of monitors' activities (Khanna 2011) – resulting in many inconsistencies around scope, cost and ultimately outcomes (Ford and Hess 2011), as well as an absence of transparency. Nevertheless, the idea of monitors intervening in firms to inject into them a particular cultural shape remains a powerful symbolic image of how culture drives regulation (Ford 2010).

Finance firms' cultures and engagement of identity

The culture within financial firms has been the subject of much speculation, following the GFC. Hector Sants, when chair of the FSA, identified 'poor cultures' within firms as one of the key drivers of the GFC (Sants 2010). Moving on from the causes debate to the 'solution' debate, questions have been asked about whether culture expressly or obliquely rewards excessive risk-taking and unethical behaviour, through compensation or a combination of compensation and affirmation (Wexler 2010: 14). Questions have also been asked as to whether the ethical mind sets of financial firm employees have been altered by the demands of shareholders in what were previously unincorporated businesses, by technical innovations and by the loosening of controls over business. Looking forward, others have asked whether a combination of regulatory intervention, a new culture of sanction and the promised efforts of individual firms would have the potential to reconstruct the cultural life of these firms (Dudley 2014). To have any answer to this last question, there needs to be some idea about what, in general terms, the broad ethical settings are inside financial sector firms and what constitutes the cultural *mores* of these firms.

Within the business ethics and economic psychology literature there are a number of recent studies that can be used to explore the ethical positions of professionals in the finance sector. In general terms, an individual's attitude to particular settings and issues is made up of a combination of their personal attributes and the environment in which they find themselves (Bandura 1991). The balance between these two is important, both for understanding the cultural life of the financial firm and for directing its reconstruction in the future. Holtbrügge and his colleagues suggest that, in the context of unethical behaviour in the workplace, the questionnaire responses they received from their sample of people employed at various levels in the German service and manufacturing sectors indicated that personal attributes such as age, gender and the 'big five' personality traits (Goldberg 1990) – conscientiousness, extraversion, emotional stability, agreeableness and openness to experience – are more important in encouraging ethical behaviour than organisational environment (Holtbrügge, Baron and Friedmann 2014). This would suggest that what is likely to be more effective in creating a new organisational culture in any workplace is a focus within the workplace on personal development rather than on the introduction of top-down codes of behaviour and best practice.

The study that Holtbrügge and his colleagues undertook examined the position of employees in a number of sectors and roles. Their findings might become relevant to financial sector professionals if we drill down into the actual values of those professionals and compare them with those studied by Holtbrügge. This would go some way towards dealing with the proposition that there is something inherently different about the values structure of those who earn their living in the financial sector. This plays into the bad apples versus bad barrels situation referred to above. If finance professionals are similar to employees in other roles, then we know that it is their personal values that are the pre-eminent force behind their behaviour. If these personal values include honesty and probity, then we could assume that in general they are good apples. This would then lead us on to thinking about how individuals are influenced by the behaviour of others – bad apples – in proximity to them, for example. If, on the other hand, finance professionals are different in their emotional settings from other employees – with organisational culture being more significant to them and their behaviour than personal attributes – then maybe organisational culture (bad barrel) plays a bigger part in their ethical responses.

Cohn and colleagues suggest that, in a controlled experimental setting, there is no observable difference between the ethical standards of finance professionals and other professionals (Cohn 2014). They both have the same standards of honesty and, indeed, other studies would support this (e.g. van Hoorn 2015; Rusch 2015). What is distinct about Cohn's study is that it goes on to suggest that, when the professional identity of bankers is engaged, they become considerably more dishonest. The concept of professional identity that Cohn employs is based loosely on the economics of identity literature (Akerlof and Kranton 2010), which is not particularly sophisticated in its delineation of identity compared with, say, the more extensive treatment offered by the disciplines of sociology and psychology (Teschl 2010). However, in this context its insight that individuals have multiple identities, operating in parallel, each of which is supported by particular social norms that define acceptable behaviours for that identity, is useful. It admits the claim that, if unethical behaviour is acceptable to finance professionals, it will be triggered by an appeal to their professional identity. The other professional groups in the same experiment do not react to the engagement of their professional identity.

Cohn's experiment, although not without its critics (Vranka and Houdek 2015), is offering a more sophisticated response around the spectrum of values versus environmental factors. Its findings are based upon responses to a financial incentives experiment involving self-reporting leading directly to financial gain. This is much closer to a replication of the real world location of bankers than the other studies that found bankers as a group to espouse values no different from those of the general population. Cohn's experiment tested their respondents for individual triggers for unethical behaviour. It was able to discount pure financial gain, without more, and competition for success (with success being framed as 'the best at what you do'), cross-checked against the sample's view of the amount of misreporting their fellow respondents were engaged in, as co-requisites for unethical behaviour.

What this seems to suggest is that achieving cultural change in the financial services sector is more complex than external regulators imposing controls designed to curb individual risk-taking, and also more complex than firms undertaking to restructure their reward mechanisms. Finance professionals operate according to a number of interconnected norms and values, rather than single imperatives. This professional identity is located within an organisational culture in which at least some of those norms will be present in the bottom two layers of Schein's pyramid. Long before Business Anthropology emerged as a field of study in its own right (Westney and van Maanen 2011), a number of high quality ethnographies set in financial sector firms emerged. They paint a picture of the motivations and social norms under which financial business is conducted. From these we can obtain a better understanding of the professional identity to which Cohn drew attention. The subjects of these studies vary; from investment bankers (Ho 2009) to floor traders (Abolafia 1996; Zaloom 2006) and each has a particular focus. For Ho, it is to examine the role that investment bankers play in shaping US corporations, as they move towards globalisation and financialisation. For Zaloom, it is to track the impact of the introduction of digital trading technologies into trading rooms. Only for Abolafia is it a desire to explore the forces that shape the world of the trader. Nevertheless, what can be gleaned from these accounts about the personal characteristics and values of financial market professionals is that there is a considerable degree of commonalty between them, despite the breadth of the occupational role.

The world of the banker

According to Ho, bankers see themselves as very different from other employees in the firm, such as those staff, accountants for example, who provide back office support functions. Those staff are portrayed as inefficient and unproductive, whereas bankers are an elite. The lack of respect for support functions, particularly human resources (HR), is confirmed by the Salz Review, which identified it as one of the reasons why HR could not successfully intervene in the running of Barclays in the years immediately before the GFC (Salz Review 2013: 8, 87 and 120).

This difference between back office functions and banking functions is captured by Cohn, who reports that the professional identity salience that his experiment identified for those in the banking industry was lower for those in support units, such as HR, than it was for those in core units. The price of the finance professionals' position is that they have little job security and work very long hours (Ho 2009: 97–99; Mandis 2013: 72–73). The reward for their labours, they acknowledge, is very good, but offset by the precariousness of their position (Ho 2009: 213–19; Mandis 2013: 79–82). Zaloom and Wexler report a similar position in relation to traders. Traders see themselves as self-reliant, self-disciplined and self-governed, living on their wits and using their individual skills to balance risk and reward (Zaloom 2006: 104–109; Wexler 2010: 15). They become totally absorbed in the logic of the market and talk of the need to cut their losses if necessary and move with the market (Abolafia 1996: 28). They need to signal confidence in themselves and their judgments to others, and so require a high degree of self-belief (Wexler 2010: 17). Vigilance, interpreted as the ability to assimilate and evaluate large amounts of information, and intuitive judgment, based on experience and careful observation of others, are seen as essential skills (Abolafia 1996: 23–27).

Traders have no stake in the organisation they work for; they do not expect career advancement within the structure of the firm they are employed by. Instead advancement, consequent upon success, is likely to mean moving to another firm with more opportunities and bigger trading limits. The absence of client relationships, as investment banks have expanded and embraced a higher reliance on proprietary trading as a profit generator and the digitalisation of trading, means an absence of socialisation in the workplace (Zaloom 2006: 55, 144; Wexler 2010: 18; cf. Beunza and Stark 2004: 378–82).

Both Mandis in his account of the demise of Goldman Sachs and the Salz Review of Barclays business practices comment on how traders had a singular view of their role and operated outwith what others saw as the prevailing organisational culture (Mandis 2013: 143,162,163; Salz Review 2013: 6, 65, 80). The demands of the organisation upon their time, and their financial interdependence (especially for investment bankers), remove them from wider social circles and thrust them into intense social networks with each other (Mandis 2013: 78, 82). Given their trust in each other, it is perhaps no great shock that the Parliamentary Commission on Banking Standards in the UK (2013: 18) found that there was an industry-wide reluctance to police or report unethical behaviour noticed in others.

Gino and Bazerman suggest that individuals accept the ethical failings of others if standards of behaviour slip, or are allowed to slip, over time rather than abruptly. A gradual erosion of ethical standards that meets with little resistance in a close-knit professional community is not particularly surprising (Gino and Bazerman 2009). Cohn's professional identity appears to be occupied by a group of independent, self-reliant and confident individuals who work very hard and see themselves as highly skilled. They value risk-taking in themselves and others and are socially self-referential. It is these occupationally demanded dispositions that have to be accommodated within the cultural reconstruction that firms in the financial sector are promising they will deliver.

A top-down perspective on the ethical settings of firms reveals what Mandis describes as 'organizational drift' (Mandis 2013: 266) in the context of Goldman Sachs. He identifies this as changes in the organisation that had not been planned for or then controlled once they occurred. The four factors that produced changes are named as four different pressures – organisational, regulatory, competitive and technological – that bore down on the Goldman Sachs business structure. The Salz Review confirms that Barclays experienced many of the same pressures, with the same drift occurring, taking Barclays away from long-established governance structures (Salz Review 2013: 6–10). The repeal of the Glass–Steagall legislation by the Financial Services Modernization Act in 1999 and the equivalent Big Bang of 1986 in the UK, otherwise known as the deregulation of the London Stock Exchange, saw the rapid expansion of financial sector firms into new trading areas and the arrival of competition for investment capital (Mandis 2013: 93–94; Salz Review 2013: 23–25).

The identity and ethos of firms changed as new and expanding ventures became silos with their own business plans and differential appetites for risk. Internal communications became difficult and diffused. There was an absence of central control and oversight (Mandis 2013: 98; Salz Review 2013: 6, 10, 109, 122). The 2008 acquisition of Lehman Brothers is identified as a key point in Barclays' loss of organisational shape (Salz Review 2013: 36) but, in the years preceding that acquisition, investment banking had steadily become a larger and larger part of its activities. By 2007, it accounted for some 30 per cent of its business. A similar shift occurred at Goldman Sachs in relation to proprietary trading (Mandis 2013: 142–49).

Shareholder pressure for profit replaced the more watchful gaze of partners carrying personal liability (Salz Review 2013: 25; Mandis 2013: 118–19, 156–62) at the same time as technology was creating information transparency, so reducing the margins available in transactions. Volume trades became hugely important. The upsurge in trading activity typifies the changes in the cultural landscape, identified from both top-down and bottom-up accounts of life in the firm – internal silos, lack of socialisation and loss of central control. There is no reason to think that Goldman Sachs and Barclays were the only financial sector firms where this occurred (Gill and Sher 2012), and where a technocratic mind-set saw reliance on legal or regulatory structures as a permissive green light for practices which the exercise of ethical judgment might have vetoed with a red light (Mandis 2013: 173–74; Salz Review 2013: 71, 82).

Achieving cultural change: not so fast

Schein offers a model of cultural change that is nested in his idea of sub-cultures (Schein 1985). He identifies three sub-cultures as being present in every organisation: executive sub-culture, operator sub-culture and professional sub-culture.

Cultural change can only come from the executive sub-culture level; in other words, it must be introduced by the *fiat* or example of the organisation's leaders. However, to be effective, new values that embody the cultural change must be absorbed into the unconscious assumptions of the organisation's culture and all three sub-cultures must be aligned. This means that those working within the organisation, outside of leadership positions, must also own the proposed new values (Schein 1984). For Schein, then, these new values have to permeate the pyramid of organisational culture and be integrated into it. This permeation is achieved not by boldly asserting that the culture needs to be changed, but by focusing on the issues that need to be addressed and how they will be addressed. Significantly for financial sector firms, Schein doubts that the deepest of an organisation's underlying assumptions can be changed (Sathe and Davidson 2000: 283).

Schein and Bennis (1965), drawing on Lewin (Lewin 1951), identify three stages in a process model for cultural change: there has to be a motivation for change (or an unfreezing, as Lewin (1951) describes it); there has to be organisational learning around new concepts and standards – a reinvigoration of judgment if you like; and an internalising of those new concepts and standards across the organisation. At the first stage, a sense of psychological safety is very important, as disconfirming evidence reveals the need for change and inevitably causes anxiety (Meyerson and Martin 1987). This anxiety is centred on the fear of loss of status and identity within the organisation. Consequently, psychological safety is secured by the organisation's leaders adopting a number of measures that address this fear: the adoption of a compelling case for change, formal and informal training, structures that support the changes and employee involvement.

Cultural change requires changing behaviours and changing attitudes. Intrinsic motivations which tend to effect attitude and value change and extrinsic motivations, which pull on behaviour change, have a role to play here. The dominant view within the psychology literature (less so from the standpoint of economic theory – see Gneezy, Meier and Rey-Biel 2011) about the relative importance of intrinsic and extrinsic motivations, is that intrinsic motivation is more important to the cultural change project (Deci, Koestner and Ryan 1999). Intrinsic motivations address the key area for cultural change, that of changing values, whilst extrinsic motivations produce only short-term change and reactive behaviour (Bénabou and Tirole 2003). Insofar as extrinsic motivation has a role in culture change, encouragement and recognition are considered to be more important than compensation (Litwin, Bray and Brooke 1996).

This position might come under pressure in the context of changing the culture of financial sector firms. There, the pre-GFC position was that compensation and recognition were synonymous with each other; high levels of compensation were used to signal personal recognition and value to the firm and were awarded for taking large risks (Rajan 2008; Mandis 2013: 136). The identification of compensation practices as problematic and needing to be redesigned (in the context of the internal structures of the firm and in addition to external regulatory requirements – see Smith 2010), does not take the agenda for cultural change very far forward in the circumstances set out above. If it is the case that compensation is not the most significant motivator vis-à-vis misconduct, then restructuring remuneration policy will not achieve the required cultural shift. However, for traders compensation would appear to be the only significant lever available, either intrinsically or extrinsically, given their place within the organisational structure and how they view themselves. Encouragement, recognition and other extrinsic motivations would not appear to be motivating factors in the accounts of their working life, as are referred to above. The dependence of many financial sector professionals on the compensation lever presents something of a difficulty for the leadership of financial sector firms. Discouraging high risk transactions and changing ideas about the function of financial products – through a change of values – would require finding other motivational tools, intrinsic ones at that, in a business sector where both symbolically and materially compensation is hugely significant (Wright 2010).

In his evidence to the Parliamentary Commission on Banking Standards (2013: 356–57), David Walker, then chairman of Barclays, was confident that cultural change could be accomplished and accomplished quickly. On closer examination, it seems that his promise of a quick rebuild of corporate culture was a promise that involved only moving through Schein's initial unfreezing stage. Other financial services sector firms have also announced that they are participating in unfreezing activities: Deutsche Bank, J P Morgan, Citigroup, Bank of America and Wells Fargo for example (Glazer and Rexrode 2015a). Typically, these activities consist of stakeholder engagement (see for example Goldman Sachs 2011: 9–11) and employee surveys to identify what is wrong with the culture of the organisation, often commissioned from professional consultancy firms and costing many thousands of dollars (Glazer and Rexrode 2015b) as, indeed, did the Salz Review (Mullin 2013). The Salz Review more realistically forecasts that moving from stage one of cultural change – unfreezing – to stage two – organisational learning – would take some considerable time, if it is achievable at all (Salz Review 2013: 94, 195).

Barclays' response to the Salz Review was published in April 2013 (Barclays 2013) and unsurprisingly it committed itself to implementing all of the Salz Review recommendations. The measures that it undertakes to put in place are very similar to those identified by Goldman Sachs, J P Morgan Chase and others in the sector (Goldman Sachs 2011; J P Morgan Chase 2014; Deutsche Bank 2013). They are relatively easy initiatives to insert into an organisation, in the hope that they form the basis of intrinsic motivations for change. A strengthened values statement and a reinforced code of conduct are promised for the whole firm, irrespective of function.

These are not new ideas. They were popular across financial sector firms before the GFC. Post GFC, these strengthened statements and codes are going to be driven into the culture of firms through an intensive training programme, beginning with the organisations' leaders – again these sorts of initiatives were common before the GFC (Treviño, Weaver, Gibson and Toffler 1999). Employees will receive training on an ongoing basis and not just as a single event. Employees will be required to state their compliance with the Code on an annual basis and employee performance assessment will be concerned with not only 'what' has been achieved but also 'how' it has been achieved. Employee recruitment will involve employees being assessed for 'cultural alignment' to values and being inducted into the organisation, by means of a values-driven induction programme. There is a place for enhanced whistle-blowing, more properly described as 'issue escalation', schemes that offer greater protection to employees.

These are all laudable attempts at cultural change. Continuing endorsement of value positions by those in leadership roles is very important (Schminke, Ambrose and Neubaum 2005), as is new employee acceptance of an organisation's values. However, there is little indication of how these things will be achieved and how they will be measured. Goldman Sachs talks about the importance of recognition for its employees (Goldman Sachs 2011: 56), presumably as a counterpoint to the promised new compensation policies, but what form that recognition will take or how it will be assessed is missing.

It seems unlikely that a values statement or code that covers the whole of a firm's operations will provide sufficient detail or material of relevance to gain employee traction (De Bruin 2014: 266), even though the problem of differential perceptions of values across different functions within firms has been identified as a core problem. Treviño and her colleagues provide some comfort on this point, by telling us that the specific contents of an ethics code matter less in terms of effectiveness than employees' perceptions of its adoption by the organisation's leadership (Treviño, Hartman and Brown 2000), and that codes' embeddedness into the organisation as values rather than as a negative protection from legal or regulatory liability are more likely to gain traction (Treviño, Nieuwenboer and Kish-Gephart 2014). However, the point about recognition of organisational membership by employees such as traders remains. A reward or compensation strategy that is linked to ethical code compliance risks jeopardising its adoption in any long-term sense as this can only be secured by the internal motivations represented by the intrinsic dimension (Treviño and Youngblood 1990). Training for ethical behaviour and ethical decision-making is considered to be far from a certain success (Waples, Antes, Murphy, Connelly and Mumford 2009) unless training is focused first on moral reasoning and then on particular situated ethical dilemmas.

Conclusion

This chapter has drawn attention to the link between firm culture and regulation. It has also looked at the setting in which financial sector professionals conduct their work lives and at how that setting might be changed by firms themselves. There has been considerable noise from within the sector in the years since the GFC and particularly since the Libor and forex scandals about culture change and the measures that were being introduced to achieve it. Until there are further scandals, which have their roots after full implementation of recent changes (and, of course, there may be no future substantial scandal, or it might takes years for one to come to light, as for example Libor did), it will be impossible to say whether any or all of these interventions have unfrozen firm culture and moved it through Schein's subsequent two stages of cultural change. Interim assessment does not give grounds for optimism.

In 2013 Goldman Sachs produced a report of its activity in relation to its review of business standards that took place in 2010 (Goldman Sachs 2013). As O'Brien points out, the report is defensive in tone. There is much discussion of reputational risk and the importance of accountability but little concrete information on whether culture and values adoption has been tested in any way. Enhanced levels of disclosure are not revealed to be as a result of regulatory intervention and regulatory settlement requirements, leaving the impression that they are voluntary initiatives (O'Brien 2014). Observers might have hoped for a more convincing and dynamic account of how operating culture has been rebuilt. In May 2015, Tenbrunsel and Thomas, as authors of a survey for Labaton Sucharow LLP, surveyed 1200 financial sector professionals in the UK and the US, a repeat of a study that they had conducted in 2012. Their context for the 2015 study was the changed regulatory climate; however, it could just as easily have been the promised culture change that was the impetus. Their findings are depressing if instructive; more than one-third of employees have knowledge of unethical behaviour occurring in their own workplace, more than one-third of employees reported that they would behave unethically to obtain a large financial benefit with a disproportionate number of these being employees with less than 10 years' service in the sector and one-third of employees considered that their employer's compensation scheme incentivised unethical behaviour (Labaton Sucharow 2015). The position reported to be adopted by relatively recent recruits to the profession is particularly troubling.

The outworking of cultural reform in financial firms may, as Tracey McDermott, Director of Enforcement and Financial Crime at the Financial Conduct Authority suggested in a speech in December 2014 at the FCA's Enforcement Conference, take a generation to become the accepted *credo* (McDermott 2014). Alternatively, the flat hierarchies and nodal structures of this type of employment, coupled with the possibilities of substantial financial gain without the personal liability of partnership, may mean that culture is firmly set and resistant to change.

References

Aalbers, M, 2008, 'The financialization of home and the mortgage market crisis', *Competition and Change*, 12(2), 148–66.

Abolafia, M, 1996, *Making Markets*, Cambridge, Mass: Harvard University Press.

Akerlof, G and Kranton, R, 2010, *Identity Economics: How our Identities Shape Our Work, Wages, and Wellbeing*, Princeton: Princeton University Press.

Alvesson, M and Sveningsson, S, 2008, *Changing Organizational Culture*, Abingdon: Routledge.

Ashforth, B and Anand, V, 2003, 'The normalization of corruption in organizations', *Research in Organizational Behavior*, 25, 1–52.

Baldwin, R and Black, J, 2008, 'Really responsive regulation', *Modern Law Review*, 71(1), 59–94.

Bamberger, K and Mulligan, D, 2011, 'New governance, chief privacy officers, and the corporate management of information privacy in the United States: an initial inquiry', *Law and Policy*, 33(4), 477–508.

Bandura, A, 1991, 'Social cognitive theory of moral thought and action', in Kurtines, W and Gewirtz, J (eds), *Handbook of Moral Behavior and Development* Volume 1, 45-103, Hillsdale NJ: Erlbaum Publishers.

Barclays, 2013, *Barclays response to the Salz Review* (25 April 2014), London: Barclays http://www.barclays.com/content/dam/barclayspublic/documents/news/471-392-250413-salz-response.pdf (last accessed 26 September 2015).

Bénabou, R and Tirole, J, 2003, 'Intrinsic and extrinsic motivation', *Review of Economic Studies*, 70, 489–520.

Bennett, R and Kottasz, R, 2012, 'Public attitudes towards the UK banking industry following the global financial crisis', *International Journal of Bank Marketing*, 30(2), 128–47.

Beunza, D and Stark, D, 2004, 'Tools of the trade: the socio-technology of arbitrage in a Wall Street trading room', *Industrial and Corporate Change*, 13(2), 369–400.

Black, J, 2012, 'Paradoxes and failures: "New governance" techniques and the financial crisis', *Modern Law Review*, 75(6), 1037–63.

Black, J and Baldwin, R, 2010, 'Really Responsive Risk-Based Regulation', *Law & Policy*, 32(2), 181–213.

Brown, A, 2005, 'Making sense of the collapse of Barings Bank', *Human Relations* 58(12), 1579–1604.

Cohn, A, Fehr, E and Maréchal, M, 2014, 'Business culture and dishonesty in the banking industry', *Nature*, 516, 86–89.

Davies, H, 2010, *The Financial Crisis: Who is to Blame?*, Cambridge: Polity.

De Bruin, B, 2014, 'Ethics management in banking and finance', in Morris, N and Vines, D (eds), *Capital Failure*, Oxford: OUP, 255–76.

de Goede, M, 2009, 'Finance and the excess', *Zeitschrift für Internationale Beziehungen*, 16 (H2), 299–310.

Deci, E, Koestner, R and Ryan, M, 1999, 'A meta-analytic review of experiments examining the effects of extrinsic rewards on intrinsic motivation', *Psychological Bulletin*, 125(6), 627–68.

Deutsche Bank 2013 'Intensified oversight of ethics', *Corporate Culture and Corporate Values*, Frankfurt am Main: Deutsche Bank AG https://www.db.com/cr/en/concrete-cultural-change.htm (last accessed 26 September 2015).

Dudley, W, 2014, 'Enhancing financial stability by improving culture in the financial services industry', Speech to the Workshop on Reforming Culture and Behavior in the Financial Services Industry, Federal Reserve Bank of New York, New York City http://www.newyorkfed.org/newsevents/speeches/2014/dud141020a.html (last accessed 26 September 2015).

Edelman, L and Talesh, S, 2011, 'To comply or not to comply – that isn't the question: how organizations construct the meaning of compliance', in Parker, C and Nielsen, V (eds), *Explaining Compliance*, Cheltenham: Edward Elgar, 103–122.

Engelen, E, Ertürk I, Froud, J, Johal, S, Leaver, A, Moran, M and Williams, K, 2012,

'Misrule of experts? The financial crisis as elite debacle', *Economy and Society*, 41(3), 360–82.

Financial Reporting Council, 2014, *The UK Corporate Governance Code* https://www.frc.org.uk/Our-Work/Publications/Corporate-Governance/UK-Corporate-Governance-Code-2014.pdf (last accessed 8 October 2015).

Financial Services Authority, 2012, Final Notice 2012: UBS AG (19 December 2012) http://www.fca.org.uk/your-fca/documents/final-notices/2013/fsa-final-notice-2012-ubs-ag-19th-dec (last accessed 26 September 2015).

Financial System Inquiry 2014, Final Report, November, Canberra http://fsi.gov.au/files/2014/12/FSI_Final_Report_Consolidated20141210.pdf (last accessed 26 September 2015).

Financial Stability Board, 'Progress report on the oversight and governance framework for financial benchmark reform: Report to G20 Finance ministers and Central Bank Governors' (Report, Financial Stability Board, 29 August 2013) 2 http://www.financialstabilityboard.org/wp-content/uploads/r_130829f.pdf (last accessed 8 October 2015).

Finch, J, 2009, 'No more Mr Nice Guy – Hector Sants is Dirty Harry', *The Guardian*, (13 March 2009).

Ford, C, 2010, 'New Governance in the teeth of human frailty: lessons from financial regulation', *Wisconsin Law Rev*, 441–87.

Ford, C and Hess, D, 2011, 'Corporate monitorships and new governance regulation: in theory, in practice, and in context', *Law and Policy*, 33(4) 509–41.

Garrett, B, 2007, 'Structured reform prosecution', *Virginia Law Rev*, 93, 853–957.

Garrett, B, 2014, *Too Big to Jail*, Cambridge, Mass: Harvard University Press.

Gill, A and Sher, M, 2012, 'Inside the minds of the money minders', in Long, S and Sievers, B (eds), *Towards a Socioanalysis of Money, Finance and Capitalism*, Abingdon: Routledge 68.

Gilligan, G, 2011, 'Jérôme Kerviel the "Rogue trader" of Société Générale: bad luck, bad apple, bad tree or bad orchard?', *The Company Lawyer*, 32(12), 355–62.

Gino, F and Bazerman, M, 2009, 'When misconduct goes unnoticed: the acceptability of gradual erosion in others' unethical behaviour', *The Journal of Experimental Social Psychology*, 45:4, 708–19.

Glazer, E and Rexrode, C, 2015a, 'What banks are doing to improve their culture', *Wall Street Journal* (2 February 2015).

Glazer, E, and Rexrode, C, 2015b, 'As regulators focus on culture, Wall Street struggles to define it', *Wall Street Journal* (1 February 2015).

Gneezy, U, Meier, S, and Rey-Biel, P, 2011, 'When and why incentives (don't) work to modify behavior', *J of Econ Perspectives*, 25(4), 1–21.

Goldberg, L, 1990, 'An alternative 'description of personality': the big-five factor structure', *Journal of Personality and Social Psychology*, 59(6), 1216–29.

Goldman Sachs, 2011, *Report of the Business Standards Committee*, (January 2011), New York: Goldman, Sachs & Co http://www.goldmansachs.com/who-we-are/business-standards/committee-report/business-standards-committee-report-pdf.pdf(last accessed 26 September 2015).

Goldman Sachs, 2013, http://www.goldmansachs.com/a/pgs/bsc/files/GS-BSC-Impact-Report-May-2013.pdf (last accessed 26 September 2015).

Gray, W and Shadbegian, R, 2005, 'When and why do plants comply? Paper mills in the 1980s', *Law and Policy*, 27, 238–61.

Gunningham, N, 2009, 'Environmental law, regulation and governance: shifting architectures', *J of Environmental Law*, 21(2), 179–212.

Gunningham, N, Kagan, B and Thornton, D, 2004, 'Social license and environmental protection: why businesses go beyond compliance', *Law and Social Inquiry*, 29, 307–41.

Heimer, C, 2013, 'Resilience in the middle: contributions of regulated organizations to regulatory success', *Annals of Am Acad Pol & Soc Sci*, 639, 139–56.

Ho, K, 2009, *Liquidated*, Durham, NC: Duke University Press.

Hofstede, G, Bram, N, Daval, O and Geert, S, 1990, 'Measuring organizational cultures: a qualitative and quantitative study across twenty cases', *Administrative Science Quarterly*, 35, 286–316.

Holtbrügge, D, Baron, A and Friedmann, C, 2014, 'Personal attributes, organizational conditions and ethical attitudes: a social cognitive approach', *Business Ethics: A European Review*, online first (14 October 2014).

Jones, T, 1991, 'Ethical decision-making by individuals in organizations: an issue contingent model', *Academy of Management Review*, 16, 366–395.

J P Morgan Chase, 2014, How We Do Business – The Report (19 December 2014), New York: J P Morgan Chase, http://investor.shareholder.com/jpmorganchase/how-we-do-business.cfm (last accessed 11 December 2015).

Kay, J, 2012, 'The Kay Review of UK equity markets and long-term decision-making: final report' (Report, HM Government, July 2012).

Keasey, K and Veronesi, G, 2008, 'Lessons from the Northern Rock affair', *Journal of Financial Regulation and Compliance*, 16, 8–18.

Khanna, V, 2011, 'Reforming the monitor', in Barkow, A and Barkow, R (eds), *Prosecutors in the Boardroom*, New York: New York University Press, 226–48.

Labaton Sucharow, 2015, 'The street, the bull and the crisis: a survey of the US and UK financial services industry' www.secwhistlebloweradvocate.com/LiteratureRetrieve.aspx?ID=224757 (last accessed 26 September 2015).

Langevoort, D, 2009, 'The SEC and the Madoff scandal: three Narratives in search of a story', *Mich St L Rev*, 899–914.

Laufer, W, 1999, 'Corporate liability, risk shifting and the paradox of compliance', *Vand L Rev*, 52, 1341–1420.

Lenglet, M, 2012, 'Ambivalence and ambiguity: the interpretative role of compliance officers', in Huault, I and Richard, C (eds), *Finance: The Discreet Regulator*, Basingstoke: Palgrave Macmillan, 59–84.

Lerner, J, 2006, 'The new financial thing: the origins of financial innovations', *J of Fin Econ*, 79(2), 223–55.

Litwin, G, Bray, J and Brooke, K, 1996, *Mobilizing the Organization: Bringing Strategy to Life*, Englewood Cliffs NJ: Prentice Hall.

Lewin, K, 1951, *Field Theory in Social Science*, New York: Harper and Row.

Mandis, S, 2013, *What Happened to Goldman Sachs?*, Cambridge, Mass: Harvard Business Review Press.

Marshall, J, Pike, A, Pollard, J, Tomaney, J, Dawley, S and Gray, J, 2012, 'Placing the run on Northern Rock', *J of Econ Geog*, 12(1), 157–81.

Matthews, K and Matthews, O, 2010, 'Controlling bankers' bonuses: efficient regulation or politics of envy', *Economic Affairs*, 30(1), 71–76.

McDermott, T, 2014, 'Learning the lessons of the past as an industry', speech, 2 December 2014, London: Financial Conduct Authority http://www.fca.org.uk/news/learning-the-lessons-of-the-past-as-an-industry (last accessed 26 September 2015).

Meyerson, D and Martin, J, 1987, 'Cultural change: an integration of three different views', *J of Man Studies*, 24(6), 623–47.

Mullin, K, 2013, 'Salz and the £15m Barclays travesty', *International Financing Review* (8 April 2013) http://www.ifre.com/salz-and-the-15m-barclays-travesty/21078296.full article (last accessed 26 September 2015).

O'Brien, J, 2013, 'Professional obligation, ethical awareness and capital market regulation: an achievable Goal or a contradiction in terms', Working Paper, *Centre for Law, Markets and Regulation* www.clmr.unsw.edu.au (last accessed 26 September 2015).

O'Brien, J, 2014, 'Professional obligation, ethical awareness and capital market regulation', in Morris, N and Vines, D (eds), *Capital Failure*, Oxford: OUP, 209–33.

O'Brien, J and Dixon, O, 2014, 'Deferred prosecutions in the corporate sector: lessons from LIBOR', *Seattle University Law Review*, 37(2), 475–509.

Parliamentary Commission on Banking Standards, 'Changing banking for good – Volume I' (Report, HM Parliament, 19 June 2013).

Rajan, R, 2008, 'Bankers' pay is deeply flawed', *Financial Times* (8 January 2008).

Rusch, H, 2015, 'Do bankers have deviant moral attitudes? Negative results from a tentative survey', *Rationality, Markets and Morals*, 6, 6–20.

Salz, A, 2013, *Salz Review: An Independent Review of Barclays' Business Practices*, London: Barclays PLC, https://www.home.barclays/content/dam/barclayspublic/documents/news/875-269-salz-review-04-2013.pdf (last accessed 11 December 2015).

Sants, H, 2010, 'Can culture be regulated?', Speech at Mansion House Conference (4 October 2010) http://www.fsa.gov.uk/pages/Library/Communication/Speeches/2010/1004_hs.shtml (last accessed 26 September 2015).

Sassen, S, 2012, 'Expanding the terrain for global capital: when local housing becomes an electronic instrument', in Aalbers, M (ed), *The Political Economy of Mortgage Markets*, Oxford: Wiley Blackwell, 74–96.

Sathe, V and Davidson, E, 2000, 'Toward a new conceptualization of cultural change', in Ashkanasy, N, Wilderom, C and Peterson, M (eds), *Handbook of Organizational Culture and Change*, London: Sage, 279–96.

Schein, E, 1984, 'Coming to a new awareness of organizational culture', *Sloan Management Review*, 25(2), 3–16.

Schein, E, 1985, *Organizational Culture and Leadership*, San Francisco, CA: Jossey Bass.

Schein, E, 1996, 'Culture: the missing concept in organization studies', *Administrative Science Quarterly*, 46(2), 229–40.

Schein, E and Bennis, W, 1965, *Personal and Organizational Change*, London: John Wiley.

Schifferes, S and Roberts, R, 2015, *The Media and Financial Crises*, Abingdon: Routledge.

Schminke, M, Ambrose, M and Neubaum, D, 2005, 'The effect of leader moral development on ethical climate and employee attitudes', *Orgainizational Behavior and Human Decision Processes*, 97(2), 135–51.

Smirich, L, 1983, 'Concepts of culture and organizational analysis', *Administrative Science Quarterly*, 28, 339–58.

Smith, N, 2010, 'Reforming the bonus culture', *Butterworths Journal of International Banking and Financial Law*, (January 2010) 37–39.

Spira, L and Slinn, J, 2013, *The Cadbury Committee*, Oxford: OUP.

Teschl, M, 2010, 'Identity economics: towards a more realistic economic agent', *J of Economic Methodology*, 17(4), 445–48.

The Economist, 2012, 'First mover disadvantage' (7 July 2012).

Tomasic, R, 2010, 'Beyond "Light touch" regulation of British banks after the financial crisis', in MacNeil, I and O'Brien, J (eds), *The Future of Financial Regulation*, Oxford: Hart, 103–24.

Treviño, L and Youngblood, S, 1990, 'Bad apples in bad barrels: a causal analysis of ethical decision-making behavior', *J of Applied Psychology*, 75(4), 378–85.

Treviño, L, Weaver, G, Gibson, D and Toffler, B, 1999, 'Managing ethics and legal compliance: what works and what hurts', *Calif Man Rev*, 41(2), 131–51.

Treviño, L, Hartman, L, and Brown, M, 2000, 'Moral person and moral manager: how executives develop a reputation for ethical leadership', *Calif Man Rev*, 42(4), 128–42.

Treviño, L, Weaver, G and Reynolds, S, 2006, 'Behavioral ethics in organizations: a review', *J of Management*, 32(6), 951–90.

Treviño, L, den Nieuwenboer, N and Kish-Gephart, J, 2014, '(Un)Ethical behavior in organizations', *Annu Rev Psychol*, 65, 635–60.

Turner, A, 2012, 'Adair Turner on BOE Job & Banking Culture' video, (24 July 2012), Bloomberg News http://www.bloomberg.com/news/videos/b/4034f4fc-8506-498d-b034-92487c40fa88 (last accessed 26 September 2015) at 1.22.

van Hoorn, A, 2015, The Global Financial Crisis and the Values of Professionals in Finance: An Empirical Analysis, *Journal of Business Ethics*, 130, 253–269.

Vranka, M and Houdek, P, 2015, 'Many faces of bankers' identity: how (not) to study dishonesty', *Frontiers in Psychology*, 6, 302.

Walker, D, 2009, *A review of corporate governance in UK banks and other financial industry entities. Final recommendations*, (26 November 2009), London: The Walker review secretariat http://webarchive.nationalarchives.gov.uk/+/http:/www.hm-treasury.gov.uk/d/walker_review_261109.pdf (last accessed 8 October 2015).

Waples, E, Antes, A, Murphy, S, Connelly, S and Mumford, M, 2009, 'A meta-analytic investigation of business ethics instruction', *JBE*, 87(1), 133–51.

Weait, M, 1994, 'The role of the compliance officer in firms carrying on investment businesses', *Butterworths Journal of International Banking and Financial Law*, 9(8), 381–84.

Westney, E and van Maanen, J, 2011, 'The casual ethnography of the executive suite', *Journal of International Business*, 42(5), 602–607.

Wexler, M, 2010, 'Financial edgework and the persistence of rogue traders', *Business and Society Review*, 115(1), 1–25.

Whittle, A and Mueller, F, 2011, 'Bankers in the dock: moral storytelling in action', *Human Relations*, 65(1), 111–39.

Wright, A, 2010, 'Culture and compensation: Unpicking the intricate relationship between reward and organizational culture', *Thunderbird International Business Review*, 52(3), 189–202.

Zaloom, C, 2006, *Out of the Pits*, Chicago: Chicago University Press.

Chapter 5

Culture as cash: from bonus to *malus*

Jay Cullen

Rebuilding trust in banks has been one of the most contentious challenges for governments across Western jurisdictions since the global financial crisis (GFC). A consequence of the massive economic costs imposed by widespread bank failures was that regulatory reform to the financial sector has taken centre stage, with politicians across countries galvanised to lead a comprehensive programme of initiatives to reform the financial system. Further, as a result of the unavoidable rescues of large financial institutions and unprecedented central bank interventions in financial markets, public interest considerations now occupy a much more significant position in the overarching legal, political and governance arrangements that apply to banking institutions and their employees.

Arguably, the United Kingdom (UK) suffered more economic damage than any comparable economy from financial institution collapses and there has been a widespread public perception that the crisis was brought about by the reckless conduct of a number of financial system insiders. It is therefore perhaps unsurprising – especially in light of revelations of further post-GFC scandals – that UK law-makers have been so proactive in addressing public concerns about banker conduct.

Reported admissions made recently by the global head of sanctions at HSBC, the UK's largest bank, concerning the 'cast-iron certainty' of future governance failures serve merely to underscore what has become regarded as a systemic problem (Davies and Ball 2015). However, there are also signs of regulatory fatigue (Goodhart and Perotti 2015) and recent comments from the UK chancellor concerning an 'end to banker-bashing' appear to signal the conclusion of the reform agenda (Parker, Binham and Noonan 2015). This therefore seems an appropriate juncture at which to provide a critical evaluation of some recent regulatory amendments.

A principal goal of corporate governance at financial institutions is to prevent or mitigate externalities from excessive risk-taking, capital manipulation and loss dissimulation. However, corporate governance failures have been cited widely as instrumental in causing the GFC. In this context there have been many claims that banking suffered a gradual erosion of ethics, and that this detachment from core principles of business contributed to the excessive risk characteristic of pre-2008 banking (Dudley 2014). On this basis, the untrammelled pursuit of earnings targets encouraged excessive risk and the pursuit of profit 'at all costs', which was valued more than client interests or institutional reputation. The effects of these perceptions are well summarised by Carney (2014a):

> In the run-up to the crisis, banking became about banks not businesses; trans-actions not relations; counterparties not clients. New instruments originally designed to meet the credit and hedging needs of businesses quickly morphed into ways to amplify bets on financial outcomes. When bankers become detached from end-users, their only reward becomes money . . . This reduc-tionist view of the human condition is a poor foundation for ethical financial institutions needed to support long-term prosperity.

According to this narrative, an inherently 'rotten' culture evolved, thanks largely to the contamination in the 1990s of commercial mega-banks by the managerial and operational styles of investment banking (Avgouleas 2015). Discussing culture, Kane (2015) notes that: 'A culture may be defined as customs, ideas, and attitudes that members of a group share and transmit from generation to generation by systems of subtle and unsubtle rewards and punishments'. In consequence, absent proper control culture tends to shape itself, with the danger that the behaviours produced will not be those desired (Salz 2013). In these circumstances, employee behaviours are instead shaped by what is perceived to be rewarded. If rewards become contingent only on financial outcomes, employees will come to believe that these outcomes are what their organisation values.

Of course, in banking financial outcomes are prioritised, particularly at high organisational levels. However, the imparting of these values may produce dam-aging behaviours – in terms of both excessive and unprincipled risk-taking. It is perhaps to be expected that empirical studies evidence that bankers are, on aver-age, more dishonest than other professionals (Cohn, Fehr and Maréchal 2014). Indeed, unethical behaviour has often been tacitly encouraged at large banks (for instance, the now infamous ABACUS CDO scheme devised by Goldman Sachs was designed to fail and inflict losses on some of its clients, whilst accounts of mort-gage brokers selling unaffordable loans to consumers are legion) and recent survey evidence suggests that practices within banking have not changed significantly since the GFC (Wehinger 2013).

In the UK, one of the main tasks of the Parliamentary Commission on Banking Standards (PCBS) (2013) established in the wake of the LIBOR rate-setting pro-cess was to investigate how deep lapses in professional standards and culture in the UK banking sector were allowed to occur. The PCBS concluded that improving standards in the financial sector required reform in four areas:

(i)   ensuring individual and collective accountability for decision-making
(ii) reforming governance standards
(iii) reformulating individual incentives and
(iv) empowering regulators (PCBS 2013).

Accordingly, thanks to the perception that dubious behaviours were rewarded – either implicitly or explicitly – reforms to incentives at financial institutions have been placed at the centre of the regulatory response to the crisis. The purpose of these reforms is to mitigate incentives for excessive risk and to align the interests of individuals with the broader interests of their firms in order to prevent and root out inappropriate behaviour, in the interests of financial stability.

The chief prescribed mechanisms to achieve these aims – compensation reform and the introduction of sanctions for egregious individual conduct – have been widely recommended as front-stop remedies to the amorphous endeavour of carving out a 'revolution' in the culture of retail banking. Certainly, bankers' pay was cited by many reports as a major contributory factor to the 2008 crisis (indicatively, see International Monetary Fund (IMF) 2014) and there was a collective failure amongst managers and shareholders to challenge certain aggressive risk-taking and overt transgression of regulatory provisions. In turn, these failures resulted in considerable public anger at the impotence to punish transgressors of the bounds of acceptable conduct, amid accusations of regulatory capture.

Naturally, if there are substantial systemic and cultural benefits to restricting bankers' pay and introducing penalties for reckless risk-taking, these reforms are worthwhile. However, as I will argue in this chapter, proponents of these reforms pay insufficient regard to some crucial drawbacks of focusing on individual incentives to effect long-term changes in behaviour.

First, there are inherent practical difficulties relating to the credibility and enforcement of sanctions, which together with defects in compensation structure mandates may undermine the effectiveness of new regulations in producing substantive change. Secondly, and more significantly, there are logical flaws in the application of prevailing corporate governance paradigms in relation to banks, which mean incentive-alignment may not be totally effective in reducing risk-taking, due in particular to the following factors: (i) the cognitive biases and limitations of market participants who may be unaware of – or rationally agnostic with regard to – materialising risks; (ii) shareholder preference, which may promote excessive risk-tolerance; and (iii) bankers' motivations for risk-taking beyond compensation targets – in particular pressures from the career market – which may themselves lead to sub-optimal capital structure choices.

An analysis of UK reforms in light of these factors – both practical and normative – reveals that it is at least arguable whether the threat of punishment for inappropriate behaviour, or restricting bankers' compensation incentives over the medium term, will reduce risk-taking behaviour to the extent that threats to financial stability recede significantly or banking culture improves.

The chapter is structured as follows. First, I perform a legal analysis of the most significant reforms made since the GFC to the regulatory framework governing bankers' compensation and sanctioning powers in the UK. Next, I critically discuss these reforms and analyse some of their limitations, in light of the observations above. The following section offers some brief thoughts on further directions that might be pursued in this area, before the chapter concludes.

UK legal reforms to sanctions and incentives

The new sanctions regime: the Financial Services (Banking Reform) Act 2013

On the basis of the recommendations of the PCBS, in 2013, Parliament enacted the Financial Services (Banking Reform) Act. The Act, inter alia, establishes a new 'senior managers' regime' (SMR) at certain financial institutions, which extend the 'approved persons' (AP) regime under the Financial Services and Markets Act 2000. The Act's provisions apply to any person at a financial institution who performs a 'senior management function' (SMF) and requires relevant firms to take reasonable care to ensure that no employees performing 'significant harm functions' as specified by the regulators do so unless the firm has certified them as fit and proper to do so.

Any application to perform an SMF must be accompanied by a 'statement of responsibilities', the purpose of which is to designate the aspects of the bank's business affairs that a senior manager will be responsible for managing, although it is likely that many areas of responsibility will not be assigned to individuals, but instead will remain within the remit of the board. The SMR at banks constitutes: the relevant firm's board and, at larger and more complex firms, the executive committee; heads of key business areas satisfying certain quantitative criteria; individuals in group or parent companies exercising significant influence on the firms' decision-making; and, where appropriate, individuals who are not otherwise approved as senior managers but who are ultimately responsible for important business, control or conduct-focused functions within the firm (Bank of England 2014).

The Act makes members of the SMR responsible for any firm conduct that constitutes a regulatory breach. Members of the SMR are subject to the full range of civil remedies available, including fines, restrictions on responsibilities, and industry bans. In early statements of its legislative intentions the government had indicated the usual burden of proof would be reversed, with members of the relevant SMR – rather than the regulator – liable to demonstrate that the individual member was not guilty of reckless misconduct. This so-called 'presumption of responsibility' would have constituted a significant change to the previous position. However in October 2015 HM Treasury rescinded this provision, instead requiring that for enforcement action to take place, the relevant manager 'did not take such steps as a person in the senior manager's position could reasonably be expected to take to avoid the contravention occurring (or continuing)' (HM Treasury 2015). This concept, known as the 'duty of responsibility', does little more than codify the existing Financial Conduct Authority (FCA) position.

Perhaps most significantly in legal terms, the Act also introduces an offence of 'reckless misconduct', which may be applied in cases of financial institution failure, and makes members of the SMR criminally liable for taking a decision which leads to the failure of a bank, or failing to prevent such a decision being taken, if the senior manager in question was aware of a risk that the implementation of the decision may have caused failure.

For the offence to be proven, three elements must be present: (i) the member of the SMR must take a decision (or fail to prevent a decision being taken) which causes the insolvency of the bank; (ii) the member of the SMR must be aware at the time that the relevant decision (or failure to prevent the decision being taken) could cause that insolvency; and (iii) the conduct in relation to the decision (or failure to prevent the decision being taken) must 'fall far below' what could reasonably be expected of a person in his or her position. Senior managers found guilty of this offence may be jailed for up to seven years (Financial Services Act 2013 section 36). In any such cases, the usual criminal standard for convictions (i.e. 'beyond a reasonable doubt') applies.

New compensation rules: the UK Remuneration Code

In light of the severe doubt cast on the capacity of market-led private contractual bargaining to constrain harmful risk-taking at financial firms, controlling compensation has been afforded special attention, with the consequence that the UK now has some of the most prescriptive compensation rules amongst developed financial centres. The work of the PCBS – together with that of the Financial Stability Board (FSB) Principles for Sound Compensation Practices (FSB 2009) and the provisions of the Fourth EU Capital Requirements Directive (CRD IV) – influenced the widespread changes made to the UK Remuneration Code ('Rem-Code') now issued jointly by the FCA and the Prudential Regulation Authority (PRA). Proposals to refine the Rem-Code further were made in June 2015 and it is anticipated that these changes will be implemented by January 2016 (Bank of England 2015).

The provisions of the Rem-Code apply to all banks, building societies, investment firms and their subsidiaries, although the FCA has reserved the right to apply it to other, smaller entities. Underpinning the Rem-Code are 12 principles covering five thematic spheres, which will now be discussed.

Scope of the rules

The Rem-Code extends the ambit of compensation rules and policies from senior management and the board of directors to include senior traders, as these traders may have significant influence on balance sheet composition and borrowing levels. To this end, the FCA has adopted the European Union (EU) approach, which defines such persons at financial institutions as 'material risk-takers' (MRTs). The European Banking Authority (EBA) issued detailed guidance, which came into force in June 2014, on the determination and categorisation of such persons for regulatory purposes (EU Commission MRT Regulation 604/2014).

Under the EBA's rules, in assessing whether an individual is to be regarded as an MRT, the following factors should be taken into consideration: (i) if the individual's total remuneration exceeds €500,000 per year, subject to the following two caveats: (a) individuals who earn up to €750,000 may be excluded from the cap if it is determined by the employer that the individual is not, in fact, taking or managing risks; and (b) individuals who earn between €750,000 and €1 million may be excluded from the cap if the exclusion is approved by the national regulator, and an individual earning €1 million or more may be excluded from the cap if the exclusion is approved by the EBA itself; and/or (ii) if the individual is part of the 0.3 per cent of staff with the highest remuneration in the institution or firm; and/or (iii) if the individual's remuneration bracket is equal to or greater than the lowest total remuneration of senior management and other risk takers (EU Commission MRT Regulation 604/2014, Article 4(1)(a)).

On this basis, the FCA defines an MRT as any:

> staff including senior management, risk takers, staff engaged in control functions and any employee receiving total remuneration that takes them into the same remuneration bracket as senior management and risk takers, whose professional activities have a material impact on the firm's risk profile.
>
> (FCA, SYSC: 19A.3.4)

Notwithstanding these reforms, recent proposals to amend the Rem-Code mean that some of its provisions will not apply to the full spectrum of employees caught by the above definition; instead, the most restrictive provisions will apply only to members of the SMR (Bank of England 2015). These exceptions are discussed further below.

Mandating long-term pay-for-performance

To promote the alignment of mangers' pay with investor interests, the Rem-Code requires that at least 50 per cent of the variable remuneration of senior executives and other 'high-end' employees be comprised of shares or equivalent instruments which reflect the credit quality of the institution as a going concern or which can be converted to equity in adverse circumstances (for example, contingent convertible bonds) (FCA, SYSC: 19A.3.47).

Linked to this requirement, compensation at large banks must also focus on the longer term. Under the Rem-Code, banks are now required to consider alternative measures of performance to traditional metrics such as earnings per share (EPS) or total shareholder return (TSR), as these may encourage a short-term focus during the life of the compensation plan, yet expose institutions to longer-term risks (FCA, SYSC: 19A.3.23). Accordingly, in assessing a financial firm's performance for the purposes of the award of variable compensation to employees, remuneration committees must have regard principally for the institution's risk-adjusted profits, rather than its earnings (FCA, SYSC: 19.A.3.22–19A.3.23, 19A.3.25).

Additionally, the Rem-Code mandates scales of deferment used to promote long-term objectives by ensuring 'the assessment of performance is set in a multi-year framework' (FCA, SYSC: 19A.3.38). To this end, the Rem-Code requires that a significant proportion of non-fixed compensation (at least 40 per cent) paid to a relevant employee (MRTs whose actions could have a material impact on a firm) is deferred over a period of three to five years (FCA, SYSC: 19.A.3.49). Proposed amendments to the Rem-Code would extend this period to five years for some relevant staff at financial institutions (PRA-designated risk managers with senior, managerial or supervisory roles) and to seven years for the most senior managers, with a further three years for senior managers whose firm is subject to a regulatory investigation (Bank of England 2015). This, as noted above, means some MRTs remain excluded from the Rem-Code's more prescriptive provisions.

In relation to the director of a firm which is particularly large, is organisationally complex and the nature, scope and complexity of its activities is significant, and the remuneration of that director is particularly high (£500,000 or more), the amount of variable pay that must be deferred rises to 60 per cent (FCA, SYSC: 19.A.3.49) (although, under its proportionality guidance, the Rem-Code excludes from these provisions employees whose variable remuneration is no more than 33 per cent of total remuneration and whose total remuneration is no more than £500,000 per annum). Limits are also placed on the vesting of equity awards following the cessation of employment ('golden parachutes') to prevent financial institution employees from simply leaving their role to procure rewards earlier than mandated.

The Rem-Code also requires that financial institutions enforce so-called 'malus', or clawback, provisions which require the relevant firms to require employees return a specified proportion of variable compensation in the event of: (a) participation in or responsibility for conduct which resulted in significant losses to the firm; and/or (b) failure to meet appropriate standards of fitness and propriety. The power to claw back previously awarded compensation may be exercised for up to seven years following the date of the relevant award (FCA, SYSC: 19A.3.51A). The main mechanism through which the clawback would operate is the reduction of unvested deferred compensation, which may be activated when, at a minimum, either there is reasonable evidence of employee misbehaviour or material error, or the firm or the relevant business unit suffers a material downturn in its financial performance or its risk management (FCA, SYSC: 19A.3.52). Recent proposals to extend the ambit of clawback or its enforcement appear to have been abandoned (Bank of England 2015).

Capping variable pay

Loosely regarded as reducing incentives for excessive risk-taking to boost bonus pay, a maximum threshold has been placed on the allowable proportion of variable compensation at financial institutions. Accordingly, the Rem-Code has been amended to reflect the 'bonus cap' provisions of CRD IV, which is applicable to EU-based banks, and all non-EU banks with EU subsidiaries. The cap applies to all MRT staff (see above) at EU banks and all staff at non-EU banks operating in the EU.

The basic operating principle underpinning the cap is the default position that variable compensation is capped at the same level as fixed compensation (1:1). The only permissible variations to the cap are that: (i) with shareholder approval (requiring a supermajority of 66 per cent of eligible shareholders to vote in favour of the higher ratio or, if less than the quorum of 50 per cent of shareholders participate in the vote, at least 75 per cent of voting shareholders approve), the relevant ratio may be raised to up to 1:2 (bonus up to twice salary); and (ii) up to 25 per cent of any bonus may be paid in long-term instruments, deferred for at least five years, valued on a discounted basis (FCA, SYSC: 19A.3.44A–3.44D).

Broadening targets

Finally, the Rem-Code also recommends that non-financial indicators of performance ought to be included in the assessment of employee performance and used as the basis for a significant portion of compensation awards. In particular, the Rem-Code recommends that compensation ought to be adjusted where it can be demonstrated that effective risk management and behavioural norms are not adhered to, and where appropriate, qualitative performance indicators should override metrics of financial performance (FCA, SYSC 19A.3.37). These moves reflect recommendations at the supra-national level (for example, the 2009 EC Commission Remuneration Recommendation states: 'When determining individual performance, non-financial criteria, such as compliance with internal rules and procedures, as well as compliance with the standards governing the relationship with clients and investors should be taken into account') although the extent to which these factors influence remuneration at high levels in banking remains open to question.

Evaluating UK reforms

There is much to be commended in the programme of reforms undertaken by the UK regulatory authorities in recent years. It is of course hoped that the granting of new sanctioning powers under the Financial Services (Banking Reform) Act 2013 to tackle individual recklessness may produce an environment in which compliance with regulation by banking professionals is more likely, and engender a shift towards more responsible banking. Arguably, building a more robust sanctioning regime in relation to the banking sector was necessary (even if its sufficiency remains doubtful). However, in spite of the ethical signposting they provide, due to practical difficulties of detection and enforcement, there is considerable doubt as to whether the new powers for regulators will be sufficient to deter the forms of conduct that the legislation aims to curb. Further, whilst it is widely acknowledged that short-termism in the financial system was exacerbated by certain compensation provisions, it is arguable whether altering remuneration incentives, *a priori*, will instigate any substantive behavioural changes over the long-term, as multi-faceted flaws in the overarching paradigmatic structure of compensation systems remain, which arguably limits their value in reducing risk-taking.

Practical obstacles to effective reform

Tackling egregious conduct

The new enforcement powers under the 2013 Act were introduced largely to combat the claims by senior banking executives during regulatory enquiries that they had no knowledge of any breaches of standards, and consequently escaped accountability for the decisions of subordinates (PCBS 2013). Naturally, these changes will certainly require financial institutions covered by these provisions to institute appropriate governance systems and controls, and improved levels of reporting and information-sharing. However, the main weakness with the imposition of heftier sanctions in relation to financial markets is the conception that these regimes lack 'credible deterrence'. In this context, successful deterrence constitutes:

> [W]hen would-be wrongdoers perceive that the risks of engaging in misconduct outweigh the rewards and when non-compliant attitudes and behaviours are discouraged. Deterrence occurs when persons who are contemplating engaging in misconduct are dissuaded from doing so because they have an expectation of detection and that detection will be rigorously investigated, vigorously prosecuted and punished with robust and proportionate sanctions.
> (International Organisation of Securities Commissioners (IOSCO) 2015)

In the context of financial market activity each of these conditions may be difficult to satisfy. Monitoring and supervisory roles require the employment of scarce resources, and there are significant asymmetries of information and expertise between regulators and supervisees. Prosecuting authorities rarely pursue individuals at firms accused of reckless or illegal conduct, and generally do not seek disgorgement from individuals, even when they have the ability to do so (Langevoort 2007). Whilst there is some evidence that financial sanctions may deter certain forms of conduct (Coffee 2006; Velikonja 2011), attempting to impose liability on individuals, especially at large firms, will be extremely difficult, thanks to the limited resources of enforcement authorities and the deep pockets of the relevant firms (Buell 2007).

Moreover, there are significant difficulties with entrusting the task of monitoring banks and prosecuting bankers to government and finance officials, who are subject to certain difficult-to-overcome biases generated by private interests. These biases render regulators susceptible to capture and manifest themselves particularly as meta-norms of 'regulator helpfulness and information supervision' (Kane 2015). For example, many banking regulators are aware of potential future career opportunities in industry and understand that these opportunities may be lost if they are perceived as being too critical or punishing of banks and their employees.

Further, government officials may put pressure on regulators to dampen the impact of legal rules for fear that banking business will migrate to less-regulated jurisdictions. Such pressures may, inter alia, lead to reluctance to prosecute individuals and to information suppression. These concerns are not without empirical foundation: HM Treasury concluded recently that the erosion of departmental experience and capability brought on by high employee turnover contributed to its failure to respond effectively to the GFC (HM Treasury 2012) and there is a widespread belief that loss concealment may in some circumstances constitute a public good because of the panic it may avert (Holmstrom 2015). The recent climbdown on the 'persumption of responsibility', discussed earlier, will only provide oxygen to accusations of regulatory capture.

The new criminal offence for reckless misconduct under the 2013 Act arguably demonstrates the accuracy of the observation that credible deterrence is absent from the new regime. In the first instance, the high standard of proof required in criminal trials is itself a substantial barrier to successful prosecutions. In this vein, it is unclear how the legal standard of 'recklessness' may be applied to individual decision-making at banks, or how it will be demonstrated that such recklessness was causative of any subsequent distress. Authorities have, perhaps inevitably, cautioned that the relevant thresholds to be met in any prosecutions under the new Act will be very high and that sanctioning powers are expected only to be utilised in very limited circumstances, namely 'in cases involving only the most serious of failings, such as where a bank failed with substantial costs to the taxpayer, lasting consequences for the financial system, or serious harm to customers' (PCBS 2013: 244).

Even in this context, however, how any prosecuting authority will prove, in any case other than one involving exceptional circumstances, that the act of a manager 'caused' the failure of his or her bank, is subject to debate. The opacity of banking business, the vast size and complexity of individual institutions, and the interconnectedness of the financial system – where decisions at one institution cannot easily be divorced from those taken at others – present huge challenges to regulators seeking to satisfy the burden of proof necessary to impose criminal liability. In the case of the GFC, for example, it is clear that many of the decisions taken prior to the banking collapses may have been 'risky' in the sense that any investment carries risk, but they were certainly not 'reckless' (Acharya and Richardson 2009). Moreover, many of the supposed colossal failures of risk management evident at banks prior to the GFC – such as the (eventually) disastrous takeover of ABN Amro by RBS – were emphatically approved by shareholders.

Certainly in the UK prosecutions against individuals in relation to unethical or reckless conduct in financial markets are rare. For example, the introduction of a criminal sanction under the Enterprise Act 2002 against individual corporate directors whose firms engage in cartel activity has resulted in just one prosecution in the last 12 years (Mehta and Bickler 2014). Similarly, recent investigations into the fixing of Libor markets resulted in (as of the time of writing) one criminal conviction in the UK, despite significant documentary evidence being available to prosecutors (Henning and Enrich 2015) and there have been extensive criticisms of the dearth of prosecutions of individuals over the banking crisis as a whole (Raymond 2013).

It is perhaps noteworthy that extreme financial scandals have universally presaged the introduction of more demanding corporate codes and legislation, and this has not prevented the incidence of grand-scale frauds and mismanagements from growing (Rockness and Rockness 2005). Accordingly, there is no guarantee that even the much-upgraded regulatory toolkit provided by the Act will deter excessive risk-taking, or significantly improve the ethical quality of banker behaviour.

Controlling compensation: flawed structures

There is a well developed literature on the link between performance-related pay and shareholder returns (Jensen and Murphy 1990; Boschen and Smith 1995) and over the past two decades the use of equity-based compensation was overtly encouraged at all public corporations (including banks) by regulators and legislatures across Western jurisdictions. In spite of this, there appears to be a glaring paradox at the centre of the Rem-Code's compensation structure requirements. On the one hand, the Rem-Code encourages boards and remuneration committees to set targets which do not provide incentives for bankers to rely wholesale on increasing return on equity (RoE) to capture higher compensation awards. In contrast, however, the Rem-Code also requires that senior executives are paid with significant chunks of equity. Whilst the two are not to be treated as analogous, both equity-based rewards and bonuses based upon RoE may lead to instability-inducing behaviours: the risk-taking incentives provided by equity-based pay are well rehearsed in the literature on compensation systems (Chen, Steiner and Whyte 2006; Mehran and Rosenberg 2007; Suntheim 2010; Cheng, Hong and Scheinkman 2013; DeYoung, Peng and Yan 2013).

Managers rewarded in equity-linked compensation or on the basis of RoE have keen incentives to increase leverage where possible, in the process generating higher gains to equity holders from identical asset returns (Minsky 1986; Bebchuk, Cohen and Spamann 2010), even as equity prices during economic booms may not necessarily reflect the total risk in banks' choices of asset portfolios (Cullen 2014). Accordingly, most of the extreme returns witnessed in the banking sector in the 2000s were a result of higher leverage, rather than more efficient use of capital (Haldane 2012; Guo, Jalal and Khaksari 2010; Moussu and Petit-Romec 2014). Similar patterns were in evidence at the global level; banks ramped up securitisation operations massively to increase leverage to – amongst other things – amplify their RoE (Clementi and others 2009).

The significance for financial stability of these incentives may be substantial. RoE targeting, naturally linked to equity-based pay, may contribute to the amplification of leverage cycles, with far-reaching consequences for financial stability (Fostel and Geanakoplos 2013; Bhattacharya and others 2011). During the GFC, the relationship between incentives and write-downs was particularly strong in highly leveraged institutions (Chesney, Stromberg and Wagner 2011) and, in general, positive relationships have been documented between the sensitivity of bank CEO compensation to short-term earnings per share (Bhattacharyya and Purnanandam 2011) and excessive speculative activity (Bolton, Scheinkman and Xiong 2006). There is substantial evidence that compensation packages with large equity-based components incentivise manipulation (Bergstresser and Philippon 2006; Burns and Kedia 2006; Efendi, Srivastava and Swanson 2007; Johnson, Ryan and Tian 2009; Cheng, Warfield and Ye 2010). As might be expected in these circumstances, higher stock-option wealth within financial firms heightens bankruptcy risk (Armstrong and Vashishtha 2012). In contrast, where top bankers receive a greater proportion of their remuneration in salary and bonuses rather than stock options, they are less likely to take high risks and their firms are more stable (Palia and Porter 2004).

As noted earlier, the UK Rem-Code also recommends that banks utilise a range of performance measures in determining variable compensation, to supplant the rather singular focus on RoE prevalent in the pre-GFC period. In particular, the observation embedded in the Rem-Code that '[p]rofits are a better measure [than earnings] provided they are adjusted for risk' seems unarguable (FCA, SYSC: 19A.3.36). Notwithstanding the imperfections of RoE, however, reliance on alternative performance measures may carry problems of its own, including issues of mis-measurement of, or excessive, risk. For example, there have been calls for variable compensation to be linked to measures such as return on assets (RoA) (Haldane 2012) or other market-based indices such as a bank's credit risk, as expressed in its credit default swaps (CDS) spread (Bolton, Mehran and Shapiro 2011). In the case of RoA, where compensation is deferred, and linked to a firm's long-run stock price or financial returns, pay-outs vary with the riskiness of firm assets which incentivises asset risk (Chason 2013).

Banks may also engage in greater levels of asset substitution and use regulatory arbitrage and risk-weight optimisation to invest in asset portfolios with higher risk in order to maximise return on capital (Koehn and Santomero 1980; Goodhart 2013). Banks' capacity to borrow heavily to alter financial risks permits them to engage in substantial levels of asset substitution and hide problems in their asset books (Merton 1977); in fact, very risky firms are characterised by higher ratios of asset turnover (Cheng and others 2013). Focusing on RoA also encourages the securitisation of assets, which increases banks' leverage capacity and adds to financial complexity (Brunnermeier and Pedersen 2009; Diamond and Rajan 2009).

In the alternative, focusing on CDS spreads in compensation systems places tremendous faith in the power of market discipline to provide warnings concerning the risk of individual institutions, which wholly failed in the run-up to the GFC. Most market-based indices were not generally predictive of potential crisis; in particular, bank CDS spreads did not react until mid-2007 (Flannery 2010) and, in spite of mounting evidence that a financial correction was becoming more likely, investors and analysts simply pushed for even greater returns at the height of the financial boom (Avgouleas 2012). Requiring the market to regulate compensation incentives in this way is therefore fraught with difficulties and certainly cannot be trusted to reduce excessive risk-taking.

There are also persistent difficulties with current Rem-Code deferral provisions, which arguably remain insufficient in duration. Deferral provides greater links between pay and performance for two reasons:

(a)　it disincentivises the manipulation of earnings or excessive risk adoption by senior managers to capture short-term rewards and

(b)　it allows for the effects of the financial cycle to be smoothed out, reducing the possibility that excessive compensation awards are captured on the basis of inflated asset prices or short-run profit-making trades.

Axiomatically, in order to be effective, deferral periods need to be lengthy enough to align the risk horizons of key individuals at financial institutions with the longer term interests of their firms, forcing them to internalise the consequences of their actions. On this basis, in 2013 the PCBS recommended 'a new power for the regulators to require that a substantial part of (variable) remuneration is deferred for up to ten years, where it is necessary for effective long-term risk management' (PCBS 2013). Recent amendments to the Rem-Code to require deferral of variable pay (then to be paid out in equal instalments) for at least five years for all MRTs, and at least seven years for members of the SMR provide some direction on this issue. In particular, by fixing the deferral periods under which these plans must be operated, they avoid the (serious) potential problem with rewarding senior executives with deferred equity where managers have significant discretion over the timing of awards.

In the case of a manager whose compensation comprises significant levels of deferred equity, the eventual pay-out is contingent on the equity price remaining above a range determined ex ante (at the time of the compensation award). Because under the previous version of the Rem-Code banks were given significant discretion as to which deferral period to choose (in the UK, anywhere from three to five years), depending upon the structure of the vesting period, managers may have had several years' pay hinging on the stock price at a single point in time, giving them incentives to push up the equity price of their firm towards the end of a deferral period in order that non-vested restricted stock maintained value, and deferred awards from previous years piled up (Spindler 2011).

However, even under the latest deferral provisions the period over which executives' decisions will have an impact on bank performance is typically much longer than the period used to judge management performance as reflected in remuneration. Evidently short-term financial cycles last between nine and 13 years (Hilbers and others 2005; Aikman, Haldane and Nelson 2015), whilst long-term credit cycles may last up to 18 years (Drehmann, Borio and Tsatsaronis 2012). Moreover, more credit-intensive booms are generally much more damaging thanks to the pattern of asset price increases and higher leverage that accompanies them (Jorda, Schularick and Taylor 2014). It follows that incentives in bankers' compensation which may incentivise credit-led economic expansion ought to be heavily restricted, and certainly be calibrated to more closely approximate the duration of the average credit cycle, a point addressed further below.

The introduction of clawback provisions under the Rem-Code, designed partially to mitigate these problems, may be ineffective for the following reasons. First, in spite of the extended period of seven years under which clawback of variable remuneration is permitted under the Rem-Code (in comparison to the three to five year mandated deferral periods), as noted above, this may not be sufficient entirely to capture the financial cycle 'window'. Secondly, there are significant practical constraints imposed on retrieving remuneration that has already been awarded as an ex post adjustment, particularly if these payments were made a significant time previously. Moreover, as the GFC demonstrated, holding senior managers accountable for bank failure or downturns in performance is extremely difficult. It follows that clawing back remuneration is unlikely to occur with frequency, especially as sophisticated lawyers have thus far proven adept at placing assets beyond the reach of regulators (Noonan and Binham 2015).

Thirdly, there is early evidence that the use of clawback may encourage earnings manipulation; specifically, there is a correlation between clawback and an increase in 'real transactions management', a method of artificially boosting earnings over the short-to-medium term (Chan and others 2015). Finally, as clawback operates only in relation to variable compensation, a likely effect will be that bonuses are simply shifted into salaries, although this may in fact be desirable, as discussed further below.

Limits to corporate governance theory

The aforementioned practical limitations are compounded by more general issues arising from behavioural and institutional features of the financial market, which offer a more pluralist explanation of banker motivations, thereby revealing significant deficiencies in relying on improving cultural conditions or altering corporate governance structures to produce behaviour which is socially optimal.

Cognitive limitations and herding

The application of corporate governance norms to financial institutions has proven extremely limited, particularly because it is assumed that banks operate in competitive markets which are structured by market forces to operate managerially in the same way as all other types of firm (Ciancanelli and Reyes Gonzalez 2000). Moreover, under modern finance theory, which underpins most financial regulation, investors are posited as strong-form utility maximisers operating under rational expectations, which assumes the following: (a) investors have access to all relevant available information about the structure of the financial market; (b) investors make optimal use of this information in forming their expectations;

and (c) aggregate investor decision-making will be optimal as systematic errors will be avoided.

However, it is becoming commonly recognised that the principal actors at financial institutions – including at managerial and trader levels – are subject to certain socio-psychological pressures, information asymmetries and cognitive boundaries, which place first-order limits on their capacity to evaluate risk (Avgouleas 2009a). First, agents face severe and often insurmountable limitations in their knowledge and understanding of markets owing to objective factors, such as complexity, ignorance and information asymmetries in financial transactions (Schwarcz 2009). In the modern financial system the opaque nature of the financial network which generates extended chains of claims and high degrees of unseen interconnectedness may result in genuine ignorance of both the risks inherent in investments and the potential correlations across certain asset markets.

Secondly, agents are profoundly susceptible to short-term behaviour-driven investment influences, which may lead to sub-optimal investment patterns. These influences include 'disaster myopia', whereby benign agents take high risks because they discount the probability of high-impact yet low-frequency events (FSA 2009) and the associated problem of agents' highly short-term memories (Shiller 2002). If conditions favour speculation, this in turn may lead to the emergence of unbalanced investment phenomena, particularly asset bubbles.

Even quasi-rational individual behaviours may cause market discipline to break down and exacerbate market instability. For instance, in light of information asymmetries and bounded rationality, individual investors, fully aware of their own informational and computational limitations will often adopt the rational strategy of mimicking the plausible judgments of others, and herd (Scharfstein and Stein 1990; Nofsinger and Sias 1999; Barber, Odean and Zhu 2009). However, herding has the potential to produce group behaviour that leads to destabilising outcomes which, if they persist, may cause significant damage to the wider economy when unwound (Brunnermeir and others 2009). In this context, Acharya and Yorulmazer (2003) provide convincing explanations of the procyclicality in bank lending patterns. During economic booms, banks herd and undertake correlated investments to increase the odds of aggregate survival, as there are strong incentives to reduce the likelihood of adverse effects from contagion following the revelation of information concerning a systematic factor that weakens a rival bank. These patterns occur notwithstanding the form of herding, which increases the probability of highly damaging system-wide failures and may even result in healthy banks being dragged down by weaker competitors.

Prior to the GFC, there was strong evidence of herding in asset markets, where institutional investors flooded into the market for structured credit products, despite their inability fully to quantify the risks involved and the knowledge that the credit ratings of those products were imperfect (Avgouleas 2009b). Further, the mutual economic dependence produced by interconnectedness may result in perverse incentives to build aggregate institutional size, since the larger the institution, the greater the likelihood its failure would drag down other institutions, thereby requiring a public rescue (Avgouleas and Cullen 2014). The difficulties inherent in obviating the effects of these behaviours, despite their propensity to produce sub-optimal decision-making, place obvious limits on the power of compensation systems to reduce risk-taking.

Shareholder preference

In spite of the prevailing view of shareholders as 'cautious, prudent, and long-term oriented' (Coffee 2011), they have few incentives to rein in risk-taking – especially excessive borrowing – at banks. Many studies demonstrate that there are strong positive correlations between comparative shareholder power and risk-taking (Jeitschko and Jeung 2005), as well as between large institutional ownership and excess risk (Erkens, Hung and Matos 2012; Beltratti and Stulz 2012).

Banks with larger management control engage in less risk-taking than banks controlled by shareholders (Saunders, Strock and Travlos 1990; Laeven and Levine 2009). These findings are arguably predictable. As shareholders' liability is capped, whereas the upside to their investment is potentially unlimited, losses arising from excessive risk will normally fall on creditors (and governments), rather than on investors or managers. This may take hold to such an extent that shareholders may become 'addicted' to debt and actually have incentives to increase borrowing as institutions approach insolvency (the so-called 'ratchet' effect) as the costs of excessive leverage in these circumstances are externalised (Admati and others 2013a).

Moreover, thanks to the differing tax treatments of debt and equity, significant transaction and bankruptcy costs, as well as the implicit government guarantees enjoyed by large too-big-to-fail institutions, operating with high leverage is often the optimal choice for financial institution shareholders (Admati and others 2013b). As long as these institutions operate under such under-priced guarantees, the value of a bank's equity increases with its risk (Carpenter and Walter 2011).

Senior managers at financial institutions are therefore under pressure to comply with shareholder risk-preferences across the board, irrespective of their individual risk appetites. The consequences of this for financial stability may be devastating: in the context of the GFC, there is convincing research which indicates that banks with optimal corporate governance regimes (i.e. where managerial and shareholder interests were most aligned) performed worst (Cullen 2014; Avgouleas and Cullen 2014).

Disproportionately large equity holdings ought to have incentivised senior bankers to act in the long-term interests of their firms; certainly, they had substantial incentives to prevent the assumption of excess risk (Fahlenbrach and Stulz 2011). However, senior management at financial institutions held significant equity positions and suffered substantial paper losses once stock prices began to fall sharply, and did not hedge their exposure to reduce any potential wealth losses, behaviour that is clearly inconsistent with compensation-induced short-termism. Accordingly, aligning individual CEOs' interests through financial incentives with those of shareholders may not reduce managerial risk-taking.

Career concerns

These factors appear to suggest that the adoption of excessive risk cannot be reduced simply to poor incentive alignment. In fact, as noted by Avgouleas and Cullen (2015) an in-depth examination of the counter-factual in relation to bankers' incentives arguably reveals a more nuanced explanation of pre-GFC banker behaviour. Rather than simply being driven by compensation structures, the combination of loose regulation and the capacity to adopt excessive leverage led bankers to pursue risky strategies because they were forced to do so; there are significant competitive pressures which result from operating in a supremely high-functioning and skills-portable market landscape. Industry peer pressure and career and reputational concerns, which are highly prevalent in the banking industry (Lakonishok, Shleifer and Vishny 1994; Chevalier and Ellison 1999; Hong and Kubik 2003; Brown, Wei and Wermers 2013) often push bankers at all levels – especially senior management – to adopt herding strategies in both capital structure and trading portfolios.

In this environment, the pressure to outperform or at least match rivals cannot be underestimated; these issues are compounded in euphoric markets by the knowledge that predicting losses may be catastrophic for long-term investment and/or job security for agents who control large volumes of finance, including bankers. In market bubbles, outward optimism (even where this optimism may not reflect fully the opinion of the relevant banker) amounts less to a bias than a competitive necessity (Brunnermeier 2001). Accordingly, even in the extreme context of the GFC, it is plausible that senior executives simply 'managed their banks in a manner they authentically believed would benefit their shareholders' (Grundfest 2009). As noted by Norris (2009) in the context of risk-taking at banks in the run-up to the GFC:

> [I]t is worth asking what would have happened if [Lehman Brothers' CEO] Mr. Fuld had somehow realized in 2005 that the mortgage business was a time bomb and had gotten Lehman out of it. Within a year, its profits would have sagged and its share price collapsed. Mr. Fuld would have been labeled a dunce, and might have lost his job. The same can be said of Jimmy Cayne of Bear Stearns and Stan O'Neal of Merrill Lynch, the two runners-up in the richest bank C.E.O. sweepstakes of 2006.

Summary

In light of these factors, it appears likely that neither encouraging shareholder-centric governance reform nor pursuing individual compensation reforms in isolation to align the interests of bankers with their principals will restrain reckless senior manager behaviour, particularly as shareholders are also anything but immune to the psychological pressures and biases discussed earlier (Dermine 2011). As bankers' motivations to take risks are much wider than greed – encompassing investment herding, shareholder pressure and the drive for competitive market-capture – compensation controls are likely to be insufficient in containing bankers' risk-seeking.

As argued by Avgouleas and Cullen (2014), a natural consequence of these observations is to conclude that the continued reliance on use of equity-based compensation is an exercise in futility. If, as contended by regulators, pre-GFC compensation systems provided incentives for short-termism (facilitated by regulatory arbitrage) prior compensation systems were an inefficient method of incentivising managers and contributed to financial instability. On the other hand, if these systems did not a priori provide inappropriate risk-taking incentives, current corporate governance arrangements remain fundamentally flawed; the use of equity-based pay and other forms of incentives did *not* guard against the build-up of excessive risk. As noted by Friedman (2009): 'None of [the pre-2008 behaviour] can be explained unless, on balance, the banks' management and risk-control systems kept in check whatever incentives to ignore risk had been created by the banks' compensation systems'.

Moreover, on this basis, the actual state of knowledge of market participants is irrelevant. Even where it can be shown that there is no overt assumption of risk linked to compensation awards, the net result will not differ, owing to market short-termism, and because, as discussed above, market participants are subject to a gamut of influences beyond individual financial incentives. Herding may be tacitly encouraged by investments which appear to provide commensurate risk-adjusted returns and regulation which requires banks to hold 'safe' capital (Friedman and Kraus 2011). Cognitive limitations may prevent market actors from recognising the dangers in financial products, or price distortions in the market. These problems are especially problematic in exuberant markets on the upward curve of the credit cycle because, as asset values increase, assets become more profitable, and collateral constraints are relaxed (Minsky 1986) or sophisticated bankers/lawyers find ways to stretch collateral to use for further asset purchases (Geanakoplos and Zame 2010). Indicatively, Turner notes:

> [If] irrational exuberance pushes the price of assets to irrationally high levels, mark to market accounting will swell declared profit in an unsustainable way. A significant element of trading book profits recorded in the years running up to the crisis proved in retrospect illusory. These illusory profits were however used as the basis for bonus decisions, and created incentives for traders and management to take further risk.
>
> (FSA 2009: 49)

This line of argument does not contradict the findings of the studies on equity-based wealth at banks cited previously; instead, it reveals limits to relying on compensation incentives to a significant extent, because in many circumstances equity-based awards provide no protection for investors. These factors place severe limits on the capacity of incentive contracts to be effective in aligning the long-term interests of managers and shareholders (financially or 'culturally') and simultaneously in safeguarding financial stability either at the institutional or systemic level.

Dealing with flawed incentives: moving forward

The above analysis suggests that approaching corporate governance reform in the banking sector either as a way of inculcating long-term change to the culture of banking or to reduce excessive risk-taking remains a difficult challenge. What, then, are the potential remuneration tools available to improve governance and reduce risk-taking? Below I canvass some possible strategies.

Amending the structure of compensation

Paying bankers in cash

As noted earlier, paying senior executives in equity presents many risks. In contrast, requiring that compensation packages comprise significant cash bonus levels reduces the incentives for high risk-taking (Cooper, Gulen and Rau 2009). Theoretical work by Smith and Stulz (1985) shows that where cash bonuses increase linearly with corporate performance they are not inherently risk-rewarding. Further, as cash bonuses may only be paid in a state of solvency, they incentivise CEOs to avoid excessive risks, which could threaten bankruptcy (John and John 1993; Duru, Mansi and Reeb 2005; Vallascas and Hagendorff 2013). Long-term cash bonus plans provide managers with incentives to exert effort (Indjejikian and others 2014) and, in the case of banks, their use reduces the likelihood of default in comparison to banks which utilise greater levels of equity-based pay (Balachandran, Kogut and Harnal 2010).

As cash bonuses are paid based on historically-delivered results, rather than forward-looking market values, they are less open to distortion, either through selective information disclosure or the adoption of short-term risk (Barclay, Gode and Kothari 2005). Further, there is substantial evidence that executives undervalue share awards – discounting them by up to 30 per cent per annum – as it becomes difficult to judge the size of the ultimate pay-out on a forward-looking basis, particularly where the instruments in question are deferred (Prudential Regulation Authority and FCA 2014, 8). The uncertainty created by these factors often leads to pay inflation, or the linking of remuneration to factors beyond the control of the executives in question, which will neither improve financial stability nor instil superior cultural conditions (Cullen 2014; High Pay Centre 2015).

Increasing deferral

As discussed, even recently-mandated changes to deferral periods under the Rem-Code for high-ranking bankers are arguably not lengthy enough to align individual and institutional interests. Whilst recent alterations to the deferral periods under the UK Rem-Code are welcome, arguably they remain too short. I proposed in 2014 the introduction of 10 year deferral periods for variable compensation, with half of that remuneration vesting after five years (Cullen 2014). This proposal was recently endorsed at high levels in the US (Dudley 2014). Given experiences during the GFC and the period subsequent, a decade would seem to be a reasonable timeframe to allow any distortions from the credit cycle to dissipate, as well as providing sufficient time for any illegal actions or violations of the firm's culture to materialise. There have been somewhat stricter proposals from Roubini and Mihm (2010), who argue for decade-long deferral periods with no element of early vesting, whilst a further variation on this proposal was proposed recently in the UK Parliament (Parker and Binham 2015).

An aggregated deferral period of 10 years would more closely align the risk horizons of managers with the duration of the business and credit cycles. Such periods of deferral would arguably make it much more difficult for managers to maintain inefficient levels of risk in their management of their financial institution, as sub-optimal returns to shareholders during that period brought on by excessive risk-averseness ought to mean they would be replaced with less risk-averse managers in the meantime (whose rewards will also be deferred and, therefore, despite their greater risk-tolerance, incentives for 'excessive' risks will remain capped).

Moreover, under the Cullen (2014) proposal, the in-building of a window where 50 per cent of the rewards could be paid at the halfway point ought to ameliorate the tendency of managers to postpone or reduce innovation in order to maintain future pay-outs, whilst simultaneously assisting financial institutions to attract and retain talented bankers. Extended deferral periods for variable compensation vesting would also avoid the costly and difficult process of risk-adjustment within the compensation system in calculating regular grants of deferred compensation, which even now present significant difficulties of calibration (International Institute of Finance 2009).

Widening targets

Whilst these considerations are not the primary focus of this chapter, a direction for further research could be to consider how, at an institutional level, compensation policies could be reformed further to focus on non-financial indicators of performance. There is substantial research to indicate that targets based on financial performance indicators may lead to narrow focus and encourage unethical behaviour (Schweitzer, Ordonez and Douma 2004; Ordonez and others 2009). Market participants are generally 'boundedly ethical' in their decision-making; that is, choices made in a business context may be limited by the set of goals regarded as desirable (such as perceived competence or success) to the extent that ethical considerations may be displaced (Bazerman and Moore 2009).

In addition, the incentive effects of compensation based on a 'bonus culture' may wane over the longer term, and actually demotivate employees (Frey and Jegen 1999; O'Reilly III, Main and Crystal 1988). In the context of banker attitudes to acceptable conduct, there is substantial evidence of the damaging effects of financial targets; at least one out of six bankers would be prepared to commit insider trading if the financial rewards were attractive enough (at least US$10 million) (Labaton Sucharow 2012).

Non-monetary based targets provide an additional benefit: by incentivising executives to deliver client-focused results, rather than concentrating their minds completely on increasing profits for shareholders, the potential to inculcate an improvement in business culture would arise. Research on corporate governance in the context of financial markets strongly suggests that long-term changes to behaviour requires a shift in performance-based compensation targets to focus instead on rewarding integrity (Erhard, Jensen and Zaffron 2009) and trustworthiness (Baker, Gibbons and Murphy 1993) in business conduct. Such measures may go some way to repairing the evident loss of public trust in financial markets, regarded as a key problem in driving future economic growth and is, of course, a cardinal motive for attempts to improve cultural and ethical norms in banking.

Currently these 'softer' targets under 'the balanced scorecard approach' form approximately one-fifth of determined bonus awards in banks for 'front office employees' (which include sales, marketing and customer services staff) (Basel Committee on Banking Supervision (BCBS) 2011), yet it remains clear that the most senior staff and MRTs at banks receive bonuses almost exclusively on the basis of the financial returns they generate. To the degree that financial institutions capture excess profits from the exploitation of asymmetries of expertise in relation to highly complex products, such actions impose costs on their less informed and non-expert counterparties (Awrey, Blair and Kershaw 2013), which ordinarily would be regarded as unsustainable behaviours. Accordingly, engaging in further research on alternative qualitative performance evaluation may be beneficial in reducing the reliance on performance measures that have dubious or insubstantial effects on conduct and lead to a dangerous obsession with short-term performance measurements.

Structural reforms to reduce risk

Of course, neither recent reforms nor the suggestions above are designed to achieve the overarching aim of improved financial stability in isolation; there have been many other structural reforms to the banking sector designed to reduce the likelihood of bank failures, which may have indirect effects on bankers' compensation. For example, the capacity of retail bankers to engage in risky trading will be curtailed by wholesale structural reforms such as ring-fencing, despite the concentration risks that these reforms pose (Goodhart 2012).

In fact, in drawing up the recommendations that eventually led to UK ring-fencing, the Independent Commission on Banking (2011) specifically concluded that newly-split operations under previously universal banks ought to 'have distinct governance arrangements, and should have different cultures'. Arguably, however, these comments reveal the naivety in much of the regulatory reform agenda, which assumes that, inter alia, culture is best produced through structures, and is something that can be imposed from above.

Furthermore, recent leverage restrictions announced by the Bank of England may go some way to reducing the dangers of excessive bank borrowing and thereby reduce the incentives of bankers to chase bonus targets through a simple leveraging-up of capital (Avgouleas and Cullen 2015), although there are indications that RoE targeting has not abated since the GFC (Pagratis, Karakatsani and Louri 2014). Arguably, controls on leverage will lead to a financial system comprised of smaller, less-interconnected banks with more robust capital structures. A knock-on effect of the reduction in size and complexity will inevitably be superior risk-management and reduced opacity. Simultaneously these reforms offer more effective checks on bankers' incentives to engage in risk-seeking manifested by excessive leverage than mere regulation of compensation systems (Avgouleas and Cullen 2015). Along these principles, it is plausible that approaching the issues from a structuralist perspective rather than relying on the ill-defined and (seemingly) impractical task of fostering cultural change in the banking sector will – at least in the short term – promote greater awareness of financial stability risks.

Conclusion

There is little consensus as to what methods may be appropriate to generate substantial ethical and cultural change in the banking sector. In this vacuum policy-makers and regulators have fallen back on traditional norms of governance – sanctions and incentives – and introduced new legal disciplining powers and a programme of amendments to compensation systems. In this vein, senior UK regulators have even threatened to attack fixed pay and salary going forward (Carney 2014b) in last-ditch attempts to help solve the cultural deficits in banking.

Of course, these may prove to be steps in the right direction and altering structural incentives that shape behaviour will arguably help in the quest for behavioural change. In many ways, recent amendments to the Rem-Code – particularly the increases in deferral of variable pay mandated in June 2015 – reveal that senior banking regulators have the stomach for sustaining a check on short-termism in financial markets. Risks emanating from compensation incentives will undoubtedly recede where bankers are forced to consider long-term investment horizons in their decision-making.

However, as this chapter has illustrated, despite strong progress, UK reforms are not entirely persuasive in this regard; in some cases they may actually contribute to financial instability because of their reliance on traditional forms of risk-management, which may not always be appropriate with regard to financial institutions. Furthermore, there are persistent dysfunctionalities in relation to the application of corporate governance norms to banks and financial market behaviour.

In light of these limitations, producing a true cultural revolution in banking – if it is even a plausible aim to pursue – may require more nuanced efforts on the part of the banking industry and regulators, and certainly a concerted commitment to enforcing sanctions against individuals guilty of misconduct. Changing a culture cannot be achieved if directed externally; true change must emerge endogenously and axiomatically emanate from senior levels. Recalibrating the tone and focus of reform will involve a long-term and sustained effort; it remains to be seen whether banking is yet at the point where this can be achieved. Waiting for this to materialise, however, is not an option: the financial system remains dangerously fragile. Instead, the maintenance of financial stability will have to be based upon tangible structural reforms, rather than vague regulatory initiatives which aspire to 'improve' banking culture.

References

Acharya, V V and Richardson, M, 2009, 'Causes of the financial crisis', *Critical Review*, 21(2–3), 195–201.

Acharya, V V and Yorulmazer, T, 2003, 'A theory of procyclical bank lending', London Business School Working Paper http://facultyresearch.london.edu/docs/bankherding.pdf (last accessed 27 September 2015).

Admati, A R, DeMarzo, P M, Hellwig, M F and Pfleiderer, P, 2013a, 'The leverage ratchet effect', *Rock Center for Corporate Governance at Stanford University* Working Paper No. 146.

Admati, A R, DeMarzo, P M, Hellwig, M F and Pfleiderer, P, 2013b, 'Fallacies, irrelevant facts, and myths in the discussion of capital regulation: why bank equity is not socially expensive', *Rock Center for Corporate Governance at Stanford University* Working Paper No. 161.

Aikman, D, Haldane, A G and Nelson, B D, 2015, 'Curbing the credit cycle', *Economic Journal*, 585(125), 1072–109.

Armstrong, C S and Vashishtha, R, 2012, 'Executive stock options, differential risk-taking incentives, and firm value', *Journal of Financial Economics*, 104(1), 70–88.

Avgouleas, E, 2009a, 'The global financial crisis, behavioral finance and financial regulation: in search of a new orthodoxy', *Journal of Corporate Law Studies*, 9(1), 23–59.

Avgouleas, E, 2009b, 'The global financial crisis and the disclosure paradigm in European financial regulation: the case for reform', *European Company and Financial Law Review*, 6(4), 440–75.

Avgouleas, E, 2012, *Governance of Global Financial Markets: The Law, the Economics, the Politics*, Cambridge: Cambridge University Press.

Avgouleas, E, 2015, 'Large systemic banks and fractional reserve banking, intractable dilemmas in search of effective solutions', in Arner, D, Avgouleas, E and Buckley, R (eds), *Reconceptualizing Global Finance and its Regulation*, Cambridge: Cambridge University Press.

Avgouleas, E and Cullen, J, 2014, 'Market discipline and EU corporate governance reform in the banking sector: merits, fallacies, and cognitive boundaries', *Journal of Law & Society*, 41(1), 28–50.

Avgouleas, E and Cullen, J, 2015, 'Excessive leverage and bankers' pay: governance and financial stability costs of a symbiotic relationship', *Columbia Journal of European Law*, 21(1), 35–80.

Awrey, D, Blair, W and Kershaw, D, 2013, 'Between law and markets: is there a role for culture and ethics in financial regulation?', *Delaware Journal of Corporate Law*, 38(1), 191–245.

Baker, G, Gibbons, R and Murphy, K J, 1993, 'Subjective performance measures in optimal incentive contracts', NBER Working Paper No. 4480.

Balachandran, S, Kogut B and Harnal, H, 2010, 'The probability of default, excessive risk, and executive compensation: a study of financial services firms from 1995 to 2008', Columbia Business School Research Paper.

Bank of England, 2014, *Strengthening the Alignment of Risk and Reward: New Remuneration Rules – PRA CP15/14/FCA CP14/1* (July 2014).

Bank of England, 2015, *Strengthening the Alignment of Risk and Reward: New Remuneration Rules – PS12/15* (June 2015).

Barber, B M, Odean, T and Zhu, T, 2009, 'Do retail trades move markets?', *Review of Financial Studies*, 22(1), 151–86.

Barclay, M, Gode, D and Kothari, S P, 2005, 'Matching delivered performance', *Journal of Contemporary Accounting Research*, 1, 1–25.

Bazerman, M H and Moore, D, 2009, *Judgment in Managerial Decision-making*, New York: John Wiley & Sons, 8th edn.

BCBS, 2011, *Range of Methodologies for Risk and Performance Alignment of Remuneration*, Basel: Bank for International Settlements, http://www.bis.org/publ/bcbs194.pdf (last accessed 13 December 2015).

Bebchuk, L A, Cohen, A and Spamann, H, 2010, 'The wages of failure: executive compensation at Bear Stearns and Lehman 2000–2008', *Yale Journal on Regulation*, 27, 257–82.

Beltratti, A and Stulz, R M, 2012, 'The credit crisis around the globe: why did some banks perform better during the credit crisis?', *Journal of Financial Economics*, 105(1), 1–17.

Bergstresser, D and Philippon, T, 2006, 'CEO incentives and earnings management', *Journal of Financial Economics*, 80(3), 511–29.

Bhattacharya, S, Goodhart, C A E, Tsomocos, D and Vardoulakis, A, 2011, 'Minsky's financial instability hypothesis and the leverage cycle', *LSE Financial Markets Group* Special Paper 202/2011.

Bhattacharyya, S and Purnanandam, A K, 2011, 'Risk-taking by banks: what did we know and when did we know it?', *AFA 2012* Chicago Meetings Paper.

Bolton, P, Scheinkman, J and Xiong, W, 2006, 'Executive compensation and short-termist behaviour in speculative markets', *Review of Economic Studies*, 73, 577–610.

Bolton, P, Mehran, H and Shapiro J, 2011, 'Executive compensation and risk-taking', *Federal Reserve Bank of New York* Working Paper No. 456.

Boschen, J F and Smith, K J, 1995, 'You can pay me now and you can pay me later: the dynamic response of executive compensation to firm performance', *Journal of Business*, 68(4), 577–608.

Brown, N C, Wei, K D and Wermers, R, 2013, 'Analyst recommendations, mutual fund herding, and overreaction in stock prices', *Management Science*, 60(1), 1–20.

Brunnermeier, M K, 2001, *Asset Pricing Under Asymmetric Information: Bubbles, Crashes, Technical Analysis, and Herding*, Oxford: Oxford University Press.

Brunnermeier, M K and Pedersen, L, 2009, 'Market liquidity and funding liquidity', *Review of Financial Studies*, 22(6), 2201–38.

Brunnermeier, M K, Crockett, A, Goodhart, C A E, Persaud, A and Shin, H S, 2009, 'The fundamental principles of financial regulation', *Geneva Reports on the World Economy*, 11, Geneva: International Center for Monetary and Banking Studies.

Buell, S W, 2007, 'Reforming punishment of financial reporting fraud', *Cardozo Law Review*, 28(4), 1611–52.

Burns, N and Kedia S, 2006, 'The impact of performance-based compensation on mis-reporting', *Journal of Financial Economics*, 79(1), 35–67.

Carney, M, 2014a, 'Inclusive capitalism: creating a sense of the systemic', Speech given at the Conference on Inclusive Capitalism, London (27 May 2014).

Carney, M, 2014b, 'The future of financial reform', Speech at Monetary Authority of Singapore (17 November 2014).

Carpenter, J and Walter, I, 2011, 'Remove the risk incentive from bankers' pay', *Financial Times*, London (15 March 2011).

Chan, L H, Chen, K C W, Chen, T Y and Yu, Y, 2015, 'Substitution between real and accruals-based earnings management after voluntary adoption of compensation claw-back provisions', *Accounting Review*, 90(1), 147–74.

Chason, E D, 2013, 'The uneasy case for deferring banker pay', *Louisiana Law Review*, 73(4), 923–77.

Chen, C R, Steiner, T L and Whyte, A M, 2006, 'Does stock-option-based compensation induce risk-taking? An analysis of the banking industry', *Journal of Banking and Finance*, 30(3), 915–45.

Cheng, Q, Warfield, T and Ye, M, 2010, 'Equity incentives and earnings management: evidence from the banking industry', *CAAA Annual Conference 2009 Paper*.

Cheng, I H, Hong, H and Scheinkman, J A, 2013, Yesterday's Heroes: Compensation and Creative Risk-Taking, New York: Columbia University http://econ.columbia.edu/files/econ/compensaton__risk_at_financial_firms.pdf (last accessed 14 December 2015).

Chesney, M, Stromberg, J and Wagner, A F, 2011, 'Risk-taking incentives, governance, and losses in the financial crisis', *University of Zurich Swiss Finance Institute* Working Paper No. 10-18.

Chevalier, J and Ellison, G, 1999, 'Career concerns of mutual fund managers', *Quarterly Journal of Economics*, 114(2), 389–432.

Ciancanelli, P and Reyes-Gonzalez, J A, 2000, 'Corporate governance in banking: a conceptual framework' http://papers.ssrn.com/sol3/papers.cfm?abstract_id=253714 (last accessed 27 September 2015).

Clementi, G L, Cooley T F, Richardson, M and Walter, I, 2009, 'Rethinking compensation at financial firms', in Acharya, V V and Richardson, M (eds), *Restoring Financial Stability: How to Repair a Failed System*, New York: John Wiley & Sons.

Coffee, J C, 2006, 'Reforming the securities class action: an essay on deterrence and its implementation', *Columbia Law and Economics* Working Paper No. 293.

Coffee, J, 2011, Presentation, cited at 10 in Bolton, P, Kogut, B, and Puschra, W, *Governance, Executive Compensation, and Excessive Risk in the Financial Services Industry*, executive summary, New York: Columbia Business School.

Cohn, A, Fehr, E and Maréchal, M A, 2014, 'Business culture and dishonesty in the banking industry', *Nature*, 516, 86–89.

Cooper, M J, Gulen, H and Rau, P R, 2009, 'Performance for pay? The relationship between CEO incentive compensation and future stock price performance' http://online.wsj.com/public/resources/documents/CEOperformance122509.pdf (last accessed 27 September 2015).

Cullen, J, 2014, *Executive Compensation in Imperfect Financial Markets*, Cheltenham: Edward Elgar Publishing.

Davies, H and Ball, J, 2015, 'HSBC is "cast-iron certain" to breach banking rules again, executive admits'. *The Guardian* (2 April 2015).

DeYoung, R, Peng, E Y and Yan, M, 2013, 'Executive compensation and business policy choices at US commercial banks', *Journal of Financial and Quantitative Analysis*, 48(1), 165–96.

Dermine, J, 2011, 'Bank corporate governance, beyond the global banking crisis', INSEAD Working Paper No. 2011/33/FIN.

Diamond, D W and Rajan, R, 2009, 'The credit crisis: conjectures about causes and remedies', NBER Working Paper No. 14739.

Drehmann, M, Borio, C and Tsatsaronis, K, 2012, 'Characterising the financial cycle: don't lose sight of the medium term!', BIS Working Paper No. 380.

Dudley, W C, 2014, 'Enhancing financial stability by improving culture in the financial services industry', Remarks at the Workshop on Reforming Culture and Behavior in the Financial Services Industry, Federal Reserve Bank of New York, New York City (20 October 2014).

Duru, A, Mansi, S A and Reeb, D M, 2005, 'Earnings-based bonus plans and the agency costs of debt', *Journal of Accounting and Public Policy*, 24(5), 431–47.

Efendi, J, Srivastava, A and Swanson, E P, 2007, 'Why do corporate managers misstate financial statements? The role of option compensation and other factors', *Journal of Financial Economics*, 85(3), 667–708.

Erhard, W, Jensen M C and Zaffron, S, 2009, 'Integrity: a positive model that incorporates the normative phenomena of morality, ethics and legality', *Harvard Business School* NOM Working Paper No. 06-11.

Erkens, D H, Hung, M and Matos, P, 2012, 'Corporate governance in the 2007–2008 financial crisis: evidence from financial institutions worldwide', *Journal of Corporate Finance*, 18(2), 389–411.

Fahlenbrach, R and Stulz, R M, 2011, 'Bank CEO incentives and the credit crisis', *Journal of Financial Economics*, 99(1), 11–26.

FCA [Financial Conduct Authority], *Handbook* (web-based), section on systems and controls (SYSC), London: FCA, https://www.handbook.fca.org.uk/handbook/SYSC/3/1.html

Financial Services Authority, 2009, *The Turner Review: A regulatory response to the global banking crisis* (March 2009), London: FSA, http://www.fsa.gov.uk/pubs/other/turner_review.pdf (last accessed 13 December 2015).

Financial Stability Board, 2009, *FSF Principles for Sound Compensation Practices: Implementation Standards* (25 September 2009), Basel: FSB, http://www.financialstabilityboard.org/wp-content/uploads/r_090925c.pdf (last accessed 13 December 2015).

Flannery, M J, 2010, 'What to do about TBTF?', Paper presented at the Federal Reserve Bank of Atlanta 2010 Financial Markets Conference, *Up from the Ashes: The Financial System after the Crisis*, Atlanta, Georgia (12 May 2010).

Fostel, A and Geanakoplos, J, 2013, 'Reviewing the leverage cycle', *Cowles Foundation Discussion Paper No. 1918*.

Frey B S and Jegen, R, 1999, 'Motivation crowding theory: a survey of empirical evidence', *University of Zurich Institute for Empirical Research in Economics* Working Paper No. 26.

Friedman, J, 2009, 'Bank pay and the financial crisis', *Wall Street Journal*, New York (28 September 2009).

Friedman, J and Kraus, W, 2011, *Engineering the Financial Crisis: Systemic Risk and the Failure of Regulation*, Pennsylvania: University of Pennsylvania Press.

Geanakoplos, J and Zame W R, 2010, 'Collateralized security markets', *Levine's Working Paper Archive*.

Goodhart, C A E, 2012, 'The Vickers Report: an assessment', *Law and Financial Markets Review*, 6(1), 32–38.

Goodhart, C A E, 2013, 'Ratio controls need reconsideration', *Journal of Financial Stability*, 9(3), 445–50.

Goodhart, C A E and Perotti, E, 2015, 'Maturity mismatch stretching: banking has taken a wrong turn', *Centre for Economic Policy Research Policy Insight*, 81, 1–6.

Grundfest, J, 2009, 'What's needed is uncommon wisdom', *New York Times*, New York (6 October 2009).

Guo, L, Jalal, A and Khaksari, S, 2010, 'Bank executive compensation structure, risk taking and the financial crisis' http://ssrn.com/abstract=1664191 (last accessed 27 September 2015).

Haldane, A G, 2012, 'Control rights (and wrongs)', Speech given at the Wincott Annual Memorial Lecture (24 October 2011).

Henning, E and Enrich, D, 2015, 'Deutsche Bank to pay $2.5 billion to settle Libor investigation', *Wall Street Journal*, New York (23 April 2015).

High Pay Centre, 2015, *No Routine Riches: Reforms to Performance-related Pay* (May 2015).

Hilbers, P, Otker-Robe, I, Pazarbasioglu, C and Johnsen, G, 2005, 'Assessing and managing rapid credit growth and the role of supervisory and prudential policies', IMF Working Paper No. 05/151.

HM Treasury, 2012, *Review of HM Treasury's Management Response to the Financial Crisis* (March 2012).

HM Treasury, 2015, Senior Managers and Certification Regime: extension to all FSMA authorised persons, 15 October, https://www.gov.uk/government/publications/senior-managers-and-certification-regime-extension-to-all-fsma-authorised-persons (last accessed 13 December 2015).

Holmstrom, B, 2015, 'Understanding the role of debt in the financial system', BIS Working Paper No. 479.

Hong, H and Kubik, J D, 2003, 'Analyzing the analysts: career concerns and biased earnings forecasts', *Journal of Finance*, 58(1), 313–51.

IMF, 2014, *Global Financial Stability Report*, International Monetary Fund: Washington DC.

Independent Commission on Banking, 2011, *Final Report: Recommendations*, London: Independent Commission on Banking.

Indjejikian, R, Matejka, M, Merchant, M and Van der Stede, W, 2014, 'Earnings targets and annual bonus incentives', *Accounting Review*, 89(4), 1227–58.

International Institute of Finance, 2009, *Compensation in Financial Services: Industry Progress and the Agenda for Change* (March 2009).

IOSCO, 2015, *Credible Deterrence in the Enforcement of Securities Regulation – FR09/2015* (June 2015).

Jeitschko, T D and Jeung, S D, 2005, 'Incentives for risk-taking in banking: a unified approach', *Journal of Banking and Finance*, 29(3), 759–77.

Jensen, M C and Murphy, K J, 1990, 'Performance pay and top-management incentives', *Journal of Political Economy*, 98(2), 225–64.

John, T A and John, K, 1993, 'Top management compensation and capital structure', *Journal of Finance*, 48(3), 949–74.

Johnson, S A, Ryan H E and Tian, Y S, 2009, 'Managerial incentives and corporate fraud: the sources of incentives matter', *Oxford Review of Finance*, 13(1), 115–45.

Jorda, O, Schularick, M and Taylor, A M, 2014, 'The great mortgaging: housing finance, crises, and business cycles', *Federal Reserve Bank of San Francisco* Working Paper Series 2014-23.

Kane, E J, 2015, 'Unpacking and reorienting executive subcultures of modern finance', Remarks prepared for the Institute for New Economic Thinking Annual Conference, Paris, France (15 April 2015).

Koehn, M and Santomero, A M, 1980, 'Regulation of bank capital and portfolio risk', *Journal of Finance*, 35(5), 1235–44.

Labaton Sucharow, 2012, *Ethics & Action Survey: Voices Carry*, 2nd Annual Integrity Survey of the American Public (September).

Laeven, L and Levine, R, 2009, 'Bank governance, regulation and risk-taking', *Journal of Financial Economics*, 93(2), 259–75.

Lakonishok, J, Shleifer, A and Vishny, R W, 1994, 'Contrarian investment, extrapolation, and risk', *Journal of Finance*, 49(5), 1541–78.

Langevoort, D C, 2007, 'Criminalization of corporate law: the impact on director and officer behavior', *Journal of Business and Technology Law*, 2, 89–90.

Mehran, M and Rosenberg, J, 2007, 'The Effect of employee stock options on bank investment choice, borrowing, and capital', *Federal Reserve Bank of New York* Staff Report No. 305.

Mehta, C and Bickler, R, 2014, 'Criminalising cartels: the new rules', Nabarro Briefing (10 March 2014) http://www.nabarro.com/insight/briefings/2014/march/criminalising-cartels-%E2%80%93-the-new-rules/ (last accessed 27 September 2015).

Merton, R C, 1977, 'An analytic derivation of the cost of deposit insurance and loan guarantees: an application of modern option pricing theory', *Journal of Banking and Finance*, 1(1), 3–11.

Minsky, H P, 1986, *Stabilizing an Unstable Economy*, New York: McGraw-Hill.

Moussu, C and Petit-Romec, A, 2014, 'ROE in banks: myth and reality', http://ssrn.com/abstract=2374068 (last accessed 27 September 2015).

Nofsinger, J R and Sias, R W, 1999, 'Herding and feedback trading by institutional and individual investors', *Journal of Finance*, 54(6), 2263–95.

Noonan, L and Binham, C, 2015, 'Bankers seek ways round bonus clawbacks', *Financial Times*, London (26 June 2015).

Norris, F, 2009, 'It may be outrageous, but Wall Street pay didn't cause this crisis', *New York Times*, New York (30 July 2009).

Ordonez, L D, Schweitzer, M E, Galinsky, A D and Bazerman, M H, 2009, 'Goals gone Wild: The systematic side effects of overprescribing goal setting', *Academy of Management Perspectives*, 23(1), 6–16.

O'Reilly III, C A, Main, B G and Crystal, G S, 1988, 'CEO compensation as tournament and social comparison: a tale of two theories', *Administrative Science Quarterly*, 33(2), 257–74.

Pagratis, S, Karakatsani, E and Louri, H, 2014, 'Bank leverage and return on equity targeting: intrinsic procyclicality of short-term choices', *Bank of Greece Working Paper* No. 189.

Palia, D and Porter, R, 2004, 'The impact of capital requirements and managerial compensation on bank charter value', *Review of Quantitative Finance and Accounting*, 23(3), 191–206.

Parker, G and Binham, C, 2015, 'Defer banker bonuses for 10 years, says MP', *Financial Times*, London (15 February 2015).

Parker, G, Binham, C and Noonan, L, 2015, 'George Osborne to signal end to "banker bashing"', *Financial Times*, London (5 June 2015).

Parliamentary Commission on Banking Standards, 2013, *Changing Banking For Good: Vol. 1*, HL 27-I; HC 175-I.

Prudential Regulation Authority and Financial Conduct Authority, 2014, Strengthening the alignment of risk and reward: new remuneration rules, Consultation Paper PRA CP15/14/FCA CP14/14 (July 2014), London: PRA and FCA, https://www.fca.org.uk/static/documents/consultation-papers/cp14-14.pdf

Raymond, N, 2013, 'Judge criticizes lack of prosecution against Wall Street executives for fraud', *Reuters* (12 November 2013).

Rockness, H and Rockness, J, 2005, 'Legislated ethics: from Enron to Sarbanes-Oxley, the impact on corporate America', *Journal of Business Ethics*, 57(1), 31–54.

Roubini, N and Mihm, S, 2010, *Crisis Economics: A Crash Course in the Future of Finance*, London: Allen Lane.

Salz, A, 2013, *Salz Review: An Independent Review of Barclays' Business Practices*, London: Barclays PLC, https://www.home.barclays/content/dam/barclayspublic/documents/news/875-269-salz-review-04-2013.pdf (last accessed 11 December 2015).

Saunders, A, Strock, E and Travlos, N, 1990, 'Ownership structure, deregulation and bank risk-Taking', *Journal of Finance*, 45(2), 643–54.

Scharfstein, David S and Stein, Jeremy C, 1990, 'Herd behavior and investment', *American Economic Review*, 80(3), 465–79.

Schwarcz, S L, 2009, 'Regulating complexity in financial markets', *Washington University Law Review*, 87(2), 211–68.

Schweitzer, M E, Ordonez L D and Douma, B, 2004, 'Goal setting as a motivator of unethical behavior', *Academy of Management Journal*, 47(3), 422–32.

Shiller, R J, 2002, 'Bubbles, human judgment, and expert opinion', *Financial Analysts Journal*, 58(3), 18–26.

Smith, C W and Stulz, R M, 1985, 'The determinants of firm hedging policies', *Journal of Financial and Quantitative Analysis*, 20(4), 391–405.

Spindler, J C, 2011, 'Mandatory long-term compensation in the banking system – and beyond?', *Cato Institute* Regulation Paper.

Suntheim, F, 2010, 'Managerial compensation in the financial service industry' http://ssrn.com/abstract=1592163 (last accessed 27 September 2015).

Vallascas, F and Hagendorff, J, 2013, 'CEO bonus compensation and bank default risk: evidence from the US and Europe', *Financial Markets, Institutions and Instruments*, 22(2), 47–89.

Velikonja, U, 2011, 'Leverage, sanctions, and deterrence of accounting fraud', *UC Davis Law Review*, 44, 1281–345.

Wehinger, G, 2013, 'Banking, ethics and good principles', *OECD Observer*, 294(1) http://www.oecdobserver.org/news/fullstory.php/aid/4017/Banking,_ethics_and_good_principles_.html (last accessed 27 September 2015).

Chapter 6

Gentlemen, players and remoralisation of banking: solution or diversion?

Ron Kerr and Sarah Robinson

In the aftermath of the Global Financial Crisis (GFC), the contribution of the British banks to the crisis has been the subject of a number of official and semi-official investigations. In the context of the crisis, in the United Kingdom (UK) the major relevant banks involved were Royal Bank of Scotland (RBS), HBOS (Halifax Bank of Scotland), Lloyds TSB, HSBC and Barclays. Of these, RBS declared a loss of £24.1 billion in 2009 and was bought out by the UK Government, HBOS declared a loss of £10.8 billion and, encouraged by the government, was merged with Lloyds TSB, whilst Barclays raised a massive loan from Qatari financial sources. In addition, certain other, smaller banks, e.g. Northern Rock, Bradford & Bingley and the Dunfermline Building Society, collapsed (Lanchester 2009; Perman 2012; Martin 2013; Fraser 2014).

Investigations into these banks' contributions to the GFC have identified problematic behaviours at all levels of these organisations, many of which have continued long after the onset of the crisis; indeed, more worryingly, unethical behaviours have continued to emerge post-crisis at banks including RBS again, HSBC, Standard Chartered and the Co-op. To date, criticisms have been levelled at bank executives both individually and as a class, including the managers and staff at the branch office level responsible for 'mis-selling' products such as payment protection insurance (PPI; see Peston 2011); derivative dealers and investment bankers; currency dealers (as Libor setters); mortgage and property lenders (offering interest rate swaps to small businesses); and foreign exchange (forex) traders (Chrispin 2015).

In the UK, official responses to these problems include the Turner review's 'Regulatory response' (Financial Services Authority 2009), the Financial Services Authority's (FSA) report on RBS (FSA 2011), the Vickers report on banking standards (Independent Commission on Banking 2011), the Wheatley review of the London interbank offered rate (Libor) fixing scandal (HM Treasury 2012) and the Tyrie Commission's report on banking standards (the Parliamentary Commission on Banking Standards 2013).

Non-official recommendations include the *Daily Mail*'s prescription of 'moral capitalism' (e.g. Heffer 2012) and the think-tank Rite-tank RespUblica's report, prescribing a return to what it calls 'virtuous banking' (ResPublica 2014). Such responses and recommendations can, we think, be categorised under two general headings: (1) improved state or supra-national regulation, e.g. increased capital ratios, the break-up of retail and investment operations, or the ring-fencing of 'casino banking'; and (2) a change in institutional culture, with the latter being seen as either in addition to, or as an alternative to, regulation (HM Treasury, Bank of England and Financial Conduct Authority 2015).

In this chapter we focus on prescriptions of the second type in order to address the following questions: in what ways can 'culture change' be conceptualised and understood in the context of banking; and to what extent is such proposed change feasible in the context of a neoliberal-dominated political economy? These questions arise from our supposition that changes in banking and finance in the UK cannot be divorced from changes in the social environment in which those organisations operate (following Bourdieu 1996). This sociological perspective allows us critically to examine these proposals and their presuppositions, in particular the way these appear to prescribe a return to what we take to be a quasi-imaginary past, in which banking was a gentlemanly profession conducted, at senior levels at least, by and between 'honourable gentlemen'.

In so doing, we also hope to shed light on the conservative moderniser's dilemma of how to hold together a society that marketisation is fragmenting, whilst at the same time promoting further marketisation: that is, what social equivalent of gravity will counteract the centrifugal force of the market by situating the moral subject in a framework of values? However, first we briefly summarise the historical events leading to the crash of 2008, focusing on changes in the field of banking and finance in Scotland that might help us to understand the major contribution of the Scottish banks, namely RBS and HBOS, to the crisis and, in particular, the contributory role of what has been understood as a culture change in the banking industry in the 1980s, which saw 'gentlemanly' values and behaviours being replaced by an acquisitive and competitive individualism (see Kerr and Robinson 2012).

From the Big Bang to the crash

The environment in which the UK banks operated changed during the 1980s. This was the period of Margaret Thatcher's ideological revolution (Hall 1988), which challenged the traditional establishment authority of the old Conservative ('Tory') elite, in favour of 'meritocracy'. Thatcherite reforms, what we now know as neoliberalism, included the 'Big Bang' deregulation of the City of London in 1986, which permitted commercial banks and investment banks to operate together in one institution, and the UK Financial Services Act (1986), which deregulated the British financial services industry, allowing, for example, building societies to demutualise and compete with the established banks for custom (Ingham 2002; Brender and Pisani 2009). This meant that the often locally embedded high-street banks began to move away from their social role as relationship-based banks, to become increasingly transactional-based 'universal banks' which, as they expanded and globalised, incorporated investment banking sections and speculation in financial instruments, allowing them to participate in high-risk 'casino banking' (Robinson and Kerr 2012).

In this period the Scottish banking and financial sector, based in Edinburgh, was the sixth biggest in Europe. Before 1990 the senior management of the major Scottish banks, namely the Bank of Scotland and RBS, had been dominated by an 'old guard' of traditionalists, moderate in ethos and conservative in outlook (Saville 1996). Senior managers followed a 'traditional' Anglo–Scottish gentlemanly social trajectory from a Scottish independent preparatory school to an English 'public' school (e.g. Eton, Harrow, Rugby, Winchester), then Oxbridge and, often, after the Second World War, a period of military service as one of the 'officer class'. These senior bankers and financiers shared a background with the dominant landed aristocratic Tory and Unionist political class of Scotland in the 1950s and 1960s. However, in addition to this traditional elite, senior management could accommodate a small number of 'bootstrap boys', who, joining the bank at 16, were socialised through and into the bank, with a few reaching senior positions (Kerr and Robinson 2011).

As Fourcade (2009: 33) notes, social distinction in England has been traditionally attained through 'social class and passage through an elite educational institution', plus the cultivation of 'interpersonal networks', rather than through formal qualifications per se. These elite institutions – the public schools, Oxford and Cambridge Universities, the armed forces – can be seen as having inculcated a sense of *noblesse oblige* or 'public spirited elitism' in social agents (Bourdieu 1989; Fourcade 2009: 33). This ethos is that of traditional 'gentlemanly capitalism' in England (see Augar 2002; Buchan 2003) and, by extension, in the Anglo–Scottish world of the Edinburgh banks, in which behaving honourably was a supreme value, *dictum meum pactum* (my word is my bond) being the motto of the London Stock Exchange.

In Scotland, individual exemplars of this traditional trajectory include Bruce Pattullo, Governor of the Bank of Scotland 1991–1998 and Michael Herries of the Royal Bank of Scotland (Oxford University Press 2009; Kerr and Robinson 2012). Pattullo's trajectory traversed Belhaven Scotland Hill School (an Edinburgh private school), Rugby (the English public school), Oxford University (Hertford College) and then the British army. Herries also followed this traditional Anglo-Scottish trajectory, educated at Eton and Cambridge (Trinity), followed by army service, with a detour as *taipan* of the Jardine Matheson trading house in Hong Kong. Pattullo's and Herries's leisure activities included those of the traditional Scottish landed elite, such as shooting (Herries) and hill walking (both). Both Herries and Pattullo were members of the Caledonian and New clubs in Edinburgh, elite social spaces that promote networking and exclusivity of social capital (see Wacquant 2002: 139).

This banking old guard can now be seen as moderates: their traditional approach to banking, their shared ethos, has been characterised as 'sticking to the knitting' and 'don't bet the bank', i.e. avoiding speculation and risk (Saville 1996: 808). The long-term strategy of the group was to protect Scottish banking independence, particularly from the City of London, through a focus on the longer term, on building local communities and developing local Scottish human capital (ibid). In Scotland, this old guard of gentlemanly bankers embodied the traditional 'Scottish' banking values of prudence, propriety, caution, discretion and 'a highly sceptical view of fashion' (Capie 1996; Saville 1996). Thus, according to George Graboys, Chief Executive Officer (CEO) of the Rhode Island-based Citizens Bank: 'Sir Michael (Herries) was an honourable man and we shared the same values about prudence in banking. This was part of Scotland's reputation' (quoted by Kemp 2011).

However, within the 'dog-eat-dog' economic environment encouraged by Thatcherite neoliberalism and increasing globalisation, there came a move away from the old Anglo–Scottish elite formation, towards an Americanised form of managerialism promoted by a new generation of general managers (Carroll 2009). Representatives of this new guard of 'modernisers' include George Mathewson, who became CEO of RBS in 1992. Mathewson came from a non-elite background, with degrees in maths and physics from Dundee (not at the time a university in its own right) and an MBA from a United States (US) college. Through a career trajectory from the aerospace industry in the US and then the oil industry in Scotland, Mathewson acquired the cultural capital of the transnational general manager who could then take on an insurgent role, importing 'modern' US management ideas into what he considered the 'dependency culture' of 'traditional' Scotland (Jamieson and Flanagan 2005).

Managerialist modernisers such as Mathewson, because they had no investment in 'the traditional culture of banking' (Fincham 2000: 186), could form 'an enlightened avant-garde, able to conceive, desire, and direct the change necessary' (Bourdieu 1979: 319). They were then able to revolutionise their organisations, in the RBS case by 'transforming the branch structure into something nearer a series of sales outlets' (Fincham 2000: 186) and 'replacing all-purpose branch managers with specialists in customer service' (Fincham 2000: 185). For banking leaders such as Mathewson and his protégé Fred Goodwin, the implication of these changes was to adapt to an 'eat or be eaten' competitive environment, through predatory expansion strategies, in the name of both self-interest and corporate interest (Kerr and Robinson 2011).

This change in elite composition from old guard to modernisers is linked to changes in what capitals count in the field. What counted in Scotland was no longer the elite cultural capital acquired in England – the shared British elite formation – but a post-Thatcher 'meritocracy' of Scottish management generalists, MBAs, cost-cutters and risk-takers, some formed by Thatcherite practices such as privatisation. This was Fred Goodwin's trajectory (Kerr and Robinson 2011). A key example of the 'new generation' of banking leaders, Goodwin was educated in Scotland at the fee-paying Paisley Grammar School, and was upwardly mobile. He was the first of his family to go to university, studying at Glasgow University, after which he operated as an accountant and management consultant and was involved in the privatisations and liquidations of the Thatcher period (Kerr and

Robinson 2012). His reputation, made in take-overs and associated cost-cutting, was one captured by his popular nickname 'Fred the shred' (i.e. shredder of jobs).

In 2000 Goodwin, until then deputy CEO, succeeded Sir George Mathewson as CEO of RBS (Warner 2006). This process of succession followed on the acquisition by RBS of the much larger London-based NatWest Bank, a struggle in which RBS had defeated its great historic Scottish competitor, Bank of Scotland, making RBS a banking power within the UK (Kerr and Robinson 2012; see also Garfield 1999; Martin 2013; Fraser 2014). This take-over, and the subsequent integration of the RBS and NatWest operations, was widely considered to be a triumph for Goodwin: see e.g., the Harvard Business School case study 'Masters of integration' (Nohria and Weber 2003) and the award of 'Businessman of the Year 2002' and 'The World's Greatest Banker' by *Forbes* (Morais 2003; Koenig 2003; Reid 2007). This prestige, or symbolic capital in Bourdieu's terms, was further confirmed by the award of a knighthood in 2004, conferred for 'services to banking'.

Within RBS itself, Goodwin's domination was maintained by what we term economic violence (Kerr and Robinson 2012). The RBS's internal culture has been characterised as a 'culture of fear' (Dey and Walsh 2009). There were, for example, rituals of humiliation when managers, watched by Goodwin, had to give karaoke performances. Morning management meetings, known as 'morning prayers' or 'morning beatings', were also used to humiliate senior managers (Dey and Walsh 2009). This kind of ritual of humiliation applied in particular to Goodwin's treatment of Johnny Cameron (CEO Corporate Markets, 2006–2009) whose trajectory was that of an old Scottish aristocratic and army family (Harrow, then Oxford), and who is reported to have been a particular target of Goodwin's attacks. In relation to Goodwin, Cameron was the dominated subordinate, thus reversing the 'old' elite order of dominant/dominated.

Under Goodwin, RBS pursued a strategy of expansion through the 'mercy killings' of rivals (Goodwin, quoted in Wachman 2004) and through further take-overs of banks and other related businesses in England and in the US (Martin 2013). Finally, in October 2007, the RBS led a consortium with Santander (Spain) and Fortis (Belgium) to take over ABN Amro, paying £49 billion (80 per cent in cash) for the Dutch bank (Lanchester 2009; Fraser 2014). Immediately after the take-over, RBS was (briefly) the biggest bank in the world.

However, at this point, the international financial system was already moving into crisis (Brender and Pisani 2009; Lanchester 2009). After a year of mounting emergency, in October 2008 the stock market collapsed and the money markets 'froze'. In the changed economic environment, ABN Amro was considered to be 'overvalued' and loaded with toxic debt (Fraser 2014). Moreover, Goodwin, apparently obsessed by the pursuit of ABN Amro in a deteriorating economic climate, had also missed problems of 'toxic assets' and bad debt in RBS itself (Lanchester 2009).

In January 2009 RBS posted the largest loss in UK corporate history, the announcement of which was followed by a UK Government bail-out and part-nationalisation (Kerr and Robinson 2012). Meanwhile HBOS, also weighed down with toxic assets and risky investments, was forced by prime minister Gordon Brown to merge with Lloyds Bank (Perman 2012). In the aftermath of the banking crisis, both Goodwin and Tom McKillop, who had replaced Mathewson as chair of RBS, and the senior leaders of HBOS resigned. So how was the role played by these 'dishonourable' banking leaders understood in the British public sphere?

Dishonourable bankers?

From the 1980s onwards, there had been an elite social and political consensus that top bankers would be recognised within the political field, as evidenced by the award of knighthoods and peerages (the latter allowing entry into the House of Lords). These 'cultural archaisms' (Corrigan and Sayer 1985) continued to serve as instruments of legitimation (Bourdieu 2012: 230–31). Bourdieu (2012, drawing on Corrigan and Sayer 1985) argues that the British honours system, including knighthoods, is one of the 'archaic' aspects of the British state that serves to integrate *arrivistes* into the elite: see e.g. the 'ennoblement of bankers' in the Edwardian period (Cassis 1994). Indeed, this 'archaic' phenomenon has ongoing contemporary relevance, with five (of six) CEOs of the Bank of Scotland from 1981 being knights (entitled to be addressed as 'Sir'), whilst for RBS, all the company's chairmen in that period have been 'Sir', as was Goodwin's predecessor as CEO, Sir George Mathewson and Mathewson's successor as chair, Sir Tom McKillop (Kerr and Robinson 2012).

However, this archaic – or pre-modern – system of honours had no provision (short of conviction in a court of law) for the possible subsequent 'degradation' of an individual who proved unworthy of 'honour'. The traditional honourable response to 'disgrace' would have been suicide (the army's 'glass of whisky and loaded pistol' solution). Today, however, there is no longer any socially-agreed system of what might be the ethical dimension of 'honour' and how honourable behaviour can be recognised. In ethical terms, honour is a somewhat empty term, its surviving function being to signal 'distinction'. Within banking as a contemporary social field (the post-gentlemanly era), there are no sustaining social or indeed professional *mores* that indicate what honourable behaviour might be. In place of *noblesse oblige*, a 'good' CEO, in neoliberal terms, is competitive, a risk-taker, a deal-maker, a cost-cutter and a job-shedder.

In the wake of the financial crisis, then, the banks had failed but no senior bankers had been punished. For the national press, in particular the populist *Sun* and the popular *Daily Mail*, the 'greedy bankers' had walked away 'Scot free' (Barrow 2011). (The *Daily Mail*, with a circulation of six million, targets a middle-class readership and is socially conservative rather than populist, i.e. it claims to represent the 'middle England' of largely suburban lower middle-class readers both to itself and to its readers: see Collins 2012.) The banking leaders, escaping with their bonuses and pension pots intact, in most cases into new jobs as managers or directors, left the taxpayers, savers and small shareholders – the *Mail*'s imagined community of readers – to pay for the crisis (Barrow 2011).

The *Mail*'s editorial approach to the banking crisis, then, was to moralise and personalise the crisis by focusing on guilty individuals – 'greedy bankers' – who had been 'rewarded for failure' after the collapse of their organisations. A search of the newspaper archives of the *Daily Mail* and of *The Sun* reveals that, in the wake of the financial crisis, the key epithets associated with 'bankers' in the press were *disgrace – shame – dishonour*. So, of the 47 occasions in the period 2009–2012 in which Goodwin was the subject of a headline or article in *The Sun*, he was identified as *shamed* on 22 occasions and *disgraced* on 20 occasions, i.e. in only five of these articles was Goodwin *not* either 'shamed' or 'disgraced'; whilst the *Daily Mail* preferred 'disgraced' (on 12 occasions) to 'shamed' (on four occasions).

This kind of stigmatisation of the bankers as 'shameful' or 'dishonourable' amounted, we might argue, to the constitution of a 'regime of opinion' (Macherey 2003), governed by symbolic categories with positive and negative poles, in this case *gloria* (glory) and *pudor* (shame) (Macherey 2003, drawing on Spinoza). This is a regime of opinion in which we, as part of the audience, are complicit in the attribution of *gloria* (glory) – which Burckhardt calls 'outward distinction' (Burckhardt 1951: 87) – and in attribution of shame. Therefore, we share in the construction and destruction of the public image of famous people (in contemporary societies, celebrities).

Thus, as a consequence of the bankers' escape from formal punishment, we can see how the *Daily Mail* began to campaign against the 'shamed' yet publicly-visible (in the press, in the wider media) Goodwin, urging the UK Government to remove his knighthood as a form of symbolic punishment. The *Mail*'s pursuit of Goodwin was, we could then argue, driven by a form of *ressentiment*, 'moral indignation' (Garfinkel 1956) or rage at 'the sinfulness and the illegality of the privileged' (Weber 1922/1966) and at the lack of any professional or legal punishment for the 'guilty' banking leaders (see e.g. Heffer 2012, writing in the *Daily Mail*). This campaign for a symbolic punishment for Goodwin finally succeeded on 31 January 2012, when the UK Government's Cabinet Office announced via press release that the Honours Forfeiture Committee, an 'occasional committee convened under the cabinet office' had recommended to the Queen that Sir Fred Goodwin's knighthood, awarded in 2004 for services to banking, be 'cancelled and annulled' (*Daily Mail* 2012).

However, the *Mail*'s campaign was also intended to have an effect on the field of banking and finance more widely, promoting a return to *noblesse oblige* and gentlemanly banking, that is, a return to what we might term a traditional regime of *honour*. For example, in a leading article entitled 'Bankers' greed and a matter of dishonour', the *Daily Mail* argued that Goodwin's punishment should constitute a warning to other bankers: 'Mr Goodwin's fate should teach (bankers) that today they have a clear choice. It lies between the dishonour of selfish greed – and their duty to help this nation out of the crisis they caused' (*Daily Mail* 2012).

However, other voices, including that of former chancellor of the exchequer

Alistair Darling, saw this punishment as an example of scapegoating. According to Durkheim, scapegoating is a way of managing anomie (Durkheim 1912/1995: 392, 404, 407, 412), an analysis based on *l'affaire Dreyfus*, in which a Jewish officer in the French army (Dreyfus) served as a sacrificial victim, in the context of the French defeat in the Franco–Prussian War. Max Weber connects scapegoating with *ressentiment*, defined by Brown (drawing on Nietzsche) as the 'imaginary revenge' of the 'weak', which takes the place of action, and serves to 'forestall substantive critique of, or intervention in, the larger systems that enable individual instances of social violence' (Brown 1995). For Weber, *ressentiment* is 'a concomitant of that particular religious ethic of the disprivileged which . . . teaches that the unequal distribution of mundane goods is caused by the sinfulness and the illegality of the privileged, and that sooner or later God's wrath will overtake them' (Weber 1922/1966: 110).

As a result of the *Daily Mail*'s campaign against Goodwin, the very signs of his public recognition, his honours, his cultural and symbolic capital, his distinction – that is, the things that elevated him, made him visible – were destroyed. In this context, we might indeed compare the way in which Goodwin was scapegoated and 'stripped of his honour' with the cashiering or public degradation of Dreyfus, who was stripped of his army rank, the symbols of his status destroyed, epaulettes torn off, sword broken, etc. For the headline writers, Goodwin was now no longer 'Sir Fred' or 'Sir Shred', but 'Fred the Pleb' or 'Mister Goodwin' (*Daily Mail* 2012). Goodwin was now counted as a member of the class of the disgraced and dishonoured: a class that includes Blunt the spy, Mugabe, Ceauşescu, Mussolini and Quisling, all of whom have had their British honours withdrawn.

However, in its campaign against 'bad apples', the *Mail* wanted to contain the financial crisis within the realm of the symbolic. Thus, certain 'bankers' were stigmatised and punished symbolically but this stigmatisation must not extend to 'business' in general (because 'Britain is open for business'). From this perspective, the story or stories of Goodwin as a 'disgraced' banker might be seen as a way of diverting attention from other ways of thinking about the crisis. Froud, Moran, Nilsson and Williams (2010), for instance, claim that the UK media's focus on 'bad' bankers contributed to the formation of an 'elite consensus' that facilitated the return to 'business as usual' for the financial system.

A gentleman's profession once again?

So how might the failure of the banks as social and economic institutions be addressed in order to avoid another crisis? What might be done at the level of individual and corporate culture? Might it be possible to reintroduce a professional regime of honour (following Macherey 2003)? In a sense, the various prescriptions for change in institutional culture mentioned in our introduction amount to *a return to the past of the gentlemanly bankers*. This medicine has been prescribed at the individual level ('get rid of the bad apples'), organisational level ('culture change') and professional level (prescriptions such as 'virtuous banking', with a 'bankers' vow'), in this last case drawing on Aristotelian virtue ethics (e.g. ResPublica 2014).

In his discussion of *noblesse oblige*, Bourdieu explains that 'there exist universes in which the search for strictly economic profit can be discouraged by explicit norms or tacit injunctions' (Bourdieu 1998: 86) and therefore 'to a certain extent, the aristocrat cannot do otherwise than be generous, through loyalty to his group and to himself as a person worthy of being a member of the group. That is what "noblesse oblige" means' (ibid: 87). Thus, 'nobility is nobility as a corporate body, as a group which, incorporated, embodied as a disposition, habitus, becomes the subject of noble practices, and obliges the noble to act in a noble fashion' (ibid: 87). The honourable man can do no other; he has no choice but to behave in this way.

However, as we have shown, with the onset of the GFC, the era of the honourable gentlemanly bankers had passed – although it may have continued to exist as an imaginary, haunting the popular imagination, including that of the press: otherwise, why this sense of disappointment at the lack of 'honour'? Indeed, Goodwin did not literally – or even metaphorically – 'fall on his sword' (to quote the *Daily Mail* 2009). That would have amounted to what Bourdieu calls a 'virtuous' or 'noble' action, one that would be expected of a defeated leader in a regime of honour (e.g. ancient Rome).

The *Daily Mail*'s campaign, although powered by *ressentiment* at the moral failings of the powerful, illustrates the dilemmas that arise for social conservatives in the political and other fields who espouse neoliberal economic policies. These difficulties arise from the social consequences of neoliberal economic policies, and they pose the problem of how to deal with the morally corrosive effects of self-interested market-based behaviours on more traditional and (no doubt in part imaginary) socially cohesive societies. So, when it turned out after 2008 that bankers were not a group of honourable gentlemen, an imaginary social contract, by means of which bankers would promote the national good in return for high remuneration, was seen to have been betrayed. Taming this destructive new world of competitive individualism would then require a reintroduction of some form of 'gentlemanly honour' or *noblesse oblige*; that is, 'the nobility that impedes the nobleman from doing certain things and allows him to do others' (Bourdieu 1998: 86).

However, we need to put this longing for a remoralised banking system in the context of the wider impact of neoliberalism – including changes in the dominant ethos at elite level. A regime of *noblesse oblige* had been replaced by a crude neoliberalism, which claimed that by pursuing individual utility (acquisitive individualism) executives would, through the magic of markets, benefit their businesses and then, through the trickling-down of wealth, society more widely. However, to ensure that executives' individual interests were aligned with those of the shareholders, understood as owners of the business, powerful incentives (bonuses) needed to be put in place (Kerr and Robinson 2011).

However, as became apparent in 2008–2009, this approach did not work; the worldview turned out to be mistaken, as evidenced by the 'shock' expressed by

Alan Greenspan, former chairman of the US Federal Reserve, that individuals and organisations pursuing their economic self-interest would not produce optimum results in a free market (Associated Press 2008). By this, Greenspan meant that agency theory (on which neoliberal-driven economics is in part based: see Rowlinson, Toms and Wilson 2006) could not account for why the bankers ended up destroying the businesses that they were charged with managing (Kerr and Robinson 2011).

We have argued that the resulting destruction of the Scottish banks can be attributed in part to a combination of leadership disconnect, predatory and competitive take-over strategies, extractive executive pay, an organisational 'culture of fear' and an unwillingness to hear bad news, in addition to the deskilling of front-line staff (Kerr and Robinson 2011, 2012). However, to address these problems solely by remaking banking as a gentlemanly pursuit would require an unthinkable social upheaval at the level of *wider* social values and practices – an upheaval that would somehow recreate an elite educational habitus and social trajectory, and which would at the same time coincide with a reversal of the supposedly unchallengeable forward march of neoliberal competitive individualism. As Bourdieu (1996: 127) notes: 'internal struggles (within a field) always depend, in outcome, on the correspondence that they maintain with the external struggles – whether struggles at the core of the field of power or at the core of the social field as a whole'.

Conclusion

In this chapter we set out to address the following questions: in what ways can 'culture change' be conceptualised and understood in the context of banking; and to what extent is such proposed change feasible in the context of a neoliberal-dominated political economy?

In tackling these questions we noted that there is a contradiction between a view of the self-seeking values of certain bankers, and the *Daily Mail*'s assumption that bankers were operating in a profession in which honour/dishonour *should have* social meaning, that is to say, that banking could and should be a field regulated by the gentlemanly values that were once displayed by the 'old guard' of *noblesse oblige*. These populist press expectations find some reply in the various prescriptions for 'culture change' and 'virtuous banking' that have been offered as solutions to the ethical problems that have arisen during and in the wake of the GFC.

We also noted the contradiction between the dominant neoliberal values of competitive individualism and traditional community, remembering that in 1821 the great conservative traditionalist Edmund Burke warned that when 'no man could know what could be the test of honour in a nation', then society is soon disconnected 'into the dust and powder of individuality' (Burke 1821: 133–34).

It would seem that, for the culture change proponents, the prescription is therefore a conservative one of *forward to the past*, an attempt to recreate the perhaps imaginary world of virtue and honour of the pre-neoliberal gentlemanly bankers

(Kerr and Robinson 2012). However, given the near-impossibility of this route back, we question whether a return to a banking culture of honourable gentlemen as an approach to controlling capitalism amounts to anything more than a pious wish to put the neoliberal genie back in the bottle from which it was released by Margaret Thatcher and her supporters.

References

Associated Press, 2008, 'Greenspan admits "mistake" that helped crisis' http://www.msnbc.msn.com/id/27335454 (last accessed 27 September 2015).

Augar, P, 2002, *The Death of Gentlemanly Capitalism*, London: Penguin.

Barrow, B, 2011, 'Fred the Shred gets off Scot free', *Daily Mail* (13 December 2011) http://www.dailymail.co.uk/news/article-2073368/Fred-Shred-gets-Scot-free-Fury-Goodwin-mentioned-just-13-times-report-RBS-collapse.html (last accessed 27 September 2015).

Bourdieu, P, 1979, *La distinction: critique sociale de jugement*, Paris: Les éditions de minuit.

Bourdieu, P, 1989, *La noblesse d'État. Grandes écoles et esprit de corps*, Paris: Les éditions de minuit.

Bourdieu, P, 1996, *The Rules of Art*, Cambridge: Polity Press.

Bourdieu, P, 1998, *Practical Reason: On the Theory of Action*, Cambridge: Polity.

Bourdieu, P, 2012, *Sur l'état: Cours au Collège de France (1989–1992)*, Paris: Raisons d'agir/Seuil.

Brender, A and Pisani, F, 2009, *Globalised Finance and its Collapse*, Belgium: Dexia SA.

Brown, W, 1995, *States of Injury: Power and Freedom in Late Modernity*, Princeton, NJ: Princeton UP.

Buchan, J, 2003, *Capital of the Mind: How Edinburgh Changed the World*, London: John Murray.

Burckhardt, J, 1951, *The Civilization of the Renaissance in Italy*, New York: Phaidon.

Burke, E, 1821, *Reflections on the Revolution in France*, London: John Sharpe.

Capie, F, 1996, 'The canny bankers of Auld Reekie', *Times Higher Education Supplement* (30 August 1996) https://www.timeshighereducation.co.uk/books/the-canny-bankers-of-auld-reekie/162257.article?storyCode=162257&sectioncode=8 (last accessed 28 September 2015).

Carroll, W, 2009, 'Transnationalists and national networkers in the corporate elite', *Global Networks*, 9(3), 289–314.

Cassis, Y, 1994, *City Bankers, 1890–1914*, Cambridge: Cambridge UP.

Chrispin, S, 2015, 'Forex scandal: how to rig the market', BBC Business News, http://www.bbc.co.uk/news/business-26526905 (last accessed 27 September 2015).

Collins, L, 2012, 'Mail supremacy: the newspaper that rules Britain', *The New Yorker* (2 April 2 2012) http://www.newyorker.com/reporting/2012/04/02/120402fa_fact_collins?currentPage=4 (last accessed 27 September 2015).

Corrigan, P and Sayer, D, 1985, *The Great Arch: English State Formation as Cultural Revolution*, Oxford: Blackwell.

Daily Mail, 2009, 'Bank crisis must not descend into anarchy' (26 March 2009) http://www.dailymail.co.uk/debate/article-1164926/MAIL-COMMENT-Bank-crisis-descend-anarchy.html (last accessed 27 September 2015).

Daily Mail, 2012, 'Let one man's shame be a symbol for all' (2 February 2012) http://www. dailymail.co.uk/debate/article-2095158/Fred-Goodwin-Let-mans-shame-symbol-all. html#ixzz1s8F63qf6 (last accessed 27 September 2015).

Dey, I and Walsh, K, 2009, 'How Fred shredded RBS', *The Times* (8 February 2009) http:// business.timesonline.co.uk/tol/business/industry_sectors/banking_and_finance/article5683436.ece (last accessed 27 September 2015).

Durkheim, E, 1912/1965, *The Elementary Forms of Religious Life*, New York: Free Press.

Financial Services Authority (FSA), 2009, *The Turner Review: A Regulatory Response to the Global Banking Crisis*, London: Financial Services Authority.

Financial Services Authority (FSA), 2011, *Board Report: The Failure of the Royal Bank of Scotland*, London: Financial Services Authority.

Fincham, R, 2000, 'Management as magic: re-engineering and the search for business salvation', in Knights, D and Willmott, H (eds), *The Reengineering Revolution: Critical Studies of Corporate Change*, London, UK: Sage, 174–90.

Fourcade, M, 2009, *Economists and Societies: Discipline and Profession in the United States, Britain, and France, 1890s to 1990s*, Princeton, NJ: Princeton UP.

Fraser, I, 2014, *Shredded. Inside RBS, the Bank that Broke Britain*, Edinburgh: Birlinn Limited.

Froud, J, Moran, M, Nilsson, A and Williams, K, 2010, 'Wasting a crisis? Democracy and markets in Britain after 2007', *The Political Quarterly*, 81(1), 25–38.

Garfield, A, 1999, 'Bank chiefs get personal in NatWest bid battle', *The Independent* (1 December 1999) http://www.independent.co.uk/news/business/news/bank-chiefs-get-personal-in-natwest-bid-battle-740904.html (last accessed 27 September 2015).

Garfinkel, H, 1956, 'Conditions of successful degradation ceremonies', *American Journal of Sociology*, 61(5), 420–24.

Hall, S, 1988, *The Hard Road to Renewal: Thatcherism and the Crisis of the Left*, London: Verso.

Heffer, S, 2012, 'If Dave truly believed in "moral capitalism", Fred Goodwin would be in jail sewing mailbags', *Daily Mail* (21 January 2012) http://www.dailymail.co.uk/debate/article-2089616/If-David-Cameron-truly-believed-moral-capitalism-Fred-Goodwin-jail.html#ixzz2erpd3IVi (last accessed 27 September 2015).

HM Treasury, 2012, *The Wheatley Review of LIBOR: Final Report*, London: HM Treasury.

HM Treasury, Bank of England and Financial Conduct Authority, 2015, 'Fair and Effective Markets Review. Final Report', London: Bank of England (10 June 2015) http://www.bankofengland.co.uk/markets/Documents/femrjun15.pdf (last accessed 27 September 2015).

Independent Commission on Banking, 2011, *The Vickers Report: Beyond the Ring-fence*, London: HM Government.

Ingham, G, 2002, 'Shock therapy in the City', *New Left Review*, 6, 152–58.

Jamieson, B and Flanagan, M, 2005, 'Money and intolerance: the Royal Bank of Scotland turn around', *The Scotsman* (16 April 2005) http://clippednews.blogspot.be/2005/04/money-intolerance-royal-bank-of.html (last accessed 27 September 2015).

Kemp, K, 2011, 'The rise and fall of the RBS American dream', *Herald Scotland* (6 January 2011).

Kerr, R and Robinson, S, 2011, 'Leadership as an elite field: the role of the Scottish banks in the crisis of 2007–2009', *Leadership*, 7(2), 153–75.

Kerr, R and Robinson, S, 2012, 'From symbolic violence to economic violence: the globalizing of the Scottish banking elite', *Organization Studies*, 33(2), 247–66.

Koenig, P, 2003, 'Special Report: Is RBS's Fred the Shred too good to be true?' *Times*

Online http://www.thesundaytimes.co.uk/sto/business/article42378.ece (last accessed 28 September 2015).

Lanchester, J, 2009, 'It's finished', London Review of Books (28 May 2009) http://www.lrb.co.uk/v31/n10/john-lanchester/its-finished (last accessed 28 September 2015).

Macherey, P, 2003, *Le couple catégoriel gloria/pudor (gloire/honte) chez Descartes et Spinoza*, Un texte de Pierre Macherey au groupe de travail 'Esprit', http://stl.recherche.univ-lille3.fr/sitespersonnels/macherey/Machereygloria.html (last accessed 28 September 2015).

Martin, I, 2013, *Making it Happen: Fred Goodwin, RBS and the Men Who Blew Up the British Economy*, London: Simon & Schuster.

Morais, R, 2003, 'Brisk and brusque', *Forbes* http://www.forbes.com/global/2003/0106/034.html (last accessed 28 September 2015).

Nohria, N and Weber, J, 2003, *Royal Bank of Scotland: Masters of Integration*, Cambridge, Mass: Harvard Business School.

Oxford University Press, 2009, *Who's Who 2009 and Who Was Who*, Oxford: Oxford University Press http://www.ukwhoswho.com/ (last accessed 28 September 2015).

Parliamentary Commission on Banking Standards, 2013, *Final Report: Changing Banking for Good*, London: House of Commons.

Perman, R, 2012, *Hubris: How HBOS Wrecked the Best Bank in Britain*, Edinburgh: Birlinn.

Peston, R, 2011, 'Banking industry gives up on PPI mis-selling battle', *BBC News* (9 May 2011) http://www.bbc.com/news/business-13330858 (last accessed 28 September 2015).

Reid, M, 2007, 'Is this man the world's greatest banker?' *The Times* (11 October 2007).

ResPublica, 2014, 'Virtuous banking: placing ethos and purpose at the heart of finance', London: ResPublica http://www.respublica.org.uk/our-work/publications/virtuous-banking-placing-ethos-purpose-heart-finance (last accessed 28 September 2015).

Rowlinson, M, Toms, S and Wilson, J, 2006, 'Legitimacy and the capitalist corporation: cross-cutting perspectives on ownership and control', *Critical Perspectives on Accounting*, 17(5), 681–702.

Saville, R, 1996, *Bank of Scotland: A History 1695–1995*, Edinburgh: Edinburgh University Press.

Wachman, R, 2004, 'Fred – in tooth and claw', *The Observer* (22 February 2004) http://www.guardian.co.uk/business/2004/feb/22/theobserver.observerbusiness7 (last accessed 28 September 2015).

Wacquant, L, 2002, 'De l'idéologie à la violence symbolique: culture, classe et conscience chez Marx et Bourdieu', in Lojkine, J (ed), *Les sociologies critiques du capitalisme*, Paris: Presses Universitaires de France, 25–40.

Warner, J, 2006, 'Sir George Mathewson: Royal Bank of Scotland saviour takes his final curtain call', *The Independent* (29 April 2006) http://www.independent.co.uk/news/business/analysis-and-features/sir-george-mathewson-royal-bank-of-scotland-saviour-takes-his-final-curtain-call-6102439.html (last accessed 9 October 2015).

Weber, M, 1922/1966, *The Sociology of Religion*, London: Social Science Paperbacks.

Williams, G and Filippakou, O, 2009, 'Higher education and UK elite formation in the twentieth century', *Higher Education*, 59(1), 1–20.

Part III

Concession: private regulation in the ascendancy

Chapter 7

Public and private financial regulation in the EU: opposites or complements?

Olha O Cherednychenko

Introduction

The European financial industry has played a major role in the regulation of financial markets across the world, including in the European Union (EU). In particular, professional associations of banks and other financial service providers set standards of behaviour to be observed by their members when dealing with (potential) clients. The last three decades or more, however, have witnessed the rise of public regulation in the area of financial services. This trend received a major boost in the aftermath of the global financial crisis that was triggered by the collapse of the subprime mortgage market in the United States (US) in 2007.

The crisis exposed the risks that lack of public regulation in the financial services field can pose, not only to individual consumers but also to the functioning of the financial markets and economy at large (Financial Services Authority (FSA) 2009). We have seen, for example, how irresponsible lending in the largely unregulated US subprime mortgage market not only hurt the house-buyers who signed up to mortgage contracts and then faced the loss of their homes but also caused widespread third-party effects around the globe, including in Europe.

In response, both at EU and at Member State level, the regulatory grip on the financial services industry has tightened in the post-crisis period. This is reflected in the introduction of new public regulatory measures in areas previously subject to private regulation, such as the CRA I Regulation (European Parliament and the Council 2009), as amended by the CRA II Regulation (European Parliament and the Council 2013) and the Payment Accounts Directive (European Parliament and the Council 2014d); the move away from the largely principles-based public regulation (that has strong resonances with private regulatory techniques) towards more prescriptive and centralised public regulation (Scott 2010: 9; Moloney 2010: 8; Moloney 2012: 180); and a paradigm shift in financial consumer protection from 'soft' paternalism (concerned with the consumer's ability to make well informed decisions) towards 'hard' paternalism (associated with restrictions on potentially harmful consumer transactions, such as financial product bans: see Cherednychenko 2014b).

In addition, with the establishment of a new institutional framework for financial supervision – the European System of Financial Supervision (ESFS), the post-crisis era has witnessed a major move towards a greater Europeanisation and centralisation of public supervision in the financial services field. The ESFS is formed of the three sectoral European Supervisory Authorities (ESAs) – the European Securities and Markets Authority (ESMA), the European Banking Authority (EBA) and the European Insurance and Occupational Pensions Authority (EIOPA) – plus the European Systemic Risk Board (ESRB) and national supervisory authorities. In particular, the ESAs avail themselves of their far-reaching powers to govern the financial services industry. This can be illustrated by using the example of ESMA, whose mission is to enhance investor protection and to reinforce stable and well functioning financial markets in the EU.

Whilst its predecessor – the Committee of European Securities Regulators (CESR) – was a network-based advisory body, ESMA's powers reach much further (see Moloney 2011a; Moloney 2011b). In particular, ESMA is conferred with considerable powers to adopt technical standards implementing the legislative measures of a more general character and to issue 'strong' guidelines and recommendations with which local supervisory authorities and financial institutions are required to 'make every effort to comply' (Busuioc 2013; Chiti 2013).

In addition, ESMA has direct supervisory powers over market actors, including the power temporarily to prohibit or restrict certain financial activities, as specified in relevant EU legislation, and extensive powers to gather information concerning financial supervision practices from local supervisory authorities. The rise of public supervision over private relationships between financial service providers and their (potential) clients at EU and Member State level has led to the emergence of 'European supervision private law' (Cherednychenko 2014a, cf. Biggins and Scott: Chapter 8 in this volume). This body of rules is made up of contract-related conduct of business rules for financial institutions, which are cast as supervision standards and are further elaborated and enforced by financial regulators.

These developments give rise to the question of the extent to which private actors still have a role to play in regulating financial services in the post-crisis era. A number of commentators have argued that, in the aftermath of the financial crisis, the pendulum has shifted away from private regulation and market discipline to a more interventionist role for the public sector (Germain 2010; Foot and Walter 2011; Pagliari 2012). In the words of the former French president Nicolas Sarkozy: 'The present crisis must incite us to refound capitalism on the basis of ethics and work . . . Self-regulation as a way of solving all problems is finished. *Laissez-faire* is finished. The all-powerful market that always knows best is finished' (*EU Observer* 2008).

In this chapter I argue that private regulation in the financial services field has not been entirely displaced by the post-crisis public regulation (cf. Moschella and Tsingou 2013; Andenas and Chiu 2014: 101 ff; see also Cafaggi and Renda 2012). Contrary to the traditional dichotomy between purely private regulation and command and control public regulation, there is still room for the interplay between public and private actors in governing financial services in a multi-level EU legal order. In fact, such an interplay is necessary in the post-crisis era, given that the financial services sector remains a 'decentred' regulatory space (Black 2002a; Black 2002b; Black 2003; see also Goodhart and others 1998) that is characterised, inter alia, by a high degree of complexity, fragmentation of knowledge, resources and capacity for control, as well as unpredictability of actor behaviour.

In this context, I will focus on two forms of complementarity between public and private regulation that are familiar from before the crisis and remain on the agenda in the post-crisis EU – co-regulation and meta-regulation – and I will discuss the major strengths and weaknesses of each form in achieving desired regulatory outcomes. The concept of private regulation is thus understood here in a broad sense, encompassing the rules for private actors that are produced and/ or enforced not only by such actors themselves alone, but also by private actors in cooperation with public actors, with varying degrees of the latter's involvement (Ogus 1995; Gunningham and Rees 1997; Sinclair 1997; Cafaggi 2011). I will conclude with some observations concerning the interplay between public and private actors in financial regulation in the EU.

Co-regulation

In co-regulation, public regulators define mandatory open norms or minimum standards, whilst private regulators fill them in (Cafaggi 2011: 107). In addition, private actors, in particular private alternative dispute resolution (ADR) bodies, may play an important role in the enforcement of regulatory standards (Meijer and Hansen: Chapter 10 in this volume). The involvement of private actors in standard-setting and/or enforcement may be explicitly mandated by the EU public regulation (formal co-regulation), or be (strongly) encouraged, or simply not precluded (informal co-regulation). In any case, private regulation contributes to the attainment of the specific objectives of public regulation in several respects, now discussed.

Standard-setting

A good illustration of the involvement of private actors in standard-setting within the statutory framework that implicitly leaves room for co-regulation can be found in the area of consumer credit. The Consumer Credit Directive currently in force (European Parliament and the Council 2008), which remained intact in the wake of the post-crisis financial reforms, aims at fostering market integration and ensuring a high level of consumer protection in simple unsecured consumer credit transactions. For this purpose, it obliges Member States, inter alia, to ensure that, before the conclusion of the credit agreement, the creditor assesses the consumer's creditworthiness (ibid: Article 8).

However, the directive does not specify the criteria on which the consumer's creditworthiness must be assessed or when the consumer can be considered as creditworthy. The open-ended nature of the creditor's duty to assess the consumer's creditworthiness laid down in this directive allows Member States considerable leeway in implementing this obligation of EU origin in national laws and does not preclude them from involving private actors in shaping its content. This is despite the fact that the Consumer Credit Directive is a full harmonisation measure that formally precludes Member States from maintaining or introducing in their national laws provisions diverging from those laid down in the directive (ibid: Article 22; on the implications of full harmonisation for private regulation more generally, see Cafaggi 2011: 101 ff). In practice, therefore, private actors in some Member States have played a significant role in elaborating the concept of consumer creditworthiness in simple consumer credit transactions.

This has been the case, for example, in the Netherlands, where the national legislator imposed a general duty on creditors to act as 'responsible lenders', so as to prevent consumer over-indebtedness; for this purpose, it only obliged creditors to assess whether the consumer is creditworthy before the conclusion of the credit agreement, and to refuse granting credit if this is not the case (Queen of the Netherlands 2006a: Article 4:34). The meaning of this open statutory norm as far as the assessment of the consumer's creditworthiness in simple consumer credit transactions is concerned is mainly fleshed out in the codes of conduct of the three branch organisations: the Code of Conduct of the Netherlands Association of Consumer Finance Companies (*Vereniging van Financieringsondernemingen in Nederland* (*VFN*)), the Consumer Credit Code of the Dutch Banking Association (*Gedragscode Consumptief Crediet van de Nederlandse Vereniging van Banken* (*NVB*)) and the Code of Conduct of the Dutch Home Shopping Organisation (*Gedragscode van de Nederlandse Thuiswinkelorganisatie* (*NTO*)).

All three codes of conduct share the same starting point for assessing whether the consumer is creditworthy and the provision of credit is thus justified: upon incurring interest- and repayment-related obligations under the credit agreement, the consumer must still have sufficient means to provide for his or her basic needs and to bear his or her recurring expenses. If this is not the case, providing credit would be considered irresponsible. What is more, the Dutch financial supervisory authority – the Netherlands Authority for the Financial Markets (*Autoriteit Financiële Markten* (*AFM*)) – regards the provisions of the codes of conduct as minimum norms for responsible lending.

If a particular lender is not bound by one of the codes of conduct, it may use other norms, provided that the latter offer the same or a higher level of consumer protection. Consequently, the disregard of the provisions of the codes of conduct by the financial institution when providing credit to consumers may result in the violation of the statutory rules on responsible lending, regardless of whether the institution is formally bound by a particular code of conduct or not. In such a case, the Dutch financial supervisory authority may impose administrative sanctions, such as an administrative fine.

In addition, civil courts could follow the norms on responsible lending embodied in the codes of conduct when interpreting and applying general private law concepts, such as the lender's duty of care towards its clients. Acting contrary to the relevant code of conduct may thus also lead to the lender's civil liability for the damage suffered by the consumer as a result of irresponsible lending or trigger other private law consequences. In this way, private regulation within the statutory framework can also be supported by the public and private enforcement mechanisms provided by the state.

Private regulation at Member State level could also play a similar, albeit more limited, role under the newly adopted Mortgage Credit Directive (European Parliament and the Council 2014a). This post-crisis EU regulatory measure aims to create a Union-wide mortgage credit market with a high level of consumer protection. Like the Consumer Credit Directive, the Mortgage Credit Directive also obliges creditors to assess the consumer's creditworthiness (ibid: Article 18(1)).

However, in contrast to the former, the latter provides more guidance as to how this should be done. This assessment should be thorough and take into account all necessary and relevant factors which could influence a consumer's ability to meet his or her obligations under the credit agreement over its lifetime (ibid: Article 18(1) and recital 55). Such factors include, on the one hand, future payments under the mortgage credit and other regular expenditure, debts and other financial commitments of the consumer and, on the other, his or her income, savings and assets (ibid: recital 55).

In addition, reasonable allowance should be made for future events, such as reduction in income or increase in the borrowing rate (ibid: recital 55). The creditworthiness test cannot rely predominantly on the fact that the value of the property exceeds the amount of the credit or the assumption that the property will increase in value, unless the purpose of the credit agreement is to construct or renovate the property (ibid: Article 18(3) and recital 55). In addition, in contrast to the Consumer Credit Directive, which does not deal with the consequences of the negative outcome of the creditworthiness test, the Mortgage Credit Directive obliges the creditor to refuse granting credit to a consumer in such a case (ibid: Article 18(5)(a)).

Whilst these provisions of the Mortgage Credit Directive reduce the room for manoeuvre for the Member States and private regulators in making responsible lending rules for consumer mortgage credit contracts, they do not altogether preclude co-regulation at the national level. All the more so, given that they are subject only to minimum harmonisation, which allows Member States to maintain or introduce more stringent rules (ibid: recital 7). Private actors could thus still draw up codes of conduct addressing the issue of responsible lending within the regulatory framework established by the EU legislator in the Mortgage Credit Directive, provided that the national implementing legislation also allows some leeway for such activities.

Enforcement

In addition to standard-setting within the regulatory framework established by the EU and/or national legislator, private actors could also be involved in enforcement activities within such a framework. The legal basis for their involvement can even be laid down in EU public regulation. Thus, for example, the Markets in Financial Instruments Directive II (MiFID II) (European Parliament and the Council 2014b), which was adopted in the aftermath of the financial crisis, obliges the Member States to ensure the setting up of extra-judicial bodies and an active cooperation of such bodies with their counterparts in other Member States in the resolution of cross-border disputes, using, where appropriate, existing cross-border cooperation mechanisms, notably the Financial Services Complaints Network (FIN-NET) (ibid: Article 75).

The Directive makes it clear that such extra-judicial bodies can be either public or private (ibid: recital 151). Whilst some Member States opted for the establishment of public bodies, such as the Financial Ombudsman Service in the UK, others chose to set up private bodies, such as the Financial Services Complaints Institute (*Klachteninstituut financiële dienstverlening (KiFID)*) in the Netherlands. The latter plays an important role in the settlement of disputes between financial institutions and consumers, inter alia, in the investment services field harmonised by the MiFID II, and thus has the potential to contribute to the attainment of the regulatory objectives pursued by the MiFID II in this area, in particular, ensuring a high level of investor protection.

Strengths and weaknesses

The involvement of private actors in standard-setting and/or enforcement within the EU public regulatory framework for financial services allows the EU legislator to address the problem of regulator/market information-asymmetry and to fine-tune a particular regulatory regime in response to the local circumstances (cf. Cafaggi and Renda 2012: 5). The need for co-regulation deepens as financial markets become more complex.

However, designing a well functioning co-regulatory arrangement in the financial services field is not an easy task. Potential problems include conflicts of interest, inadequate accountability and insufficient compliance. It may prove particularly difficult to ensure that a private regulatory regime set up within the public regulatory framework offers an optimal level of consumer protection, so as to avoid the need for command and control public regulation. For example, in the aftermath of the financial crisis, the Dutch Government largely replaced the provisions on responsible consumer mortgage lending laid down in the Mortgage Financing Code of Conduct (*Gedragscode Hypothecaire Financieringen (GHF)*) (drawn up by the Dutch Banking Association) with much more prescriptive and protective provisions of the delegated act – Temporary Mortgage Credit Regulations of 12 December 2012 as amended on 30 October 2013 (*Tijdelijke regeling hypothecair krediet*) (Minister of Finance of the Netherlands 2012; see Cherednychenko 2014b: 414). Private regulation in the area of consumer mortgage credit was considered to have failed to provide a sufficient level of consumer protection against over-indebtedness.

Not only private but also public regulation, however, faces difficulties in terms of designing an optimal regulatory regime. In particular, over-protective public regulation may not perform well in markets characterised by consumer heterogeneity (Epstein 2008: 810). A related concern is that highly paternalistic public regulation may backfire against consumers and thus prove ineffective in practice. Restrictive rules on responsible lending, for example, may prevent consumers from gaining credit from licensed creditors and force them into the arms of shady lenders, who charge much higher interest rates (Epstein 2008: 831).

Therefore, the substitution of co-regulatory rules in the financial services field by hard core public regulation and/or public soft law produced by financial watchdogs is not without risk. In fact, private regulation within the statutory framework may be better equipped to strike the right balance between freedom and protection, particularly if both financial institutions and consumer associations are involved in the process of private rule-making. Good governance arrangements for private rule-making are essential in this context.

Meta-regulation

In addition to co-regulation, complementarity between public and private regulation in the EU may develop through meta-regulation. Meta-regulation stimulates modes of self-organisation within financial institutions so as to achieve certain public goals (on meta-regulation in general, see Parker 2002; Gunningham 2010; Coglianese and Mendelson 2010; Gilad 2010; Scott 2012). This means that rather than regulating prescriptively (by telling the regulated entities precisely what measures to take), public regulation provides an explicit framework for systems, procedures or controls that must be introduced within financial institutions. The primary role of public regulators is to rely upon the financial institutions themselves to put in place appropriate systems and oversight mechanisms and to take the necessary measures to ensure that these mechanisms are effective. By establishing their own systems of internal control and management, financial institutions in their turn could contribute to the attainment of the specific regulatory objectives pursued by the EU public regulation.

Framework-setting

Meta-regulation has not been entirely rejected by EU post-crisis reforms. In fact, in some areas, post-crisis financial services regulation heavily relies on this approach. Thus, for example, MiFID II (European Parliament and the Council 2014b) explicitly lays down a new product governance regime, which involves regulatory oversight of the product design process aimed at preventing investment firms from developing dangerous investment products. Thus, the MiFID II obliges management bodies of investment firms to define, approve and oversee a policy as to such products in accordance with the firms' risk tolerance and the characteristics and needs of their clients, including carrying out stress testing, where appropriate (ibid: Article 9(3)).

In particular, investment firms that manufacture investment products for sale to clients should maintain, operate and review a process for the approval of each product or significant adaptations of existing products before they are marketed or distributed to clients; the product approval process should specify an identified target market of end clients for each product, ensure that all relevant risks to such market are assessed, and that the intended distribution strategy is consistent with it (ibid: Article 16(3)).

ESMA appears ready to play an active role in clarifying the content of these organisational requirements (ESMA 2014). By imposing such requirements on investment firms, MiFID II enables supervision over product development processes within the firms by national financial supervisory authorities. It opens up possibilities for regulatory intervention where these processes are not organised in a manner which promotes the interests of clients and the integrity of the financial market. The legal basis for such actions is provided by Article 69 of the MiFID II concerning supervisory powers.

Moreover, although some Member States, including Germany for example, remain cautious about resorting to product governance without explicit prompting by EU harmonisation, other Member States, including the Netherlands and the UK, have already introduced robust product governance regimes. In the Netherlands, the financial supervision requirements for financial institutions to have product development and approval processes in place came into force on 1 January 2013 (see Queen of the Netherlands, 2006b: Article 32). The new product governance regime aims to prevent mass consumer detriment resulting from defective financial products and it covers all financial products developed and offered by financial institutions, including investment products. The main rule is that, when developing a particular financial product, financial institutions should have appropriate procedures and regulations in place to ensure that balanced consideration has been given to the interests of the consumers of the financial product and that the financial product is demonstrably the result of this consideration of interests.

In particular, the required internal procedures and regulations within financial institutions should delineate a target group of consumers for the product and should conduct tests to establish that the product performs in a way that does not impair consumers' investment objectives. In the event that a particular product harms consumer interests, the financial institutions should adjust the product as quickly as possible, or cease to offer it.

What is more, based on these regulations, the Dutch financial regulator actively supervises not only the product development *processes* but also the resulting *products*. This supervisory body assesses the products from the consumer's perspective based on the four criteria: (1) cost efficiency (does the product offer value for money?); (2) usefulness (does the product fulfil a predefined need of a specific target group of consumers?); (3) safety (does the product do what it is supposed to do in different situations and is the outcome acceptable for the target group?); (4) understandability (is the product not needlessly complicated and can the consumer adequately judge its quality and suitability for his needs?) (Netherlands Authority for the Financial Markets 2013).

If the product fails to meet one or more of these criteria, it can be considered to be harmful for consumers, which can trigger enforcement action against the product provider for failure to comply with the relevant financial supervision requirements. Whilst the Dutch financial regulator has the power to take formal, essentially punitive, enforcement action against the financial institutions in order to ensure that the latter refrain from introducing potentially detrimental financial products, it currently tends to resort to informal enforcement actions for this purpose, in particular, by actively engaging in dialogue with the financial institutions (Ottow and Svetiev 2014: 538).

A similar product governance regime has also already been introduced in the UK, with a view to preventing potential consumer detriment before it develops. In the same way as the Netherlands Authority for the Financial Markets, the UK's Financial Conduct Authority (FCA) – the successor of the Financial Services Authority (FSA) – avails itself of extensive powers to supervise the product governance processes and the investment products that these deliver (for an overview, see FSA 2011: 32 ff; for an example of the FSA approach, see FSA 2012).

In addition, a meta-regulation approach features prominently in the EU's Credit Rating Regulation (CRA I), as amended by the CRA II (European Parliament and the Council 2009). In order to ensure independence and integrity of credit rating agencies and their credit rating activities in the EU, this regulation lays down a number of framework principles for the internal organisation of credit rating agencies. In particular, it obliges such agencies to be organised in a way that ensures that their business interest does not impair the independence or accuracy of the credit rating agencies (European Parliament and the Council 2009: Annex I, Section A para 2); to have sound administrative, accounting, internal control and risk management systems and procedures (ibid: Annex I, Section A para 4); to establish appropriate and effective organisational and administrative arrangements to prevent, identify, eliminate or manage and disclose any conflicts of interest (ibid: Annex I, Section A para 7); to employ appropriate systems, resources and procedures to ensure continuity and regularity in the performance of its regulatory activities (ibid: Annex I, Section A para 8); and to monitor and evaluate the adequacy and effectiveness of its systems, internal control mechanisms and arrangements and take appropriate measures to address any deficiencies (ibid: Annex I, Section A para 10).

Strengths and weaknesses

Such open-textured organisational requirements allow regulated financial institutions to shape their governance structures according to their own needs but in the spirit of the public regulatory regimes, and to engage in self-critical evaluation and learning about their regulatory performance in an uncertain environment. Here lies the major strength of meta-regulation, compared with traditional command and control public regulation. This is confirmed by the findings from organisational psychology, in particular the self-determination theory developed by Deci and Ryan (1985). These authors argue that the optimal human condition is one where individuals develop both a sense of positive motivation and responsibility; the contextual factors that lead to this are those that promote autonomy, feelings of competence and relatedness (Deci and Ryan 1985).

Based on these contextual factors identified by self-determination theory, Rupp and Williams, for example, have argued that when regulation develops in a principles-based fashion, with cooperative relationships between regulator and regulated becoming part of the regulatory environment, then regulated entities can be expected to engage more deeply with the values and goals of the particular regulatory instrument than when regulation lays down narrow requirements strictly regulating their behaviour (Rupp and Williams 2011; see also Williams and Conley 2014).

In my view, this may be particularly true for meta-regulation. By encouraging the financial industry to put in place effective modes of self-organisation with a view to realising certain public goals, meta-regulation has the potential to prompt a cultural reorientation towards public values within the financial institutions. Without such cultural change, it is highly doubtful whether more prescriptive public regulation aimed at ensuring a high level of client protection in financial services will be able to realise this goal.

However, in delivering public value, meta-regulation faces major challenges. One of the biggest challenges is how to ensure its effectiveness, particularly when meta-regulation is in place alongside with prescriptive command and control regulation. This is the case, for example, under the MiFID II which, in addition to a product governance regime, also comprises a range of product intervention techniques targeted at potentially dangerous investment products themselves. In particular, national financial supervisory authorities are given the power to suspend the marketing or sale of investment products where the investment firm has not developed or applied an effective product approval process as described above (European Parliament and the Council 2014b: Article 69(2)(t)).

Moreover, such authorities may also prohibit, suspend or restrict the marketing or sale of investment products in or from its Member State where significant investor protection concerns arise, or a threat is posed to the orderly functioning and integrity of financial markets or to the stability of the whole or part of the financial system within at least one Member State (European Parliament and the Council 2014c: Article 42 and European Parliament and the Council 2014b:

Article 69(2)(s) in conjunction with European Parliament and the Council 2014c: Article 42). In addition, ESMA may intervene in national markets by temporarily prohibiting or restricting the marketing or sale of investment products in similar circumstances (European Parliament and the Council 2014c: Article 40).

This power of ESMA relates to the general clause in ESMA's founding regulation, which empowers ESMA temporarily to prohibit or restrict certain financial activities in the cases specified in relevant EU legislation or in the case of an emergency situation (European Parliament and the Council 2010: Article 9(5)). By combining *indirect* product control through process-based organisational requirements for investment firms with *direct* product control and product banning powers in serious cases, the post-crisis EU regulation aims to prevent potential consumer detriment resulting from the purchase of dangerous investment products. But does such a combination of regulatory instruments foster a cultural reorientation within the financial institutions towards taking the consumers' interests more seriously? As Andenas and Chiu aptly put it:

> Bright line rules and prohibitions often entail a compliance mindset that is focused on the boundary between what is compliant and not compliant. But meta-regulation requires the application of a different mindset, that of understanding and willingness to achieve the spirit and purpose of regulatory regimes. Will senior management be able to embrace the requirements of both types of regulatory regimes?
>
> (Andenas and Chiu 2014: 209)

In this context, the role of financial regulators in supervising and enforcing compliance with meta-regulation becomes particularly important. However, meta-regulation may not be straightforward to enforce, and financial regulators have accumulated little experience in this area, especially when it comes to product governance arrangements. Thus, there is a risk that regulators will exercise only passive compliance monitoring and resort to formal enforcement actions with the use of punitive administrative sanctions such as pecuniary penalties. As Hopkins and Wilkinson have emphasised, however, the regulator's job under the meta-regulation approach involves *actively* challenging the regulated entities to demonstrate that their systems really work in practice (Hopkins and Wilkinson 2005).

This, in my view, could be done more effectively if there is a clear link between organisational frameworks and the achievement of regulatory outcomes, such as better quality financial products or accurate credit ratings. The Dutch and UK approaches – whereby, as mentioned above, the financial regulator actively supervises not only the product development *processes* but also the resulting *products* – may provide useful insights for EU regulation, where the link between the two is much less straightforward. What is more, the 'innovation hub' developed by the UK's FCA in 2014, with a view to supporting both small and large business in developing innovative financial products that would suit consumer needs, provides an excellent example of collaborative governance between public and private actors in this area. In the words of the FCA's chief executive, Martin Wheatley (FCA 2014): 'This work levels the playing field by giving all firms eager to innovate access to our expertise so that the process of joining the financial markets or introducing new products does not seem so daunting'.

The need for promoting a dialogue between the financial industry and regulators has also been recently emphasised in the UK's Fair and Effective Markets Review, launched by the Chancellor of the Exchequer and the Governor of the Bank of England with a view to reinforcing confidence in the wholesale Fixed Income, Currency and Commodities (FICC) markets and influencing the international debate on trading practices in this area (HM Treasury and others 2015).

In fact, given that the product governance regimes in the EU Member States are still largely untried and insufficiently specific, it is highly questionable to what extent they actually lend themselves to formal enforcement actions, with the use of pecuniary penalties and other punitive administrative sanctions as envisaged in the MiFID II (European Parliament and the Council 2014b: arts 70–72). It is notable in this context that national financial supervisory authorities across the EU do not exclusively rely on formal enforcement actions against investment firms but increasingly engage in informal enforcement practices, particularly when it comes to product governance (see Ottow and Svetiev 2014). The Europeanisation and centralisation of public supervision and enforcement, however, may significantly limit the possibilities for national supervisory authorities to experiment with a variety of techniques within meta-regulation. This in turn could seriously jeopardise the realisation of regulatory objectives.

Concluding remarks

The preceding analysis has explored the interplay between public and private actors in regulating financial services in the EU in the post-crisis era. It has shown that, despite the rise of public regulation and supervision after the crisis, private regulation has not lost its significance in governing financial services in the EU. The conventional opposition between self-regulation by the financial industry (commonly associated with its freedom) and public regulation produced by the EU or national public authorities (commonly associated with control over the financial services industry) fails to capture a number of options for regulating financial services, which lie between these polar extremes and which remain open in the post-crisis period. Such options include co-regulation and meta-regulation, both of which are based on the idea of cooperation between public and private actors in facing regulatory challenges.

It is submitted that, in view of the increasing complexity of financial products and services and the risk of government failure to achieve the regulatory objectives through intrusive public intervention in this area, there is a need to ensure the interplay between private regulation and public regulation, under the auspices of the latter, in a multi-level system of governance such as the EU. It is only where there is complementarity between the two that major breakthroughs in our understanding of the way in which financial markets operate could be achieved – breakthroughs which could increase effectiveness of financial regulation. In order to ensure a cooperative relationship between public and private actors in standard-setting and enforcement, states must become, to use the words of Van Waarden, 'responsive to regulatory initiatives of markets and civil society and vice versa, with responses varying from banning or blocking, to support or even adoption' (Van Waarden 2012: 367). The meaning of 'responsive' regulation in this sense is thus different from the one given to it by Ayres and Braithwaite (regulation 'responsive' to the reactions of regulatees) (Ayres and Braithwaite 1992).

However, as other contributors to this volume also make clear in relation to specific issues and fields, co-governance arrangements between public and private actors face major challenges. Potential problems include, inter alia, conflicts of interest, an uneasy relationship with more intrusive public regulatory techniques, inadequate enforcement by financial watchdogs and insufficient compliance by financial institutions. In fact, developing complementarity between public and private regulation in the financial services field requires revisiting and recasting pre-crisis notions of co-regulation and meta-regulation.

More research is needed into how the effectiveness of such co-governance arrangements can be assessed and under what conditions they can be effective. The findings on the dynamics and effects of co-governance by public and private actors in the provision of common goods in other policy fields could be particularly interesting in this context. Analysis of the interplay between public and private actors in the financial services field could in turn provide valuable insights into the potential of co-governance arrangements to deliver public value in other policy areas such as healthcare, energy and telecommunications. The interplay between public and private actors in financial regulation in the EU thus provides important opportunities for policy experimentation and research.

References

Andenas, M and Chiu, I-H, 2014, *The Foundations and Future of Financial Regulation: Governance for Responsibility*, London & New York: Routledge.

Ayres, I and Braithwaite, J 1992, *Responsive Regulation: Transcending the Deregulation Debate*, Oxford: Oxford University Press.

Black, J, 2002a, 'Critical reflections on regulation', *Australian Journal of Legal Philosophy*, 27(1), 1–35.

Black, J, 2002b, 'Mapping the contours of contemporary financial services regulation', *Journal of Corporate Law Studies*, 2(2), 253–87.

Black, J, 2003, 'Enrolling actors in regulatory systems: examples from UK financial services regulation', *Public Law*, (Spring), 63–91.

Busuioc, M, 2013, 'Rule-making by the European financial supervisory authorities: walking a tight rope', *European Law Journal*, 19 (1), 111–25.

Cafaggi, F, 2011, 'Private regulation in European private law', in Hartkamp, A and others, *Towards a European Civil Code*, 91–126, Alpena an den Rijn: Kluwer Law International.

Cafaggi, F and Renda, A, 2012, 'Public and private regulation: mapping the labyrinth',

CEPS Working Document 370, October 2012, Brussels: Centre for European Policy Studies.

Cherednychenko, O O, 2014a, 'Public supervision over private relationships: towards European supervision private law?', *European Review of Private Law*, 22(1), 37–67.

Cherednychenko, O O, 2014b, 'Freedom of contract in the post-crisis era: *Quo Vadis?*', *European Review of Contract Law*, 10(3), 390–421.

Chiti, E, 2013, 'European agencies' rulemaking: powers, procedures and assessment', *European Law Journal*, 19 (1), 93–110.

Coglianese, C and Mendelson, E, 2010, 'Meta-regulation and self-regulation', in Baldwin, R, Cave, M and Lodge, M (eds), *The Oxford Handbook of Regulation*, Oxford: Oxford University Press http://www.oxfordhandbooks.com (last accessed 29 September 2015).

Deci, E and Ryan, R, 1985, *Intrinsic Motivation and Self-Determination in Human Behaviour*, New York: Plenum.

Epstein, R, 2008, 'The neoclassical economics of consumer contracts', *Minnesota Law Review*, 92(3), 803–835.

ESMA, 2014, *Structured Retail Products – Good Practices for Product Governance Arrangements: Opinion*, ESMA/2014/332, Brussels: European Securities and Markets Authority.

EU Observer, 2008 '"Laissez-faire" capitalism is finished, says France' (26 September) https://euobserver.com/political/26814 (last accessed 28 September 2015).

European Parliament and the Council, 2008, Directive 2008/48/EC of the European Parliament and of the Council of 23 April 2008 on credit agreements for consumers and repealing Council Directive 87/102/EEC, *OJEU* 2008 L133/66–92 (Consumer Credit Directive).

European Parliament and the Council, 2009, Regulation (EC) No. 1060/2009 of the European Parliament and of the Council of 16 September 2009 on credit rating agencies, *OJEU* 2009 L302/1–31 (CRA I Regulation).

European Parliament and the Council, 2010, Regulation (EU) No. 1095/2010 of the European Parliament and of the Council of 24 November 2010 establishing a European Supervisory Authority (European Securities and Markets Authority), amending Decision No. 716/2009/EC and repealing Commission Decision 2009/77/EC, *OJEU* 2010 L331/84–119.

European Parliament and the Council, 2013, Regulation (EU) No. 462/2013 of the European Parliament and of the Council of 21 May 2013 amending Regulation (EC) No. 1060/2009 on credit rating agencies, *OJEU* 2013 L146/1–33 (CRA II Regulation).

European Parliament and the Council, 2014a, Directive 2014/17/EU of the European Parliament and of the Council of 4 February 2014 on credit agreements for consumers relating to residential immovable property and amending Directives 2008/48/EC and 2013/36/EU and Regulation (EU) No. 1093/2010, *OJEU* 2014 L60/34–85 (Mortgage Credit Directive).

European Parliament and the Council, 2014b, Directive 2014/65/EU of the European Parliament and of the Council of 15 May 2014 on markets in financial instruments and amending Directive 2002/92/EC and Directive 2011/61/EU (recast), *OJEU* 2014 L173/349–496 (MiFID II).

European Parliament and the Council, 2014c, Regulation (EU) No. 600/2014 of the European Parliament and of the Council on markets in financial instruments and amending Regulation (EU) No. 648/2012, *OJEU* 2014 L173/84–148 (MiFIR).

European Parliament and the Council, 2014d, Directive 2014/92/EU of the European Parliament and of the Council of 23 July 2014 on the comparability of fees related to payment account switching and access to payment accounts with basic features, *OJEU* 2014 L257/214–46 (Payment Accounts Directive).

FCA, 2014, 'Innovation hub now open for business, says FCA', London: Financial Conduct Authority http://www.fca.org.uk/news/innovation-hub-now-open-for-business (last accessed 28 September 2015).

FSA, 2009, *The Turner Review: A Regulatory Response to the Global Financial Crisis*, London: Financial Services Authority http://www.fsa.gov.uk (last accessed 28 September 2015).

FSA, 2011, *Product Intervention: Discussion Paper 11/1*, London: Financial Services Authority (January 2011).

FSA, 2012, *Retail Product Development and Governance: Structured Product Review. Finalised Guidance*, London: Financial Services Authority (March 2012).

Foot, R and Walter, A, 2011, *China, the United States, and the Global Order*, New York: Cambridge University Press.

Germain, R, 2010, *Global Politics and Financial Governance*, Basingstoke: Palgrave Macmillan.

Gilad, S, 2010, 'It runs in the family: meta-regulation and its siblings', *Regulation and Governance*, 4(4), 485–506.

Goodhart, C, Hartmann, P, Llewellyn, L, Royas-Suárez, L and Weisbrod, S, 1998, *Financial Regulation: Why, How and Where Now?* London & New York: Routlegde.

Gunningham, N and Rees, J, 1997, 'Industry self-regulation: an institutional perspective', *Law & Policy*, 19(4), 363–414.

Gunningham, N, 2010, 'Enforcement and compliance strategies', in Baldwin, R, Cave, M and Lodge, M (eds), *The Oxford Handbook of Regulation*, Oxford: Oxford University Press, http://www.oxfordhandbooks.com (last accessed 28 September 2015).

HM Treasury, Bank of England and Financial Conduct Authority, 2015, 'Fair and Effective Markets Review. Final Report', London: Bank of England (10 June 2015) http://www.bankofengland.co.uk/markets/Documents/femrjun15.pdf (last accessed 28 September 2015).

Hopkins, A and Wilkinson, P, 2005, 'Safety case regulation for the mining industry', Working Paper 37, National Research Centre for Occupational Health and Safety Regulation, Canberra: Australian National University.

Minister of Finance of the Netherlands, 2012, Temporary Mortgage Credit Regulations of 12 December 2012 as amended on 30 October 2013 (*Tijdelijke regeling hypothecair krediet*), *Staatscourant* 2012 No. 26433.

Moschella, M and Tsingou, E, 2013, 'Regulating finance after the crisis: unveiling the different dynamics of the regulatory process', *Regulation and Governance*, 7(4), 407–416.

Moloney, N, 2010, 'Financial services and markets', in Baldwin, R, Cave, M and Lodge, M (eds), *The Oxford Handbook of Regulation*, Oxford: Oxford University Press http://www.oxfordhandbooks.com (last accessed 28 September 2015).

Moloney, N, 2011a, 'The European Securities and Markets Authority and institutional design for the EU financial market – a tale of two competences: part (1) Rule-making', *European Business Organization Law Review*, 12(1), 41–86.

Moloney, N, 2011b, 'The European Securities and Markets Authority and institutional design for the EU financial market – a tale of two competences: part (2) Rules in action', *European Business Organization Law Review*, 12(2), 177–225.

Moloney, N, 2012, 'The investor model underlying the EU's investor protection regime: consumers or investors?', *European Business Organization Law Review*, 13(2), 169–93.

Netherlands Authority for the Financial Markets, 2013, Explanations relating to Market Conduct Supervision (Financial Institutions) Decree 2006, art. 32 http://www.afm.nl/nl/professionals/regelgeving/thema/productontwikkeling/toetskaders.aspx (last accessed 28 September 2015).

Ogus, A, 1995, 'Rethinking self-regulation', *Oxford Journal of Legal Studies*, 15(1), 97–108.

Ottow, A and Svetiev, Y, 2014, 'Financial supervision in the interstices between private and public law', *European Review of Contract Law*, 10(3), 496–544.

Pagliari, S, 2012, 'Who governs finance? The shifting public–private divide in the regulation of derivatives, rating agencies and hedge funds', *European Law Journal*, 18(1), 44–61.

Parker, C, 2002, *The Open Corporation*, Cambridge: Cambridge University Press.

Queen of the Netherlands, 2006a, Financial Supervision Act (*Wet op het financieel toezicht (Wft)*), *Staatsblad* 2006, No. 475.

Queen of the Netherlands, 2006b, Market Conduct Supervision (Financial Institutions) Decree (*Besluit Gedragstoezicht financiële ondernemingen (BGfo Wft)*), *Staatsblad* 2006, No. 520.

Rupp, D and Williams, C, 2011, 'The efficacy of regulation as a function of psychological fit', *Theoretical Inquires in Law*, 12(2), 581–602.

Sinclair, D, 1997, 'Self-regulation versus command and control? Beyond false dichotomies', *Law & Policy*, 19(4), 529–59.

Scott, C, 2010, 'Standard-setting in regulatory regimes', in Baldwin, R, Cave, M and Lodge, M (eds), *The Oxford Handbook of Regulation*, Oxford: Oxford University Press, http://www.oxfordhandbooks.com (last accessed 28 September 2015).

Scott, C, 2012, 'Regulating everything: from mega- to meta-regulation', *Administration*, 60(1), 61–89.

Waarden, T van, 2012, 'The governance of markets: on generating trust in transactions', in Levi-Faur, D (ed), *The Oxford Handbook of Governance*, Oxford: Oxford University Press, 355–71.

Williams, C and Conley, J, 2014, 'The social reform of banking', *Journal of Corporation Law*, 39(3), 101–134.

Chapter 8

Resolving the gaps: embedding ISDA in states' responses to systemic risk

John Biggins and Colin Scott

Introduction

'If you owe the bank $100 that is your problem. If you owe the bank $100 million that is their problem.' John Paul Getty neglected to add that if you owe the bank US$100 billion, then this goes beyond the bank and becomes the state's problem, and possibly even the problem of a wider transnational community.

For many commentators, the regulatory weaknesses that were demonstrated with such calamitous effects in the global financial crisis (GFC) were, at least in part, a product of excessive delegation to private and self-regulatory organisations (Quinn 2009). It has been surprising, perhaps, then to see some spheres in which there has since actually been an enhanced role for private regulation. We have highlighted elsewhere how the contractual character of the dominant private regulatory standard for over-the-counter (OTC) derivatives had not prevented the main trade body, the International Swaps and Derivatives Association (ISDA), from successfully embedding industry norms in national legislation prior to the financial crisis (Biggins and Scott 2012).

Hence, ISDA had a key role in defining the regulatory architecture, both public and private in character, prior to the GFC. In the wake of the GFC, it is clear that, despite contrary expectations in some quarters (Tett 2010), ISDA has in fact further expanded its role so as to assume significant new decision-making tasks, for example through its Credit Derivatives Determinations Committees (Biggins and Scott 2015).

Governments at national and supranational level have at minimum facilitated, if not encouraged, this accretion of additional powers to ISDA, with a capacity to exert significant third-party effects. Here we seek to illustrate and conceptualise a more recent manifestation of this tendency, arising from certain cross-border implementation challenges associated with legislation enacted post-crisis governing the resolution of distressed banks. In this regard, public regulators had identified potential gaps in the resolution processes arising from the cross-border character of certain transactions, such as OTC derivatives.

In one sense, ISDA contractual norms arguably lay at the heart of this challenge, and thus ISDA itself was seen as pivotal to finding a solution. Accordingly, leading public regulators sought out ISDA which, not least because of its trans-national reach, can set standards and processes with a territorial scope which is not readily attainable by any governmental body. This process of complementary public and private action led to the issuance of the ISDA Resolution Stay Protocol (RSP) in 2014 and the development of accompanying procedures under which banks voluntarily declared their adherence to the instrument, which adjusts their legal rights under derivatives contracts.

In this chapter we outline first of all ISDA's genesis and key activities, which have included embedding OTC derivative industry norms within public legisla-tive and regulatory processes, with considerable success. In this regard, we par-ticularly surface ISDA's traditional support for so-called 'safe harbours' for OTC derivatives in bankruptcy (insolvency), given the relevance of such safe harbours for the subsequent public policy challenges of interest in this chapter. We then examine the character of, and the reasons for, certain gaps in public regulatory initiatives with respect to the orderly resolution of cross-border systemically sig-nificant institutions following the GFC. Specifically, we illustrate how ISDA came to be seen as a major part of the solution to certain of these challenges in the eyes of public regulators.

We follow up on this by examining the character of the RSP. Given that its origins lie in a form of public delegation, we consider whether it should be characterised as 'private soft law' and what the significance of this might be. We analyse also the relationship between public and private actors in a context where the public actors acting alone lack complete *de iure* capacity. In the absence of such capacity, we thus illustrate how public actors are nevertheless able to engage ISDA in furthering what is, in essence, a public regulatory task. We contextualise this engagement in terms of the complementarity between ISDA, as a private actor, and public actors more broadly.

ISDA and safe harbours

Given the contractual origins of ISDA as a purely private trade association and predominant standard-setter for OTC derivatives markets, it is remarkable that it has taken on significant roles first in policy-making around national legislation and, more recently, in issuing soft law instruments somewhat akin to that of a governmental body, with what is effectively a loan of public authority.

ISDA was officially founded in the mid-1980s (initially named the International Swaps Dealers' Association), at a time when new OTC derivative products and pricing models were emerging (Partnoy 2009: 43–45). ISDA was established by, and for, the largest OTC dealer banks but its membership has since expanded to encompass a much wider constituency of market participants and interested others. ISDA's early key objective was to oversee and defend an industry-developed standard ('boilerplate') (Choi and Gulati 2006) contract for OTC derivatives transactions, now known as the ISDA Master Agreement, as well as related documentation such as product definitions.

The earliest form of the Master Agreement resulted from, at times, fractious negotiations between the major OTC derivative dealer banks, with a common concern to enhance legal certainty and minimise transaction costs in the emerging OTC financial derivatives markets (Flanagan 2001; Golden 1994). Today, the ISDA Master Agreement and ancillary documentation remain centrally important for governing transactions across the main OTC derivative trading centres. This remains the case despite revamped market infrastructure for OTC derivatives following the GFC (Financial Stability Board (FSB) 2014b), to which ISDA has adapted; albeit not wholeheartedly in all respects (ISDA 2015).

Since its foundation ISDA has also engaged in lobbying activities aimed at bolstering the cross-border legal integrity of its contractual standard, as well as encouraging hospitable public regulatory frameworks for OTC derivatives more broadly. This lobbying was clearly an important factor in the enactment of OTC derivatives-friendly legislation in major jurisdictions in the late 1990s and early 2000s (Stout 2011; Greenberger 2011; Partnoy 2009). However, of most interest for present purposes is ISDA's success in encouraging national governments to enact so-called 'safe harbours' for OTC derivatives (Schwarcz and Sharon 2014).

These safe harbours have had the effect of shielding OTC derivatives from the full force of bankruptcy (and gambling) laws by substantially exempting them, for instance, from 'automatic stays' on contractual termination that may otherwise apply to other types of contracts. This effectively permits derivative counterparties to leapfrog the creditor queue in the event of bankruptcy, or where there is a perceived risk of bankruptcy, and to net out contracts, as well as to seize any available collateral (Roe 2011; Duffie 2010).

Broadly speaking, ISDA's (contestable) (Duffie and Skeel 2012; Bergman and others 2004) posture has historically been that these safe harbours are crucial for guaranteeing legal certainty that OTC derivatives can be smoothly settled, irrespective of an adverse default event and, therefore, they serve to enhance overall systemic stability (ISDA 2010). However, this has been disputed in certain quarters (Campbell 2005) and some commentators have not found a systemic risk-based justification for bankruptcy safe harbours to be convincing (Lubben 2010).

By way of example, it has been suggested that, even prior to the more recent GFC, policy options for dealing with a distressed systemically significant hedge fund in the late 1990s (Long-Term Capital Management) were narrowed precisely owing to a risk that the hedge fund's counterparties could legitimately elect to terminate derivative contracts *en masse*. It was feared this could in fact have prompted broader instability in markets (Edwards and Morrison 2005). Others have pointed to the possibility that safe harbours may degrade market discipline ex ante (Roe 2011).

Aside from a systemic risk-related rationale, enactment of safe harbour legislation has also tended to be positioned by ISDA as being conducive to financial services businesses and, in particular, the growth of OTC derivatives markets (ISDA 2012). In this respect, ISDA offers model legislation (ISDA 2006) as a template for enacting safe harbours and there are clear examples of national legislators having followed the substance, if not the form, of this instrument (Riles 2000: 29–30; Biggins and Scott 2012). As such, ISDA can be considered to have created a 'political burden that discouraged alternative views' (Schwarcz and Sharon 2014: 1741). Therefore, although ostensibly a 'technical' matter, as we have argued elsewhere, these interactions have had a strong normative dimension (Biggins and Scott 2012).

Gaps in public regulation

In this section we explore why it has been difficult for public regulators alone to put in place norms and processes with entirely effective reach across jurisdictions, using the particular example of resolution mechanisms installed by legislators following the GFC.

The context of the resolution stay protocol

It quickly became clear at the outbreak of the GFC, and illustrated most starkly in the case of Lehman Brothers, that placement of a large, complex and interconnected financial institution into bankruptcy could have the capacity to seriously exacerbate systemic stress (Acharya and others 2009; Brunnermeier 2009). This occurred irrespective of – and, some would argue, partly because of (Wiggins and Metrick 2014) – the existence of bankruptcy safe harbours (Roe 2011: 554). At minimum, the availability of the bankruptcy safe harbour appears to have facilitated opportunistic behaviour on the part of some of Lehman's derivative counterparties (Faubus 2010: 832).

The cautionary lesson of Lehman Brothers, in turn, further incentivised authorities with few other options to provide public financial support to ailing systemically significant institutions (Sjostrum 2009), rather than risk disorderly insolvencies and broader financial shocks. In Europe such interventions had the effect of shackling banks to sovereigns (Mody and Sandri 2011), heaping pressure on some sovereigns to seek external financial assistance. Evidently, more bespoke and effective approaches for dealing with financial institution distresses would be required in future.

Aside from extolling the need for fundamental reform of OTC derivative market regulation generally, the 2008 Group of Twenty (G20) Summit in Washington also acknowledged the potential virtues of revamped bank resolution processes, declaring that: 'National and regional authorities should review resolution regimes and bankruptcy laws in light of recent experience to ensure that they permit an orderly wind-down of large complex cross-border financial institutions' (Group of Twenty 2008).

This was further elaborated at the 2009 G20 Summit in Pittsburgh, culminating, for example, in Recommendations of a Cross-Border Bank Resolution Group (Basel Committee on Banking Supervision 2010) under the auspices of the Basel Committee on Banking Supervision (BCBS) in 2010: a cooperative forum and international standard-setting body comprising public financial regulators. As well as encouraging the establishment of effective national powers for the orderly resolution of financial institutions, the recommendations also promoted coordination in the resolution of cross-border financial institutions; coupled with procedures to facilitate mutual recognition of crisis management and resolution measures across jurisdictions (Basel Committee on Banking Supervision 2010: 1–3).

Even at this relatively early stage, the BCBS recognised that ISDA contractual mechanisms could help to bolster the effectiveness of resolution regimes. In particular, the BCBS prodded national authorities to encourage ISDA to explore the possibility of facilitating delays in the termination of OTC derivative contracts where certain resolution actions are initiated (Basel Committee on Banking Supervision 2010: 42). In one sense, this was effectively a concern about remedying a potential right to automatic termination subsisting within existing ISDA contracts and norms, and thus ISDA was logically seen as best placed to solve an ISDA-related issue – or, put differently, to 'suggest "solutions" to problems they themselves helped define' (Mügge 2006). Nonetheless, it can also be read as an early recognition of the potential limitations of public measures alone to underpin coherent cross-border resolution measures more generally in the event of a crisis.

Subsequently, the FSB, an umbrella body for national financial authorities and international standard-setting bodies, promulgated *Key Attributes of Effective Resolution Regimes* (Key Attributes). The Key Attributes expanded, inter alia, on appropriate conditionality for delaying contractual termination rights where resolution powers are activated. The Key Attributes also specifically canvassed for:

> . . . transparent and expedited processes to give effect to foreign resolution measures, either by way of a mutual recognition process or by taking measures under the domestic resolution regime that support and are consistent with the resolution measures taken. . . .
>
> (Financial Stability Board 2014c: 13)

Disjointed statutory responses

Post-crisis legislation enacted in the European Union (EU) and United States (US) has embedded more dedicated and coherent frameworks in those jurisdictions for the resolution of distressed financial institutions and has broadly given expression to the main principles outlined by the BCBS and FSB. In the EU, this came in the form of Directive 2014/59/EU establishing a framework for the recovery and resolution of credit institutions and investment firms, known as the Bank Recovery and Resolution Directive (BRRD) (European Union 2014), which was due to be transposed into the national laws of the EU Member States by 31 December 2014. However, BRRD was predated by national legislative initiatives in individual EU jurisdictions, such as the United Kingdom (UK). In the US, Title II of the Dodd-Frank Wall Street Reform and Consumer Protection Act (United States 2010) introduced a regime for the 'orderly liquidation' of relevant financial institutions.

Regulatory requirements and tools introduced by these frameworks include, inter alia, the possibility of transferring rights and liabilities to 'bridge' institutions, installing special management, extending maturities of liabilities and 'bailing in' certain creditors. Of most interest for present purposes, in certain circumstances both frameworks permit the relevant public regulators to suspend temporarily (stay) termination rights under contracts (e.g. OTC derivatives) to which the institution under resolution is a party. However, there are certain differences in approach between these frameworks. For example, the applicable time periods for such temporary suspensions appear to differ between Article 71 of Directive 2014/59/EU (European Union 2014) and Section 210(c)(10)(B) of Title II of the Dodd-Frank Wall Street Reform and Consumer Protection Act (United States 2010).

Therefore, whilst the requirements and powers heralded by both of these frameworks are undoubtedly considerable when surveyed separately, they simultaneously give rise to thorny operational questions in relation to cross-border cooperation and recognition – particularly where resolution actions may be pursued in relation to globally systemically important financial institutions (G-SIFIs). According to the FSB, such challenges around cross-border recognition could arise in at least three circumstances:

- where an institution undergoing resolution in its home jurisdiction operates a foreign branch or
- where an institution undergoing resolution in its home jurisdiction controls a subsidiary in another jurisdiction or
- where assets, liabilities or contracts of an institution in resolution are located or booked in, or subject to the law of, another jurisdiction in which the firm is not itself established

(Financial Stability Board 2014a: 4–5).

To concretise further the potential difficulty here, suppose that an internationally active institution were placed into resolution in its 'home' jurisdiction and a temporary stay has been imposed on certain contractual obligations of that institution. Absent a sufficient degree of statutory alignment between jurisdictions and/ or formal arrangements for legally robust recognition, it may not necessarily be guaranteed that a third country (host) regulator with jurisdiction over affiliates of the institution under resolution would (or could) fully recognise the stay imposed by the 'home' regulator (ICI Global 2014: 4–5). Local financial stability, creditor and legal factors, for instance, can weigh heavily on host regulators (Financial Stability Board 2014a; Bank of England 2014: 9). As such, foreign affiliates of the parent institution may face immediate termination of contracts by counterparties, potentially exerting further pressures on overall group stability and depleting resources that may otherwise have assisted with orderly resolution.

More broadly, it has also been suggested that such disconnects between jurisdictions may generate perverse incentives ex ante. For example, the US Systemic

Risk Council, an agglomeration of former government officials, financial and legal experts, has pointed out that:

> Counterparties that might otherwise engage in a swap within the same legal jurisdiction might have an incentive to simply establish swaps with entities or affiliates in other jurisdictions simply to benefit from the potential ambiguity during a crisis.
>
> (Systemic Risk Council 2014: 2)

Overall, this was a classic manifestation of a 'regulatory gap', conceptualised by Joel Trachtman as 'underlaps' in regulatory coverage that 'make possible regulatory arbitrage, avoidance or evasion' (Trachtman 1997: 643). As Robert Wai has pointed out, such gaps present a serious challenge for the regulation of international business actors that are 'often adept at operating in, and indeed taking advantage of, decentralised international markets where there are gaps and conflicts among national regulatory regimes' (Wai 2002: 253).

Whilst a dialogue between EU and US regulatory authorities is underway with respect to cross-border resolution, the common EU legal framework and institutional architecture in this area have only recently been finalised under the BRRD and the Single Resolution Mechanism Regulation (European Union 2014a). However, bilateral discussions between US and UK regulators appear to be relatively more developed, illustrated by publication of a joint paper on G-SIFI resolution in 2012 (Federal Deposit Insurance Corporation and Bank of England 2012) and the undertaking of detailed simulation exercises (Federal Deposit Insurance Corporation 2015).

Nevertheless, indicative of ongoing concerns regarding the operationalisation of cross-border resolution more broadly, in late 2014 the FSB published a consultative document, with particular emphasis on the development of appropriate statutory recognition procedures and support mechanisms (Financial Stability Board 2014a: 5–11). Here the FSB recognised that further alignment of public statutory initiatives could take some time and that an interim contractual solution would be warranted. Identifying cross-border recognition clauses for resolution-related stays within financial contracts was seen as being of high priority (Financial Stability Board 2014a: 11). Enter ISDA.

Delegating to ISDA

ISDA had been formally approached by financial regulators of the UK, Germany, Switzerland and the US by way of a joint letter in 2013 (Federal Deposit Insurance Corporation and others 2013). In that letter the regulators first outlined their concerns around the risk of disorderly terminations of derivatives, stemming from the exercise of termination rights in ISDA contracts in the event of resolution or insolvency. Whilst the letter went on to acknowledge work underway between public regulators to harmonise statutory regimes further, it also suggested that a change in the underlying contracts for derivative instruments would be a 'critical step' for providing certainty. The letter concluded that ISDA had 'the opportunity to play a pivotal role' and continued:

> As resolution regimes are developed and implemented in an increasing number of jurisdictions, ISDA is in a unique position to link these regimes by providing consistent and enforceable contractual provisions related to termination.
>
> (Federal Deposit Insurance Corporation and others 2013: 2)

In response, ISDA issued the RSP in late 2014. The RSP was developed by an ISDA working group, comprising ISDA members as well as other trade associations. According to ISDA, the working group actively engaged with regulators and developed the RSP in coordination with the FSB.

Where adopted, the RSP amends the ISDA Master Agreement and supporting documentation. As ISDA itself explains, fundamentally the RSP debars adherents from immediately terminating outstanding derivatives contracts only by reason of, for example, the resolution of their counterparty or certain of its affiliates; thereby 'giving regulators time to resolve the troubled institution in an orderly way' (ISDA 2014). This is primarily achieved under the RSP by contractually subjecting RSP adherents to the resolution regime, including any stays, applicable to their counterparty, as well as each 'related entity' (i.e. relevant affiliates as defined in the RSP) of their counterparty, should the counterparty or related entity become subject to resolution proceedings. Accordingly, under the RSP, an adherent's capacity to exercise termination rights is rendered subject to the resolution regime applicable to their counterparty and that counterparty's relevant affiliates.

The RSP at minimum covers the 'pre-qualifying' resolution regimes of France, Germany, Japan, Switzerland, the UK and the US. The RSP may also be invoked to cover the resolution regimes of other FSB member jurisdictions meeting certain conditions. In addition, opt-out and sunset clauses are included in the RSP. Interestingly, an opt-out is available, for example, where a relevant resolution regime has been amended such that the regime is deemed by an RSP adherent to affect 'materially and adversely' its ability to exercise default rights (ISDA 2014a). This could therefore potentially be read as another instance where an ISDA contractual mechanism is signalling industry-acceptable parameters for public legislative action.

The G18 global dealer banks were initial adherents to the RSP and the list has since expanded to include a broader range of market participants. With a view to widening the RSP's industry-penetration, public regulators have also actively promoted it, including by way of rule-making aimed at creating disincentives for non-adoption of the RSP. For instance, in May 2015 the UK Prudential Regulation Authority (PRA) issued a consultation paper (CP) on *Contractual Stays in Financial Contracts Governed by Third-Country Law* (Bank of England 2015). This CP proposed a public regulatory rule which would:

[P]rohibit firms from creating new obligations or materially amending an existing obligation . . . unless the counterparty has agreed in writing to be subject to similar restrictions on early termination and close-out to those that would apply as a result of the firm's entry into resolution . . . if the financial contract were governed by the laws of the United Kingdom.

(Bank of England 2015: 5)

The PRA has positioned this as feeding into a broader 'co-ordinated effort' with other public regulatory authorities, with the common objective of supporting ISDA's RSP initiative (Bank of England 2015; 6). Similarly, the chairman of the US Federal Deposit Insurance Corporation has indicated that the US Board of Governors of the Federal Reserve System is also likely to issue rules to 'codify' compliance with the RSP (Federal Deposit Insurance Corporation 2015; 12). These supplementary initiatives by public regulators could at least partly be interpreted as an effort to mitigate the risks associated with a contractual solution alone. As observed by the FSB, contractual fixes have 'yet to be tested in the courts' and 'limitations on their enforceability (for example, on public policy grounds) may not always be clear' (Financial Stability Board 2014a: 11).

This concern would appear to chime with Robert Wai's observation that, in the present international environment, it is not necessarily possible for transnational commercial transactions to 'lift-off' entirely from the constraints of national legal systems (Wai 2002: 264–68). Hence, as we have argued elsewhere, the back-up role of the public regulators in relation to the RSP could be construed as another indicator that the ISDA regime is not purely 'anational' (Michaels 2007). Rather, it is a regime beyond, but not necessarily without, the backstopping capacity of the nation state (Biggins 2012: 1318; Michaels 2007: 465–68).

Conceptualising complementarity of public and private roles

The issuance and effects of the RSP raise significant conceptual and practical questions about the instruments for effective governance, both in financial markets and more generally. We are increasingly accustomed to public authorities issuing instruments that lack formal public authority, but which are both intended to, and do, have effects (Snyder 1993). The reference to law in the 'soft law' term given to this wide range of instruments refers to the fact of public authority lying behind, and being deployed in, the instrument to give it weight and normative force, even though it is not legally binding. The origins of the RSP lie in the request of the public regulators to ISDA to assist in developing an instrument that the regulators could not develop themselves because of the transnational character of the problem.

Within soft law instruments, traditionally conceived, it is the public authority that issues the instrument and gives the instrument its power. The term soft law is sometimes used to refer to privately issued instruments, even though they lack a key ingredient of public authority (Abbott and others 2012). In many cases, privately issued instruments, to be effective, are rendered binding through contractual commitment, and thus lack the softness associated with soft law, in addition to lacking the public authority. The RSP is one of an increasing number of instruments that are ostensibly non-binding and privately issued, but which have public encouragement or backing.

We suggest that, in the case of the RSP, the public regulators may be thought of as loaning their authority to ISDA, creating a form of 'private soft law' (Senden and Scott 2015). Such instruments are key examples of the complementarity of the actions of public and private actors in contemporary governance of financial markets (Cafaggi 2011).

Superficially, the RSP might be regarded as a mutually agreed amendment to the Master Agreement, and thus just another dimension of the contractual governance of the sector. However, its source, in a request from national regulators and the FSB makes it different in character. Parties to derivatives contracts incorporate and follow the terms of the Master Agreement as a matter of choice in entering into their transactions and are bound by the terms of the Master Agreement to the extent that they agree to be bound. At first glance, the RSP also appears to be non-binding on the banks. However, the banks and other market actors are invited to confirm adherence to the RSP, not only as a matter of bilateral negotiation between themselves and another contractual party, but rather in a letter to ISDA itself. Thus, ISDA's role with the RSP is not simply to set standards for others to use, but rather is to persuade banks and others to confirm adherence to the rules it has set down.

The source and origins of the RSP are also very different from the Master Agreement, albeit the two are inherently related. The Master Agreement originates in the needs of the banks for certainty in transactions, enabling them to rely on accepted and tested contractual terms. The RSP originates in requests from national regulators and from the FSB that ISDA should address matters that national regulators could not adequately address, because of transnational elements to the transactions. The FSB is an inter-governmental body, but not a treaty organisation, and it lacks the power to make binding rules. For these reasons we cannot regard the RSP as only a bilateral contractual instrument. The character of the RSP is that it is intended to affect the behaviour of the banks, through their agreement to adhere to its terms in transactions with other adherents. Nevertheless, non-adherence or cessation of adherence in certain circumstances are possibilities.

Therefore, if the RSP is not binding, and if the banks cannot fully bind themselves to compliance, then what is giving the instrument normative force, such that the major banks not only commit to adhering but also, in practice, do follow the norms? The involvement of the public regulators and the FSB is significant. We suggest that the involvement of the public regulators is a key factor in giving the RSP normative power with the banks. There are at least two potential dimensions to this public involvement.

First, there is the authority of the public regulators. Public authority is recognised as a central ingredient in the making of this wider variety of governance instruments referred to as 'soft law'. The public empowerment of private regulators is not unprecedented and occurs in a number of different ways. Formal delegations of public authority may be made through legislation, as when a professional body has statutory authority to license and discipline members or when a self-regulatory body takes on wider regulatory functions through a statutory delegation (Scott 2002). Frank Partnoy has characterised the latter tendency as amounting to a 'regulatory licence' (Partnoy 2006). We have explored elsewhere the extent to which Partnoy's regulatory licensing analogy can be applied to the establishment of the ISDA Credit Derivatives Determinations Committees (DCs) (Biggins and Scott 2015).

The ISDA DCs heralded, inter alia, centralised industry panels for issuing binding interpretations of triggering events for the purposes of ISDA's credit derivatives contracts. These industry-based governance structures were also established by way of ISDA Protocols. We have found that, whilst the DCs were not created through an explicit statutory delegation, public regulators were nevertheless a substantial driving force behind enhanced private governance structures in that segment of the market. As such, public regulators explicitly welcomed the ISDA Protocols underpinning the DCs and encouraged market participants to adopt them (Federal Reserve Bank of New York 2009).

We have also previously seen public regulators rely upon private regulatory capacity for the purposes of engaging in what can be thought of as soft law-type activities engaging the hybrid or co-regulatory capacity of private and public actors (Peters and Pagotto 2006). Anna Gelpern (2009) has illustrated this in the context of the public policy response to the distressed Japanese Long-Term Credit Bank (LTCB) in 1998. The Japanese authorities had become concerned that if they were unilaterally to take LTCB into 'special public administration', this could trigger an event of default under the ISDA Master Agreements to which LTCB was party, resulting in LTCB's counterparties simultaneously terminating ('closing out') their contracts. In turn, it was feared that this could have the potential to exert further instability in the Japanese financial markets, as well as the wider international financial system (Nakaso 2001).

The Japanese authorities therefore liaised with ISDA, explaining the substance of the public measures that would be invoked to ensure that LTCB met its obligations under outstanding OTC derivatives contracts. The authorities also undertook to use terminology different from the triggering language under the ISDA Master Agreements, agreeing to characterise the rescue of LTCB as 'temporary nationalisation', rather than 'special public administration'. In return, ISDA issued a statement which confirmed that it 'understood and welcomed' the intention of the Japanese authorities (Nakaso 2001: 13). Gelpern (2009: 61) has conceptualised this as a 'private "no action letter" of sorts – that pre-empted a rush for the exits'. If a national government were to issue such comfort letters, they would be regarded as a key instrument of soft law.

Aside from examples such as this, as noted above it is frequently regarded as questionable to use the term soft law to describe self- (or private-) regulatory regimes, as self- (private-) regulation is not necessarily soft in character, but rather may be legally binding on those who have signed up to the regime (Bernstein 2001). The RSP is of a different type, soft in character (at least until the point at which it is incorporated into contracts), but arguably with loaned public authority underpinning its normative power, which extends beyond ISDA but does not formally require them to act. The question of the character of the RSP is somewhat distinct from its actual effects. Its character is one of intending to have behavioural effects. When we look at the actual effects we find that the key market participants pledge adherence to it, in a deviation from their strict legal rights. So, a question arises, why do the banks profess adherence and follow the RSP?

In some contexts we might think that respect for the trade association (ISDA), of which most major OTC derivative market participants are members, is sufficient to command adherence. However, it is equally plausible in this case that the complementarity of the private action of ISDA with the encouragement of the public regulators is significant. The banks are in regulatory relationships with the public regulators and, whilst they do not risk formal enforcement of the RSP against them, they may be vulnerable to other regulatory actions which are adverse to their interests – such as compensating systemic changes to financial regulation, should the banks fail to toe the line on stays. So the public regulators could not issue the instrument, but they could speak softly to ISDA and to the banks, indicating that a fix was required and that the banks should sign up to it.

A further possibility is that the position of banks in networks with public actors makes it possible for regulators to act, even where they lack the power, and to expect the support of the banks. Thus, the behaviour of the banks can be seen as part of a wider phenomenon in which participation in networks which take on, to a degree, shared objectives, may result in behavioural alignments in order to comply with network expectations and to achieve outcomes that could not be delivered by the network participants acting alone (Abbott and Snidal 2009; Lazer 2005).

Conclusions

Private regulation is commonly adopted as a response to a gap identified by the private actors who then initiate a regime. This may be true of businesses, as with the origins of ISDA, which was established to provide reasonable certainty around the adoption and implementation of standard terms in derivatives agreements, to the benefit of the market and the actors within it. In some cases private regulation originates with a non-governmental organisation, concerned for example that environmental or employment standards are too low, or are not adequately enforced. Where governments identify governance gaps, a common response is to act directly through new or adapted regulation. In the case of the RSP, the option to act directly and effectively was not immediately open to the public regulators nor to the FSB. The issue of a private instrument, the RSP, was not driven by the ISDA members (as is true for ISDA's other instruments) but rather at the request of the regulators.

The adherence to the RSP of the main banks cannot be understood as a purely private matter, as it would appear that the willingness to treat themselves as being bound derives not only from their relationship with ISDA but also from their ongoing relationships with the public regulators within what are, at least implicitly, network governance arrangements. Therefore, we suggest it may be correct to think of the RSP as a pragmatic solution to a problem, where the outcome is neither wholly private nor public, but rather a species of 'private soft law', a particular form of public–private complementarity in governance, which we are likely to see more of in the future.

Acknowledgements

This chapter derives from a broader research initiative: 'Transnational Private Regulation in the OTC Derivatives Industry', which the authors were involved in as part of an international collaboration funded by the Hague Institute for the Internationalisation of Law and coordinated by Fabrizio Cafaggi at the European University Institute: *Constitutional Foundations of Transnational Private Regulation*. Opinions expressed in this chapter are the personal views of the authors alone and do not necessarily represent the views of any other individuals or organisations to which the authors are affiliated. Errors remain the authors' alone. This article was largely drafted in early June 2015 and is not reflective of subsequent developments. We are grateful to Kate Moloney for research assistance.

References

Abbott, K and Snidel, D, 2009, 'The governance triangle: regulatory standards institutions and the shadow of the state', in Mattli, W and Woods, N (eds), *The Politics of Global Regulation*, Princeton: Princeton University Press, 44–88.

Abbott, K, Marchant, G and Corley, E, 2012, 'Soft law oversight mechanisms for nanotechnology', *Jurimetrics*, 52, 279–312.

Acharya, V, Philipon, T, Richardson, M, and Roubini, N, 2009, 'The financial crisis of 2007–2009: causes and remedies', *Financial Markets, Institutions and Instruments*, 18(2), 89–137.

Bank of England, 2014, *The Bank of England's Approach to Resolution* London: Bank of England http://www.bankofengland.co.uk/financialstability/Documents/resolution/apr231014.pdf (last accessed 30 September 2015).

Bank of England, 2015, *Contractual Stays in Financial Contracts Governed by Third-Country Law*, Consultation Paper, CP19/15 London: Bank of England http://www.bankofengland.co.uk/pra/Documents/publications/cp/2015/cp1915.pdf (last accessed 30 September 2015).

Basel Committee on Banking Supervision, 2010, *Report and Recommendations of the Cross-Border Resolution Group* http://www.bis.org/publ/bcbs169.pdf (last accessed 30 September 2015).

Bergman, W, Bliss, R, Johnson, C, and Kaufman, G, 2004, *Netting, Financial Contracts and Banks: The Economic Implications*, Federal Reserve Bank of Chicago Working Paper 2004-02.

Bernstein, L, 2001, 'Private commercial law in the cotton industry: creating cooperation through rules, norms and institutions', *Michigan Law Review*, 99, 1724–90.

Biggins, J, 2012, "'Targeted touchdown' and 'partial liftoff': post crisis dispute resolution in the OTC derivatives markets and the challenge for ISDA', *German Law Journal*, 13(12), 1297–328.

Biggins, J and Scott, C, 2012, 'Public–Private relations in a transnational private regulatory regime: ISDA, the state and OTC derivatives market reform', *European Business Organization Law Review*, 13(3), 309–346.

Biggins, J and Scott, C, 2015, 'Licensing the gatekeeper? Public pathways, social significance and the ISDA Credit Derivatives Determinations Committees', *Transnational Legal Theory*, 6, (forthcoming).

Brunnermeier, M, 2009, 'Deciphering the liquidity and credit crunch 2007–2008', *Journal of Economic Perspectives*, 23(1), 77–100.

Cafaggi, F, 2011, 'New foundations of transnational private regulation', *Journal of Law and Society*, 38, 20–49.

Campbell, R, 2005, 'Financial markets contracts and BAPCPA', *American Bankruptcy Law Journal*, 79(3), 697–712.

Choi, S and Gulati, G, 2006, 'Contract as statute', *Michigan Law Review*, 104, 1129–74.

Duffie, D, 2010, 'The failure mechanics of dealer banks', *Journal of Economic Perspectives*, 24(1), 51–72.

Duffie, D and Skeel, D, 2012, *A Dialogue on the Costs and Benefits of Automatic Stays for Derivatives and Repurchase Agreements*, University of Pennsylvania Institute for Law & Economics Research paper 12-02, http://papers.ssrn.com/sol3/papers.cfm?abstract_id=1982095 (last accessed 30 September 2015).

Edwards, F and Morrison, E, 2005, 'Derivatives and the Bankruptcy Code: why the special treatment?', *Yale Journal on Regulation*, 22(1), 91–122.

European Union 2014, Directive 2014/59/EU of the European Parliament and of the Council of 15 May 2014 establishing a framework for the recovery and resolution of credit institutions and investment firms and amending Council Directive 82/891/EEC, and Directives 2001/24/EC, 2002/47/EC, 2004/25/EC, 2005/56/EC, 2007/36/EC, 2011/35/EU, 2012/30/EU and 2013/36/EU, and Regulations (EU) No 1093/2010 and (EU) No 648/2012, *Official Journal of the European Union*, L173, 12/6/2014, 190–348.

European Union, 2014a, Regulation (EU) No. 806/2014 of the European Parliament and of the Council of 15 July 2014 establishing uniform rules and a uniform procedure for the resolution of credit institutions and certain investment firms in the framework of a Single Resolution Mechanism and a Single Resolution Fund and amending Regulation (EU) No. 1093/2010, *Official Journal of the European Union*, L225, 30/7/2014, 1–90.

Faubus, B, 2010, 'Narrowing the bankruptcy safe harbor for derivatives to combat systemic risk', *Duke Law Journal*, 59(4), 801–42.

Federal Deposit Insurance Corporation, 2015, A Progress Report on the Resolution of Systemically Important Financial Institutions, Martin J. Gruenberg, Chairman, Federal Deposit Insurance Corporation, Speech to the Peterson Institute for International Economics; Washington, D.C. https://www.fdic.gov/news/news/speeches/spmay1215.pdf (last accessed 30 September 2015).

Federal Deposit Insurance Corporation and Bank of England, 2012, *Resolving Globally Active, Systemically Important, Financial Institutions* http://www.bankofengland.co.uk/publications/Documents/news/2012/nr156.pdf (last accessed 30 September 2015).

Federal Deposit Insurance Corporation, Bank of England, German Federal Financial Supervisory Authority and Swiss Financial Market Supervisory Authority, 2013, Joint Letter to ISDA (5 November 2013) Washington: Federal Deposit Insurance Corporation https://www.fdic.gov/news/news/press/2013/pr13099a.pdf (last accessed 30 September 2015).

Federal Reserve Bank of New York, 2009, *New York Fed Welcomes CDS Auction Hardwiring* http://www.newyorkfed.org/newsevents/news/markets/2009/ma090312.html (last accessed 30 September 2015).

Financial Stability Board, 2014a, *Cross-Border Recognition of Resolution Action: A Consultative Document* http://www.financialstabilityboard.org/wp-content/uploads/c_140929.pdf?page_moved=1 (last accessed 30 September 2015).

Financial Stability Board, 2014b, *OTC Derivatives Market Reforms: Eighth Progress Report on Implementation* http://www.financialstabilityboard.org/wp-content/uploads/r_141107.pdf (last accessed 30 September 2015).

Financial Stability Board, 2014c, *Key Attributes of Effective Resolution Regimes for Financial Institutions* http://www.financialstabilityboard.org/wp-content/uploads/r_141015.pdf (last accessed 30 September 2015).

Flanagan, S, 2001, 'The rise of a trade association: group interactions within the International Swaps and Derivatives Association', *Harvard Negotiation Law Review*, 6, 211–64.

Gelpern, A, 2009, 'Commentary: public promises and organizational agendas', *Arizona Law Review*, 51(1), 57–74.

Golden, J, 1994, 'Setting standards in the evolution of swap documentation', *International Financial Law Review*, 13(5), 18–19.

Greenberger, M, 2011, 'Overwhelming a financial regulatory black hole with legislative sunlight: Dodd-Frank's attack on systemic economic destabilization caused by an unregulated multi-trillion dollar derivatives market', *Journal of Business and Technology Law*, 6(1), 127–68.

Group of Twenty, 2008, *Declaration of the Summit on Financial Markets and the World Economy*, G20 Information Centre Washington: United Nations http://www.un.org/ga/president/63/commission/declarationG20.pdf (last accessed 30 September 2015).

ICI Global, *Cross-Border Recognition of Resolution Action* (25 November 2014) http://www.financialstabilityboard.org/2014/12/public-responses-to-the-september-2014-consultative-document-cross-border-recognition-of-resolution-actions/ (last accessed 30 September 2015).

ISDA, 2006, *2006 Model Netting Act* http://www.isda.org/docproj/model_netting.html (last accessed 30 September 2015).

ISDA, 2010, *The Importance of Close-Out Netting* http://www.isda.org/researchnotes/pdf/Netting-ISDAresearchNotes-1-2010.pdf (last accessed 13 December 2015).

ISDA, 2012, *ISDA Submission on Consistency of Netting Application to Spur Market Growth*, ISDA Submission to Indian Authorities http://www2.isda.org/search?headerSearch=1&keyword=submission+on+consistency+of+netting (last accessed 30 September 2015).

ISDA, 2014, *ISDA 2014 Resolution Stay Protocol*, Frequently Asked Questions http://www2.isda.org/functional-areas/protocol-management/faq/20/ (last accessed 30 September 2015).

ISDA, 2014a, *ISDA 2014 Resolution Stay Protocol* http://assets.isda.org/media/f253b540-25/958e4aed.pdf/ (last accessed 30 September 2015).

ISDA, 2015, *derivatiViews* http://isda.derivativiews.org/ (last accessed 30 September 2015).

Lazer, D, 2005, 'Regulatory capitalism as a networked order: the international system as an informational network', *The Annals of the American Academy of Political and Social Science*, 598, 52–66.

Lubben, S, 2010, 'Repeal the safe harbors', *American Bankruptcy Institute Law Review*, 18(1), 319–36.

Michaels, R, 2007, 'The true *lex mercatoria*: law beyond the state', *Indiana Journal of Global Legal Studies*, 14(2), 447–68.

Mody, A and Sandri, D, 2011, *The Eurozone Crisis: How Banks and Sovereigns Came to be Joined at the Hip*, IMF Working Paper 11/269.

Mügge, D, 2006, 'Private–Public puzzles: inter-firm competition and transnational private regulation', *New Political Economy*, 11, 177.

Nakaso, H, 2001, *The Financial Crisis in Japan in the 1990s: How the Bank of Japan Responded and the Lessons Learnt*, Bank for International Settlements Papers, 6 http://www.bis.org/publ/bppdf/bispap06.pdf?noframes=1/ (last accessed 30 September 2015).

Partnoy, F, 2006, 'How and Why credit ratings agencies are not like other gatekeepers', in Fuchita, Y and Litan, R (eds), *Financial Gatekeepers: Can They Protect Investors?*, Washington DC: Brookings Institution Press, Tokyo: Nomura Institute of Capital Markets Research.

Partnoy, F, 2009, *Infectious Greed: How Deceit and Risk Corrupted the Financial Markets*, Philadelphia: Public Affairs.

Peters, A and Pagatto, I, 2006, 'Soft law as a new mode of governance: a legal perspective', Basel: New Modes of Governance Project.

Quinn, B, 2009, 'The failure of private ordering and the financial crisis of 2008', *New York University Journal of Law & Business*, 5, 549.

Riles, A, 2000, *The Transnational Appeal of Formalism: The Case of Japan's Netting Law*, Stanford/Yale Junior Faculty Forum Research Paper 00-03 http://ssrn.com/paper.taf?abstract_id=162588 (last accessed 30 September 2015).

Roe, M, 2011, 'The derivative market's payment priorities as financial crisis accelerator', *Stanford Law Review*, 63(3), 539–90.

Schwarcz, S and Sharon, O, 2014, 'The bankruptcy-law safe harbor for derivatives: a path-dependence analysis', *Washington and Lee Law Review*, 71(3), 1715–56.

Scott, C, 2002, 'Private regulation of the public sector: a neglected facet of contemporary governance', *Journal of Law and Society*, 29, 56–76.

Senden, L and Scott, C, 2015, *The Onward March of Soft Law in the EU: From Core Institutions to Network and Private Governance Regimes*, EUSA Conference 2015: Boston.

Sjostrum, W, 2009, 'The AIG bailout', *Washington and Lee Law Review*, 66(3), 943–94.

Snyder, F, 1993, 'The effectiveness of European Community law: institutions, processes, tools and techniques', *Modern Law Review*, 56(1), 19–54.

Stout, L, 2011, 'Derivatives and the legal origin of the 2008 credit crisis', *Harvard Business Law Review*, 1, 1–38.

Systemic Risk Council, 2014, *Submission to the Financial Stability Board: Cross-Border Recognition of Resolution Action Document* http://www.systemicriskcouncil.org/wp-content/uploads/2014/12/FSB-Cross-Border-Letter.pdf (last accessed 30 September 2015).

Tett, G, 2010, 'Calls for radical rethink of derivatives body', *Financial Times*, (26 August) http://www.ft.com/cms/s/0/f7794d1c-b13d-11df-b899-00144feabdc0.html (last accessed 30 September 2015).

Trachtman, J, 1997, 'Externalities and extraterritoriality: the law and economics of prescriptive jurisdiction', in Bhandari, J and Sykes, A (eds), *Economic Dimensions in*

International Law: Comparative and Empirical Perspectives, Cambridge: Cambridge University Press, 642.

United States, 2010, *Dodd-Frank Wall Street Reform and Consumer Protection Act*, Title II, PubL 111–203, HR 4173.

Wai, R, 2002, 'Transnational liftoff and juridical touchdown: the regulatory function of private international law in an era of globalization', *Columbia Journal of Transnational Law*, 40(2), 209–276.

Wiggins, R and Metrick, A, 2014, *The Lehman Brothers Bankruptcy G: The Special Case of Derivatives*, Yale Program on Financial Stability Case Study 2014-3G-11 http://papers.ssrn.com/sol3/papers.cfm?abstract_id=2593080 (last accessed 30 September 2015).

Chapter 9

Virtuous vultures: hedge funds as private regulators

Nicholas Dorn

Introduction and scope

This chapter looks at three strategies of hedge funds which, in the course of doing their business, make wide claims about their contribution to the good functioning of markets, their enhancement of investors' returns and their policing of competence, honesty and decency in markets and even in sovereign states. Ironically, such claim-making reminds us of the roles of public regulators in respect of conduct, effectiveness and fairness issues. It evokes a variety of responses from other market participants and from regulatory communities, including embarrassment, outrage and counter-strategies. The chapter explores hedge funds' positioning of themselves as 'quasi-regulatory' in relation to three strategies: activism, shorting and litigation vis-à-vis distressed debt. It concludes with some suggested agendas for research at this intersection of politics, law and markets.

An 'activist' hedge fund strategy involves intervening in target companies and disciplining management in order to push up the share price, justifying this in terms of promotion of good governance and enhancement of value for shareholders. The hedge fund strategy summarised as 'short and shout' seeks to close down firms whose managers are claimed to be misleading markets through misrepresentation or fraud, thus removing undesirables and making the market cleaner and better functioning. A final hedge fund strategy examined here targets the distressed debt of firms or sovereign states that seek to renegotiate terms and to repay less than 100 per cent at maturity. All strategies involve a mix of investigation, market position-taking, legal work, public relations, moral claims-making and attempts to drag media and public regulatory agencies or other branches of government into the fray, as allies of the hedge fund. There are many other hedge funds strategies; however, these three clearly invoke public interest claims.

In the eyes of some observers, hedge funds add to the efficiency and stability of markets. For others, they are unsettling in both economic and normative senses. We touch on the origins of hedge funds and the range of strategies that they pursue, before focusing on claims made by some hedge funds that their actions improve governance and integrity in the markets. On origins, according to Partnoy and Thomas (2007: 23–24)

Scholars attribute the development of the first hedge fund to Alfred Winslow Jones, a sociologist and journalist who in 1949 established a private investment partnership that reduced risk by buying one stock while shorting another in the same industry. Winslow's approach had several advantages. First, the investment partnership form was flexible and the partnership could trade positions quickly, using leverage to make large bets on the movements of individual stocks. Second, the partnerships were not subject to regulation under the Investment Company Act of 1940, and thus could act outside of government scrutiny. Finally, and perhaps most importantly, instead of charging a fixed fee, Winslow's compensation was set at 20 percent of profits, aligning his interests with those of his investors by giving him strong incentives to maximize fund value.

On the development of hedge funds as global actors, the renowned United States (US) sociologist Robert K Merton holds some responsibility for fathering Robert Cox Merton, an economist who became a director of and strategist for one of the biggest post-war hedge funds. Created in 1994, Long Term Capital Management (LTCM) exceeded its objective of 20 per cent profit in its first year of operation, doubled that in years two and three, and took on more leverage (up to 100 to one at one stage), before being blind-sided by the 1997 Asian financial crisis and the 1998 Russian crisis. Citing systemic risk if the situation was not managed, and despite some concerns over moral hazard, the New York Federal Exchange orchestrated a private sector bail-out of the firm. Following the demise and rescue of LTCM, the industry has expanded.

Some commentators make claims that hedge funds increase the efficiency and stability of markets, by identifying and filling 'governance gaps' within the private sector. Put briefly, that view builds upon a perception that, in the economy generally, the functioning of many companies' boards and managements leaves much to be desired. Hence, for example, 'activists' such as hedge funds might compensate for such shortfalls in governance.

This we take to be a claim for private regulation – not in the form of self-regulation (firms and/or their associations regulating aspects of their own conduct) but rather inter-sectoral regulation: elements of the financial sector regulate the wider political economy. In the years immediately following the financial market crisis of 2007–2009, such claims would hardly wash; however, they do not go away.

Activists: assist the meek

Hedge funds concerning themselves with the governance and strategy of target companies include 'activists', which seek an upward movement in a target's net worth (whilst others, to be discussed later, seek the opposite).

Activist hedge funds have a short- or medium-term temporal span of attention – in contrast with some other market participants, for example private equity, which engage over a longer period of time. It has been suggested that, in private equity, 'People are contemplating longer careers here, so that means more of a relationship, less the transactional' (interviewee cited by Froud and others 2012: 17). The long-term orientation in private equity stems from the fact that it might take many years, even a decade, for private equity to develop and sell on its investments. This would contrast with, for example, investment banking, which looks for shorter term trades and which, according to some in private equity, has 'lost its moral bearings' and in which 'treading on people as they go past is considered fine', owing to an orientation to 'short-term gain' (ibid: 11). Participants in investment banking, which has been the focus of much criticism, might wish to question that characterisation or at least to move on from it. The point for present purposes is that activist hedge funds share the short-term orientation of investment banking; however, they manage their public relations more actively, indeed frenetically, by imputing a mix of incompetence and immorality to reluctant or resistant target managements.

Talking of activists, Dionysia Katelouzou (2014: 5–6) identifies a game-plan as having four stages:

> An activist hedge fund manager first selects a target company that presents high-value opportunities for engagement (entry); it accumulates a nontrivial stake (trading); it then determines and employs its activist strategy (disciplining); and, finally, it exits (exit). While the entry and trading stages will be also present to other forms of value investing, the readiness to take a hands-on role and lobby for changes (disciplining stage) is the crucial additional dimension to hedge fund activism.

Explicit in this is that hedge funds 'operate to improve corporate performance and value' or, more precisely, a hedge fund purchases the equity of a firm from which it aims to 'extract value' (Katelouzou 2014: 7–9). Within this context, the management and board are 'disciplined' – and indeed so might be the workforce, suppliers and other stakeholders – with the objective of moving the share price up, at least in the short to medium term. In the vast majority of cases, a hedge fund has capacity to acquire only a small proportion of the equity of a target company. Lacking sufficient fire power to act alone, it puts propositions before market commentators (analysts, media) and elicits support from bigger shareholders in order to discipline management, in some cases reconfiguring the board along the way (ibid: 61).

As other work points out, activism of this sort is conditional on legislation having accorded certain rights to shareholders and on the shareholders having internalised certain dispositions, notable 'shareholder value' – thus creating a 'market for corporate influence' (see inter alia Cheffins and Armour 2011: 58). Absent such shareholder rights and dispositions, a hedge fund would not be able to leverage its minority stake into real influence. An alternative or adjunct strategy may be to call in other activists/hedge funds, in what has been termed a 'wolf pack', each taking a stake (Zetzsche 2010). Such alliances may also be entered into when a hedge fund wishes to keep its strategy non-public (for a period of time) and so keeps its stake below the level that would trigger disclosure under the relevant legislation.

The amount of equity that can be purchased by a hedge fund limits its potential take-away, whilst 'free riders' (that is, say, passive investors who own the majority of the equity) may also benefit from a rise in the share price. This potential injustice (from the hedge fund point of view) stimulates hedge funds to employ leverage: borrowing to acquire more equity, the use of derivatives, or both. That implies some risk for hedge funds in cases where there is no quick resolution, since delay increases the hedge funds' borrowing costs. Greater risk arises if, after a period of time the target company refuses to be disciplined, yet its corporate profile has been wounded by the hedge fund's campaign, leading to a loss of share price. In that case a hedge fund that is heavily invested suffers accordingly. More generally, a general market down-turn hits activist hedge funds twice: once through increased costs of borrowing, and again through declines in their targets' equity prices.

> A key feature of the financial crisis was that the credit 'bubble' of the mid-2000s was replaced by a credit crunch. For hedge funds that relied on borrowing as an element of their investment strategy, a by-product was increased funding costs . . . Moreover, hedge funds specializing in shareholder activism were among those worst affected during the market turmoil. Activist hedge funds suffered because they tend to hedge less than other hedge funds, meaning they were fully exposed to the falling stock prices that characterized 2008, and because the small and midcap companies in which they typically invest suffered outsized share price declines as compared with large cap companies.
>
> (Armour and Cheffins 2009: 33–34)

The onset of financial market and Eurozone crises led one activist investor to complain that activism was 'hard' and 'unpredictable and expensive' (Armour and Cheffins 2009: 34). However, stabilised and rising markets and very low costs of borrowing in the mid-2010s provided good conditions for hedge fund activism, causing an estimated 10-fold increase in funds under management over a decade (JP Morgan 2015: 1). It has been suggested that such growth raises 'questions about overcrowded trades. In recent years, the sector has produced annual returns of more than 20 per cent. However, after a decade of frenetic growth, much of the lowest-hanging activist fruit in the American corporate world may already have been plucked. The pressure is thus rising for the sector to find new frontiers to explore' (Tett 2015: 9). In the 2010s, Asia provided one such frontier for US activists. European Union (EU) Capital Markets Union (CMU) and the European Strategic Investment Fund (ESIF) should also support activism, as the authorities encourage international investors to engage with small and medium-sized enterprises (SMEs). Academic research can be expected to be drawn to the space that is being co-produced by CMU, the ESIF, cheap credit and investors seeking returns in a low interest rate environment (Dorn 2016; Miller and Thomas 2013).

Going forward, views about activist hedge funds vary markedly. Focusing on hedge funds that go long on their targets' equity, Katelouzou describes their role as 'promising', noting the view of Brav and others (2008: 1733) that:

> [A]ctivist hedge funds occupy an important middle ground between internal monitoring by large shareholders and external monitoring by corporate raiders. Activist hedge funds are more flexible, incentivized, and independent than internal monitors, and they can generate multiple gains from targeting several companies on similar issues. Conversely, activist hedge funds have advantages over external corporate raiders, because they take smaller stakes, often benefit from cooperation with management, and have support from other shareholders. This hybrid internal-external role puts activist hedge funds in a potentially unique position to reduce the agency costs associated with the separation of ownership and control.

Some would go further, heralding the hedge fund phenomenon as a 'shining beacon of hope on an otherwise bleak landscape' of corporate governance, which might fill 'the governance gap created by the passive credit–rating agencies, the moribund market for corporate control, the rational ignorance in shareholder voting, and the captured directors and self-interested management' (Macey 2010: 248). Thus, hedge funds might make up for deficient aspects of private governance within markets. Moreover, for those who focus on profit maximisation and shareholder value as the proper concerns of companies, and who are more sympathetic to private governance than to public regulation, investors are better custodians of private goods than public regulators (Macey 2010: 11 and 227).

On the other hand, activists have been portrayed as one of the many unacceptable faces of the market – a danger to market governance rather than a godsend to it – and requiring to be controlled. In the run-up to the parliamentary elections in the United Kingdom (UK) in 2015, the then Labour leader Edward Miliband alleged that: 'Of course [the Conservatives] can't act on hedge funds because they bankroll the Tory party. He can't act because they own them lock, stock and barrel. The Conservative party is now just the political wing of the tax avoidance industry' (Marriage 2015). Indeed, anti-hedge fund rhetoric has some history in European electoral campaigning.

> In the midst of a heated election campaign, Franz Müntefering of Germany's Social Democratic Party (SPD) offered a metaphor that would resonate widely throughout continental Europe when he described hedge and private equity funds as 'locusts' who were set on devouring valued national companies with negative consequences for the future of the economic and social models of organized market economies. Underscoring that this was neither a partisan issue nor one that was only a German priority, newly elected Conservative

Chancellor Angela Merkel announced that her government, with French backing, had the intention of replacing the international non-regulatory regime that had prevailed since the 1990s and to broker an agreement on a formal regulatory regime for hedge funds when she chaired the G7 in 2007.

(Fioretos 2010: 710)

The Franco-German initiative was supported by the financial industry in those countries. In the event, however, it was the transatlantic financial crisis, rather than European concerns over locusts, which brought a degree of public regulation to hedge funds. In 2011 the EU passed the Alternative Investment Fund Managers Directive (AIFMD), which covers a range of non-retail finance, principally in relation to registration, competition, capital requirements, documentation and transparency (Ferran 2011). Previously, the US and UK had blocked action in principle, saying that driving the hedge fund industry out of the US and EU and into other jurisdictions could only make the situation worse. Following the crisis, the US became more amenable to modest forms of action, notably registration of hedge funds with the public authorities, so the latter could begin to build a picture of activities and risks.

Paradoxically, the tentative steps taken towards bringing hedge funds into the public regulatory space may have emboldened hedge funds, creative creatures that they are, to reiterate their claims to be providers of a public good: regulation itself. Stimulating the managements of target firms to improve firm performance is held to be beneficial not only for shareholders but also for trading partners and for the wider market and stakeholders: collective private goods are portrayed as constituting a public good. As the very least, activist hedge funds project a cosier public relations profile than those pursuing either shorting or distressed debt strategies.

Short and shout: devour sinners

Hedge funds practising shorting strategies do so because they have reason to believe that the firms that they target are doing badly and will do worse in future, especially if given a little push.

This is the strategy of 'short and shout': first, go short the target firm's equity and/or debt (if the strategy is to cause insolvency), then make the shorting public, giving reasons for it. Adverse media attention upon the target firm discourages its trading partners and customers, worries investors in its equity and debt, puts pressure on its margins and raises the possibility of regulatory scrutiny of the target. These factors combine to create pressure on the target, creating profit for the hedge fund's short positions.

The ideal situation from the hedge fund's point of view is that its exposés concern not simply alleged weaknesses in the target firm's business model, results and management but some also alleged misconduct. That allows a hedge fund to pose as a private regulator of conduct, serving the public good. In such circumstances, a hedge fund seeks to enlist public regulators as (ambivalent and wary) helpmates and partners. Bill Ackman, founder of Pershing Square Capital Management, speaking in an interview, cited in Bloomberg Business (2015), said:

> I have a lot of confidence, frankly, in the Department of Justice. We hired someone recently from there. I've had friends who've worked there. They are extremely capable lawyers. They know good from bad, right from wrong. Look, I think it's very important that the accuser, us, it is not making up stuff like that—when we're explaining that a company is harming people. But I can tell — well, I can't [tell] you the nature of the discussions, but we have very proactively worked with the government agencies here in assisting them in understanding the company. And we have had many private meetings with the government and conversations and shared documents.

Pershing Square is a US hedge fund well known for investigating companies in which not all may be well, shorting their shares, making public allegations about the companies, creating an impression that the public authorities should investigate the companies or are already doing so and thus (when things run as expected by Pershing Square) causing the shares of the target companies to decrease and the short position to become profitable.

This strategy is sometimes called 'short and shout' or, less colloquially, forensic short-selling, insofar as highly negative public presentations about the alleged state of affairs at target companies are based on work done by forensic accountants, investigative journalists and the like, employed by or contracted by the hedge fund. The media and the public authorities can be expected to look at the allegations raised against the target company but, equally, will look at the tactics employed and 'facts' deployed by the shorting hedge fund, which can expect its actions to be closely scrutinised. It therefore pays the hedge fund to get its facts right, to create a believable storyline and to be ready to counter suspicions that it itself (rather than its target) may be manipulating the market.

Such work may be likened to strategic intelligence in international relations, foreign policy and national security: what was hidden is rendered visible, by assembling all the information that is available or can be made available and using it to spot incoherencies and contradictions in the target's market 'story'. Thus for example, before the fall of the Soviet Union, it was noted by a Shell research team that the Soviet Union's statistics on economic output did not fit well with statistics on inputs such as energy use (Schwartz and Randall 2007: 94–96). Since the energy statistics where more verifiable and the overall economic statistic opaque (to outsiders), this implied that the Soviet Union was economically weaker than it was presenting itself as being and closer to collapse than previously thought. Such insights allowed Shell to prepare for a period of disruption but also opportunity in oil markets.

Broadly similarly, Gotham City Research looked at various published and publically visible aspects of Gowex, a Spanish wifi facilities provider: the latter's claimed revenues (too large), number of employees (too few), number of mobile phone masts (fewer than claimed), inwardly-facing governance (family dominated) and accountancy arrangements. Gotham said that claimed revenues were higher than could be accounted for by the numbers of employees and wifi masts; that the management of the company had falsified its position; and that the company was actually in bad shape. Gotham predicted that Gowex's share price would go to zero, which then happened (*Economist* 2014a). Having exposed Gowex, Gotham retreated to obscurity (Chung 2014). Subsequent commentary has blamed regulators for being sloppy, for not keeping company (self-)governance standards up sufficiently (Martinez 2015).

Key to short and shout is the construction of two moral constituencies. On the one side are *them*, the villains of the story: the target company and its senior management, who are alleged to lie about the company's business model, ethics and profitability. On the other side are *us*, the virtuous ones, who include the hedge fund, media that take up its story, public authorities whose investigation (or mooted investigation) of the target company might find wrongdoing, and the broad church of investors – who are portrayed by the hedge fund in having an interest in seeing the wheat separated from the chaff.

Sometimes, short and shout evolves as a neat process that succeeds in a reasonably short time-frame, as was the case in Gowex. In other cases, however, it is a more protracted, more strongly contested and messier process. Pershing Capital's attack on Herbalife proved lengthier (2013–2015) than the hedge fund might have originally expected, and also proved trickier, as a contractor assisting Pershing came under investigation by the Federal Bureau of Investigations. In some cases, other investment funds and hedge funds may weigh in on the opposite side, betting that the target company will not only survive but also prosper, so supporting the company's share price and causing the shorting hedge fund some financial distress.

All parties may enlist the help of others – not only technical consultants, who look at the target company's accounts and regulatory filings or go round the country scrutinising its visible assets, but also public affairs consultants, seeking to prod a range of public agencies, such as market regulators and justice departments, into action in favour of one side or the other. That is what Mr Ackman alludes to in the quote above (Bloomberg Business 2015): the sparring market actors seek to enlist not only market sentiment but also public agencies, 'assisting them in understanding' (ibid).

Short and shout normally takes the form of an assault from outside. However, a refinement of the strategy involves involvement as a shareholder, for example asking questions and voting at general or special meetings of the company. In such cases, the hedge fund has to have possession of shares in order to have voting rights. The hedge fund can, however, either borrow shares, or can purchase them but offset the economic risk by holding corresponding or greater short positions, in which case 'the hedge fund might ultimately be able to pursue goals that are quite opposed or even detrimental to the company's interests' (Ringe 2013: 1033).

Combinations of internal activism and external criticism and shorting would be difficult for target companies to decode, if indeed they would be aware of them. It may even be unclear to a hedge fund, when taking up such positions, how things will eventually play out: possibly the hedge fund would lean to activism (e.g. if management of the targeted company is cooperative) or, alternatively, the hedge fund might increase its shorts (if bad news and dirt can be found). At first sight, indecision and keeping one's options open might seem to be at odds with the buccaneering image of hedge funds. However, as their strategies become mainstreamed in the market – or to put it another way, as mainstream investors become more 'sophisticated' – so such flexibility may become more common. If so, hedge funds and hedge fund-*like* market participants will increasingly defy classification as activists or shorters; rather, market participants' thinking and activities pulse across those possibilities.

Debt holdouts: litigation as an asset class

As discussed above, activist hedge funds seek to increase the market value of companies in which they have purchased a positive interest. Hedge funds following a shorting strategy seek to decrease the market value of their targets, preferably to zero. The forms of discipline invoked by the hedge fund are, respectively, power-sharing (activists typically demand board representation for the hedge fund and/ or its allies, changes in senior management and changes in corporate direction and execution) and frontal attack (shorters use all available means to convince its trading partners and holders of its assets that it has no future).

What those forms of discipline have in common is that both are framed by the *market* and by the forms of governance that the market provides. Other market participants have to be convinced by the hedge fund to take on board its economic logic. Other resources – forensic research, allegations, alliance-building, publicity battles, even legal actions – may be deployed, but as supporting elements within a market framing of the issues.

We now turn to the third and final hedge fund strategy to be discussed here, in which *litigation* is the framing device. All manner of other resources – research, allegations, alliances, publicity and economic pressure – are typically also deployed here, but as elements in a conflict in which litigation is central and is touted as a game-changer. This is the case in relation to some notable battles around distressed sovereign debt. In such cases, the creative, determined and often controversial use of legal resources may disrupt established market logics. This not only causes further distress to the sovereigns concerned; it can also annoy and evoke responses from some powerful market interests. Where the latter are not able to return the situation to the *status quo ante*, they seek to neutralise specific elements of hedge funds' legal strategies.

The background is that hedge funds purchase distressed, low-priced assets such as bonds, that may be corporate or sovereign, with the intention of obtaining repayment at par. Distressed assets can be bought cheaply by a hedge fund when the wider market considers that the debtor, being in no condition to redeem at par, presents an uncertain and unattractive future. There may be prospects of renegotiation, involving considerable delay and expense, followed at best by partial settlement (interest payment suspension, repayment of the debt at a few cents on the dollar, roll-over into other instruments or a mix of these) and, at worst, total default. Leaving aside those rare conditions when the debtor may be excused (such as in the case of odious debt, issued by a non-democratic regime that has now fallen), there is a wider acceptance that sometimes, due either to bad luck or bad management, an issuer of debt is unable to pay according to the contract. In such cases, the market norm is for the creditors to form a negotiating committee and to do a deal with the debtor, so as to get something, rather than continuing with the messy situation. If reasonable prospects of that cannot be established, then better to sell the debt and the attached, apparently uncashable legal rights, to whoever will buy them.

When the prospects of debt being fully redeemed have sunk, the instruments in question can be bought for a fraction of their face value, and this attracts scrutiny by specialised buyers of distressed debt. Buyers follow a variety of strategies. Some are prepared to play a waiting game: having constructed a diverse portfolio of distressed debt, they hope that over the long run their gains will outweigh losses and financing costs. A few buy in a highly targeted fashion, being in possession of information, or at least speculation, about the future of specific corporate or sovereign debtors. Of interest here, however, are those who do not simply wait for something favourable to them to happen but aggressively seek to make it happen, believing that they can force better terms (ideally, repayment at 100 cents on the dollar).

Such a strategy is referred to as a holdout strategy because the aim is to hold out for the full 100 per cent, or as close to that as may be achievable. The holdout strategy typically involves litigation, which may be quick or may extend over many years. In the estimation of most investors, such rights have little economic value in practice, under (what appear to be) settled points of law. By contrast, holdouts' aim is to transform legal points of law. In addition to a capacity for litigation, the holdout strategy also requires certain social characteristics that are lacking in most investors (and indeed only partially developed in most hedge funds): aggressivity, a positive liking for conflict and uncertainty, a disregard for or possibly a liking of unpopularity, and a political willingness to inconvenience sovereign states.

Leaving aside those corporate/cultural/political characteristics (cf. chapters 4, 5 and 6 in this volume), what is of interest in the holdout strategy is the conception that it advances about the relation of law and markets: law is seen as a commodity. In the words of advocates for this strategy: 'Litigation and litigation rights are, therefore, an emerging asset class – one that is gaining growing recognition in the market' (Harrison and Huntriss 2015: 135). Thus, when buying distressed assets, a hedge fund need not simply be taking a punt on economic value, as the latter might be defined by and realisable within the marketplace. The buyer is also acquiring litigation rights, referring to the contractual terms as interpretable in certain jurisdictions. If these litigation rights can be converted into actual and successful litigation, then they may be worth considerably more than their purchase price.

Far from trying to engage with and influence the wider market and its economic logics, the strategy of litigious holdouts is to chart a course that is independent from that of other market participants, and frequently is antagonistic to their interests. Not only the issuer of debt but also other holders may suffer, finding themselves legally constrained from reaching a settlement. The holdout strategy therefore calls forth considerable concern and opposition, not only from its targets but also from other holders of the relevant debt (who may suffer delays and losses), from powerful market associations (representing interests that accept occasional debt restructuring in the interest of maintaining an orderly market) and from regulatory authorities and international organisations (that become particularly concerned when sovereign debt is disrupted over the long term). In the face of such pressure, holdouts, their legal representatives and public relations agents deploy moral and political claims.

> Defaulting corporates are being held accountable by litigation; challenges through litigation and investment treaty arbitration to wrongful acts of states, provide an important check and balance against the creep of expropriation; directors and insolvency administrators are forced to focus carefully on their duties, where there is a litigious hedge fund creditor base. Indeed, sometimes the mere presence of certain experienced hedge funds in the capital structure can be sufficient to impose this.
>
> (Harrison and Huntriss 2015: 136)

That is a claim that litigious hedge funds not only restore market disciplines after lapses have occurred; their 'mere presence' also has preventative effects. Such approbation chimes in with the content of some chapters in this book, whilst constituting grounds for criticism by others. Widening our reference points, the litigious holdout strategy invokes questions about the relationship between law and markets. According to mainstream institutionalist thinking, political and legal frameworks make markets possible: after a formative period, law becomes settled in its broad outlines and therefore so are the terms of market functioning. Market conflicts are then institutionalised, being contained within a framework. However, if the legal pot is not simply stirred but is broken – in the sense that a series of court judgments quite radically changes what hitherto was widely thought to be the applicable legal framework – then the market is returned to its formative moment, with all affected participants (not only the immediate parties) seeking new containers.

A high profile example involves Argentinean government debt, a number of hedge funds including New York-based Elliott Management (Elliott) and the courts of New York. A brief account of this long-running dispute follows. After purchasing Argentinean sovereign debt, Elliott brought and won several court cases in the courts of New York (under whose jurisdiction the bonds had been issued by Argentina). Argentina had offered settlement terms that were acceptable to many of its creditors but not to Elliott and other 'holdouts'. After earlier sovereign debt cases against Peru, Ghana and the Congo, Elliott had been able to sell its stakes at several times the prices paid for them and it aimed for the same result here.

In a controversial series of judgments, the New York courts barred Argentina from settling with other creditors (the majority of whom were prepared to settle), on the grounds that such settlement could be adverse to Elliott's claim (see *Economist* 2014b for a pro-holdout account, Stiglitz and Guzman 2014 for the converse and Doyran 2014 for a wider critical account). The US Supreme Court declined to hear appeals from Argentina and pushed the issue back to the lower courts. Subsequently, Argentina took the US to the International Court of Justice (2014); however, that case could only proceed with the consent of the US Government, which (no surprise) was not forthcoming.

The stand-off attracted international attention and, indeed, consternation, since the position of the US courts and of the political circles supporting Elliott runs contrary to legal understandings hitherto, and since allowing a small block of hold-out creditors to block settlement by all other creditors would seem to block future resolutions of distressed debt (Salmon 2014). Others have warned of damage to the US as a jurisdiction for issuance of debt in future. Nevertheless, credit rating agencies flagged Argentina's actions as constituting selective default, increasing the country's difficulties in raising further funds and increasing the pressures upon it.

As a result of such holdout actions there has been disquiet amongst issuers of sovereign debt, investors and international institutions, followed by legal and market counter-moves to curtail future holdouts (International Monetary Fund (IMF) 2014). First, there has been a general tendency to rewrite terms, so as to force a settlement upon a recalcitrant minority of bondholders when a large majority wishes to settle: the so-called Collective Action Clauses (CACs). Secondly, there has been a preference for jurisdiction outside US law; although that is easier said than achieved, given the presence of so much financial infrastructure in the US. Thirdly, other market participants have weighed in on various sides, including hedge funds that variously follow the strategy of buying distressed assets cheap but are willing to settle for an available profit rather than going for the full 100 per cent.

Such hedge funds include that of George Soros which, together with other 'non-holdouts', brought a case concerning certain euro-denominated bonds to the High Court of England and Wales. The holdouts held aloof from the case (Bloomberg Business 2014), resting on the position that, in any matter of actual payment, any bank or clearing system cutting across the judgment of the US court would find itself in contempt. In its decision, the High Court (2015) affirmed that the Eurobonds in question fell under English law (there being no doubt of that). The English court was at pains not to give an impression of cutting across ongoing US litigation; however, it whispered some concerns to the US courts and implicitly invited plaintiffs to construct grounds for further exploration of the issues.

> It would be quite wrong for this court to make, and I do not make, any comment on such orders as may be appropriate and their effect as a matter of US law. The only comment I would make is that, as a matter of English law, I can

see no basis on which any such order could of itself give either the Republic of Argentina or the holdout creditors any proprietary interest in the funds held by the trustee with the Central Bank. More problematic is the state of 'paralysis', as leading counsel for both the claimants and the trustee described it, in the operation of the trust caused by the injunction. A continuing state of paralysis may have a number of consequences in English law. Such consequences may not arise, at this time at any rate, and they have not been the subject of any submissions to the court. They are at most issues which may arise in the future.

(High Court 2014: paras 45–46)

In other words, watch this space. In closing the discussion on holdouts and distressed debt, it is notable that Elliott's founder Paul Singer has also criticised other sovereigns – including Saudi Arabia – on grounds that it may have driven down oil prices (thus damaging one of his investments). He has also criticised financial market firms, such as J P Morgan Chase, on grounds that their public documentation of their trading positions is hard to understand. Those countries and financial entities would, however, be big fishes for any hedge fund to fry, as they can mobilise considerable financial, political and legal resources. Middle-range countries and corporates present more vulnerable targets.

The shape of things to come

As the above pages have illustrated, economic and competency arguments are central to hedge fund activist strategies; moral and conduct arguments are central to shorting; and (re)shaping the legal sphere is central to sovereign debt holdouts.

Having made such distinctions, each of the strategies to some extent mobilises all three forms of claims-making. Each strategy involves investigation, evidence-getting, legal work and public relations.

On public relations, it has been pointed out by other authors (Eshraghi and Taffler 2012) that the larger hedge funds do not advertise – reasons being that advertising could destroy their *cachet*, could suggest accessibility and weakness rather than exclusivity and strength, thus putting off potential investors. Be that as it may, hedge funds certainly know about public relations, controversy being both their weapon vis-à-vis targets and their claim to serve the public good: improving governance, punishing wrongdoing and bringing debtors to account. There are many occasions when stories find their way into the financial press about allegedly incompetent or immoral leaders of companies or countries that are being targeted by hedge funds. The present author's impression is that, whilst financial journalists are wary of being manipulated, they are reluctant to miss juicy news and may be drawn into what are in effect long-running campaigns (for example on the Chinese company Hanergy and on the left-leaning country Argentina). Such sagas engage readers on economic, legal, moral and populist levels, linking private profit-seeking with public (or at least national) good.

Specific campaigns of hedge funds take place against the background of sustained engagement by hedge funds with policy-makers, government officials and regulators. Lobbying of the European Parliament is conspicuous (Corporate Observatory 2014). So too is lobbying of the US Congress. Rather than being specific to hedge funds, there is a continuous barrage by financial firms and associations. Hedge funds are noted contributors to election funds and to philanthropic causes: it would be difficult to maintain that all this is in vain.

What then about the institution, practice and culture of the law, particularly around apparent shifts in doctrine? Relations between hedge funds and the legal profession may be subject to less transparency than relations with elected officials. This seems to be one of several under-researched areas. Sitting between elected officials and judges are financial regulators, at city, national and federal/ European levels. Here again there are contacts, which could be better understood, particularly in the light of the suggestion being made here that hedge funds are acting *as if* regulators, *with* them or *in place of* them. It would be interesting to know more about how such claims are negotiated and digested by public regulators.

Clearly, hedge funds' strategies are not mere technical accomplishments. They raise central issues about relationships between markets, law and politics. Some hedge fund spokespersons maintain that their relations with each other are cooperative rather than competitive, since they often support each other's actions against non-hedge funds (*Institutional Investor* 2014). Thus they may form a relatively cohesive *bloc* within the political economy (but see reference above to conflict between the Elliott and Soros funds). If the sector is indeed more cohesive than other sectors of finance (as well as being more cohesive than the wider economy), and if it is growing, then the implications merit attention. Some research agendas are now indicated.

Agenda 1: purposes of financial markets

There is scope for a public debate over desirable objectives of hedge funds (from a public policy point of view) and over any 'red lines' required in relation to their strategies – and indeed in relation to similar strategies when deployed by other market participants that may or may not fall into the admittedly fluid category of hedge fund.

In the recent past, such debates have been driven by short-term electoral considerations and typically have been phrased in hyperbolic terms – recalling for example Mr Müntefering's and others' references to 'vultures' – which invert and yet ironically echo the high-toned moral claims-making of hedge funds. Going back some decades, one can find broadly similar debates in the UK on 'asset stripping' (activities broadly corresponding to today's more sanitised and indeed laudatory discourse on activism).

What is striking, if understandable, about such debates is their defensive tone: the offended speakers would like things to stay the same and for firms, employment, localities and communities not to fall victim to changes that render them vulnerable. Citizens might well say the same about their no-longer-sovereign countries. Resistance and, if it can be managed, defiance seem reasonable responses (without doubt, hedge funds have the means and the spirit to fight back when their own interests are threatened). However, resistance generally arises late in the day. From a democratic point of view, a wider and more proactive debate over what citizens want from financial markets is merited.

Agenda 2: market-government relations

Financial market participants have an interest in shaping and directing countries' political atmospheres, departmental dispositions, legal case law, regulatory rule-books and, of course, specific legal and regulatory findings. However, having an interest is one thing: success is contingent.

One question then is how public policy-makers in general and regulators in particular manage situations in which they are besieged and beseeched to think and act in one manner or another. Whilst there is a considerable literature on such questions in the broad (within political economy, politics and EU studies, for example), there seems to be scope for a research agenda specific to hedge funds and to their strategies of influence.

To be clear, what is mooted here is not research on hedge funds as subjects of regulation but rather research on what one might characterise as a shifting and barely coherent net of co-regulation by hedge funds and arms of government, looking at tensions around the agenda-setting and regulatory intervention.

Agenda 3: resolution and conflict of law issues

Throughout the Eurozone crisis, senior creditors of tottering banks were bailed out, at the insistence of the European Central Bank. The transfer of debt from private investors to public treasuries, from the Irish banking crisis onwards, has been one of the drivers of austerity policies in Europe. Bail-outs may have led to a degree of complacency as to the future – and even expectations that similar bail-outs would be available not only for senior bondholders of banks but also for senior bondholders of specialist vehicles that had been specifically created to hold distressed assets.

However, such an expectation would run counter to policy intentions concerning resolution (see for example Directive 2014/59/EU (European Union 2014)). As an illustration of the change in tone, consider Heta Asset Resolution AG, which was formed by the Austrian Government as a 'bad bank' in order to work out the distressed assets of Heta Alpe Adria. The senior bonds of Heta Asset Resolution AG were underwritten by the government of the Carinthian region within Austria. Subsequently, once Austria adopted domestic legislation corresponding to EU resolution legislation, the regulator – the Financial Markets Authority – publicly contemplated using such powers (Austrian Financial Markets Authority 2015). This is said to have come as a shock to some in the market – although that seems curious insofar as holders of Heta senior debt include the large fund Pimco, owned by Allianz (Johnson 2015). Conceivably, some of the bonds had been bought at a price then thought to be favourable, amidst hopes that political and legal considerations might result in an eventual sale that would leave room for profit.

In entertaining such hopes for distressed debt, large financial firms and insurers find themselves in the same negotiating space as hedge funds. Such circumstances raise the question of to what extent a distinction-in-principle can continue to be made between mainstream financial market entities and hedge funds. The new resolution regimes in the EU and in the US may attract a number of legal actions, as dissatisfied asset owners contest resolution authority decisions. In the EU, the Court of Justice of the European Union (CJEU) is the final appeal court on issues of principle. The CJEU's style, the body of law and the political atmosphere are all very different from those of New York State. Nevertheless, the potential litigants are broadly the same. Despite efforts hitherto by European courts not to get into a tangle with US courts, the potential is rising. Resolution cases could constitute a messy legal frontline.

Agenda 4: sovereign debt and rotten boroughs

As the situation concerning Greece illustrates, challenges remain in relation to sovereign debt. It is widely accepted that, in principle, reforms might be led by the market or by states. In practice, market-based solutions to the use of US law by litigious holdouts have made faster progress than public policy. Nevertheless, some interesting and indeed provocative public law proposals have been put forward, with the aim of 'changing the calculus that makes vulture litigation a viable and profitable option' (Miller and Thomas 2013: 755–57).

One proposal is for an EU legislative programme to 'immunise' assets against actions brought by holdouts, such that enforcement orders of foreign (typically US) courts would not apply within the EU (ibid). A limitation of that would be that it could not prevent retaliatory actions against any entity that has US presence or uses financial channels to which US law applies.

Other proposals, looking to fundamental restructuring of the notion of sovereign debt, would address the question of renegotiation by linking debt payments to a country's economic health, as measured for example as GNP (Barr and others 2014). That could lessen burdens on sovereign issues in hard times, whilst providing less scope for arguments with (and between) creditors. Going further along that path, if sovereigns were to issue equity rather than debt, then fixed interest payments would be replaced by variable dividends and repayment of principal would also be contingent. Creditors would presumably demand a higher coupon/rate of interest and – on the analogy with equity ownership in corporate finance – could seek a direct and formal invoice in policy-making.

Such proposals blur the lines between corporates and countries, making the latter more like the former. Already one sees in the Eurozone the famous 'conditionality' vis-à-vis Member States that in preceding decades was applied by the International Monetary Fund to emerging countries. Sovereign debt of countries in distress, if in future issued on the basis of co-governance – broadly on the model of activist investors – would root conditionality more deeply in market logics. The emerging system of economic governance in the Eurozone reminds one of pre-modern English parliaments – constituted through wealth-holders, trade guilds and corporate bodies.

References

Armour, J and Cheffins, B, 2009, 'The rise and fall (?) of shareholder activism by hedge funds', ECGI-Law Working Paper No. 136 http://papers.ssrn.com/sol3/papers. cfm?abstract_id=1489336 (last accessed 1 October 2015).

Armour, J and Cheffins, B, 2009, 'The rise and fall (?) of shareholder activism by hedge funds', *The Journal of Alternative Investments*, 14(3), 17–27.

Austrian Financial Markets Authority, 2015, *Resolution of Heta Asset Resolution AG*, Vienna: Finanzmarktaufsicht (23 March 2015) https://www.fma.gv.at/en/special-topics/heta-asset-resolution-ag.html (last accessed 1 October 2015).

Barr, D, Bush, O and Pienkowski, A, 2014, 'GDP-linked bonds and sovereign default', Working Paper 484, London: Bank of England http://www.bankofengland.co.uk/research/Documents/workingpapers/2014/wp484.pdf (last accessed 1 October 2015).

Bloomberg Business, 2014, *NML Won't Participate in London Case Over Argentine Bonds* (9 December 2014), New York: Bloomberg http://www.bloomberg.com/news/articles/2014-12-08/nml-won-t-participate-in-london-hearing-over-argentine-bonds (last accessed 1 October 2015).

Bloomberg Business, 2015, *Ackman Says FBI Hasn't Contacted Anyone at Pershing* New York: Bloomberg http://www.bloomberg.com/news/videos/2015-03-13/ackman-says-fbi-hasn-t-contacted-anyone-at-pershing (last accessed 1 October 2015).

Brav, A, Jiang, W, Partnoy, F and Thomas, R, 2008, 'Hedge fund activism, corporate governance, and firm performance', *The Journal of Finance*, 63 (4), 1729–75.

Cheffins, B and Armour, J, 2011, 'The past, present, and future of shareholder activism by hedge funds', *Journal of Corporate Law*, 37, 51–104.

Chung, J, 2014, 'Gotham City research unmasks Gowex but stays in shadows', *Wall Street Journal* (9 July 2014) http://www.wsj.com/articles/gotham-city-research-works-in-the-shadows-1404842379 (last accessed 1 October 2015).

Corporate Observatory Europe, 2014, *The Fire Power of the Financial Lobby*, (April 2014) Brussels: Corporate Observatory Europe http://corporateeurope.org/sites/default/files/attachments/financial_lobby_report.pdf (last accessed 1 October 2015).

Dorn, N, 2016, 'Capital cohabitation: EU Capital Markets Union as public and private co-regulation', *Capital Market Law Journal*, 11(1), 00–00.

Doyran, M, 2014, 'The Argentine dilemma: 'Vulture funds' and the risks posed to developing economies', *Class, Race and Corporate Power*, 2(3), 1–20.

Economist, 2014a, 'Got 'em, Gotham', *The Economist* (12 July 2014) http://www.economist.com/news/business/21606838-company-accounts-detectives-collar-another-suspect-got-em-gotham (last accessed 1 October 2015).

Economist, 2014b, 'Argentina's bonds: a good week for some investors: vulture funds win a legal victory over Argentina's government' (21 June 2014) http://www.economist.com/news/americas/21604612-vulture-funds-win-legal-victory-over-argentinas-government-good-week-some-investors (last accessed 1 October 2015).

Eshraghi, A and Taffler, R, 2012, 'Hedge funds and unconscious fantasy', *Accounting, Auditing & Accountability Journal*, 25(8), 1244–65.

European Union, 2014, *Directive 2014/59/EU of the European Parliament and of The Council: a framework for the recovery and resolution of credit institutions and investment firms* (12 June 2014) Brussels: Official Journal of the European Union.

Ferran, E, 2011, 'After the crisis: the regulation of hedge funds and private equity in the EU', *European Business Organization Law Review (EBOR)*, 12 (03), 379–414.

Fioretos, O, 2010, 'Capitalist diversity and the international regulation of hedge funds', *Review of International Political Economy*, 17(4), 696–723.

Froud, J, Green, S and Williams, K, 2012, 'Private equity and the concept of brittle trust', *The Sociological Review*, 60(1), 1–24.

Harrison, N and Huntriss, F, 2015, 'Hedge funds and litigation: a brave new world', *Capital Markets Law Journal*, 10(2), 135–41.

High Court of Justice, Chancery Division, 2015, *Knighthead Master Fund LP and Others v The Bank of New York Mellon and Anor*, Decision of 13 February 2015 [2015] EWHC 270, before Mr Justice David Richards (ChD) http://www.bailii.org/ew/cases/EWHC/Ch/2015/270.html (last accessed 1 October 2015).

IMF, 2014, *Strengthening the Contractual Framework to Address Collective Action Problems in Sovereign Debt Restructuring*, Washington: International Monetary Fund http://www.imf.org/external/np/pp/eng/2014/090214.pdf (last accessed 1 October 2015).

Institutional Investor, 2014, How Hedge Funds Influence Philanthropy: Culture of Cooperation (video), New York (19 September 2014) http://www.institutionalinvestor.com/media/3381760/how-hedge-funds-influence-philanthropy-culture-of-cooperation.html (last accessed 1 October 2015).

International Court of Justice, 2014, *The Argentine Republic Seeks to Institute Proceedings against the United States of America before the International Court of Justice. It Requests US to Accept the Court's Jurisdiction*, Press release, The Hague: ICJ http://www.icj-cij.org/presscom/files/4/18354.pdf (last accessed 1 October 2015).

Johnson, S, 2015, 'Possible default of Austrian bad-bank bond rattles Europe', *Financial Times* (22 March 2015) http://www.ft.com/intl/cms/s/0/3fd97fb0-ce48-11e4-9712-00144feab7de.html (last accessed 9 October 2015).

J P Morgan, 2015, 'The activist revolution: understanding and navigating a new world of heightened investor scrutiny', New York: J P Morgan Chase (January 2015) https://www.jpmorgan.com/directdoc/JPMorgan_CorporateFinanceAdvisory_MA_TheActivistRevolution.pdf (last accessed 1 October 2015).

Katelouzou, D, 2014, *The Legal Determinants of Shareholder Activism: A Theoretical and Empirical Comparative Analysis*, King's College London Dickson Poon School of Law Legal Studies Research Paper Series paper 2014-8 http://papers.ssrn.com/sol3/papers.cfm?abstract_id=2357547 (last accessed 1 October 2015).

Macey, J, 2010, *Corporate Governance: Promises Kept, Promises Broken*, Reprint edition, Princeton, NJ: Woodstock: Princeton University Press.

Marriage, M, 2015, 'Labour tax plan "damaging" to UK funds', *Financial Times* (22 March 2014) http://www.ft.com/intl/cms/s/0/3c9b7e9e-cf19-11e4-b761-00144feab7de.html (last accessed 9 October 2015).

Martínez, A, 2015, 'Alternative investment markets under criticism: reasons to be worried? Lessons from Gowex', *Journal of Financial Regulation*, 1(1), 164–68.

Miller, M and Thomas, D, 2013, 'Eurozone sovereign debt restructuring: keeping the vultures at bay', *Oxford Review of Economic Policy*, 29(4), 745–63.

Partnoy, F and Thomas, R, 2007, *Gap Filling, Hedge Funds, and Financial Innovation*, Brookings–Nomura Papers on Financial Services http://papers.ssrn.com/abstract=931254 (last accessed 1 October 2015).

Ringe, G, 2013, 'Hedge funds and risk decoupling: the empty voting problem in the European Union', *Seattle University Law Review*, 36 (2), 1027–115.

Salmon, F, 2014, 'Hedge fund vs. sovereign: how U.S. courts are upending international finance', *Foreign Affairs* (24 June 2014) http://www.foreignaffairs.com/articles/141588/felix-salmon/hedge-fund-vs-sovereign (last accessed 1 October 2015).

Schwartz, P and Randall, D, 2007, 'Anticipating strategic surprise', in *Blindside*, Fukuyama, F (ed), Washington: Brookings Institution Press, 93–108.

Stiglitz, J and Guzman, M, 2014, 'Argentina's Griesafault', *Project Syndicate* (7 August 2014) http://www.project-syndicate.org/commentary/joseph-e--stiglitz-and-martin-guzman-argue-that-the-country-s-default-will-ultimately-harm-america (last accessed 1 October 2015).

Tett, G, 2015, 'Samsung reveals limits to activist powers', *Financial Times* (23 July 2015) http://www.ft.com/intl/cms/s/0/64cc31ce-3148-11e5-8873-775ba7c2ea3d.html (last accessed 9 October 2015).

Zetzsche, D, 2010, *Challenging Wolf Packs: Thoughts on Efficient Enforcement of Shareholder Transparency Rules* SSRN http://papers.ssrn.com/abstract=1428899 (last accessed 1 October 2015).

Chapter 10

Arbitration and financial services

Gerard J Meijer and Richard H Hansen

Introduction

In recent years, increasing attention has been given to arbitration as a desirable means of resolving financial services disputes (Blanshard 2013). Numerous factors have contributed to this growth, amongst them being 'the globalisation of financial markets and the increasing involvement of parties from emerging market jurisdictions in particular, concurrently with the recent financial depression, [which] have caused stakeholders to seek alternative methods of dispute resolution' (Karampelia 2013; see also Park 2006: 560–61). Furthermore, courts seem to be less familiar with cases involving complex financial products and therefore often lack the required expertise. Particularly troublesome is the fact that, recently, a serious difference in views was expressed by the English and New York courts on certain subjects – and there is no 'supreme court' to reconcile such differences (Meijer and Perera 2012: 74).

Another important reason for arbitration's growing popularity in the financial sector during such a time of internationalisation is that it offers advantages in comparison with court litigation. Such advantages include the expertise of the arbitrator(s), the ability to keep the proceedings confidential, and broad international enforceability under the 1958 Convention on the Recognition and Enforcement of Foreign Arbitral Awards ('New York Convention': United Nations 1958). As regards broad enforceability under the New York Convention, see e.g. Briner and Hamilton 2008.

However, although arbitration as a form of dispute resolution in the financial sector has been growing, it still accounts for a small percentage of the number of disputes filed, with court litigation in London or New York still being more prevalent. Because many market parties still shy away from arbitration as a form of dispute resolution, this chapter will focus on the first step that such parties need to take in order further to embrace arbitration as a form of dispute resolution: the conclusion of a valid and well-drafted arbitration agreement. Through the conclusion of such an arbitration agreement, parties to financial transactions agree to submit disputes that may arise under the legal relationship in question to arbitration and, in this way, can be sure that they will be able to benefit from the special advantages arbitration has to offer.

General notions regarding drafting arbitration clauses

Although national laws differ regarding the basic features that an arbitration clause must contain in order to be valid, there are a number of general elements which should be included in all arbitration clauses in order to be sure that any applicable local laws are complied with and that disagreement about the elements of the arbitration clause does not arise after a financial services dispute has begun (for an extensive discussion of the content and validity of arbitration agreements, see Meijer 2011: 737–858). According to Born (2014: 203–209), these general elements should include:

- a specific, express reference to 'arbitration' including a provision that the resolution of the dispute 'shall be finally resolved' through the arbitration;
- a clear indication of what types of disputes arising under the legal relationship in question are to be seen as falling under the arbitration clause (i.e. all disputes, only contract law disputes, etc?);
- a choice of either an arbitration institute and its arbitration rules, or a choice for a specific set of rules which can be used in *ad hoc* arbitration (such as the UNCITRAL Rules);
- an indication of the seat or place of arbitration;
- an indication of the number, selection method and qualification criteria for the arbitrator(s);
- an indication of the language in which the arbitration is to be conducted; and
- a choice-of-law clause (i.e. a clause in which it is explicitly stated which legal system is applicable to the arbitration clause, as this can be different from that applicable to the rest of the agreement, seeing that in most legal systems, the arbitration clause is seen as separable from the rest of the agreement).

Additionally, drafters of arbitration clauses for use in financial services contracts may find it especially attractive to include language covering one or more of the following 'optional' elements also mentioned by Born (ibid: 209–210):

- legal fees;
- interest and/or the currency of the award;
- discovery;
- fast-track and/or 'escalation' clauses;
- sovereign immunity waivers; and
- confidentiality.

Model arbitration clauses

A number of well regarded arbitration institutes have noticed the growing focus on arbitration as a method for resolving financial services disputes. To that end, some of these institutes have developed specialised model arbitration clauses for use in financial contracts. Other institutes, focusing especially on the resolution of financial services disputes, have developed model clauses that are also well suited for use in financial contracts. In any event: '[i]t is strongly recommended not to use self-designed arbitration clauses, but rather to insert one of these practice-tested Model Clauses, which have been published by a recognised arbitration institution, directly into the contract, without any changes. Alternatively, the UNCITRAL Model Clause can be used' (Cologne University 2015).

The UNCITRAL model clause

The basic UNCITRAL model clause, which can be used generally for arbitrations under the UNCITRAL Rules (which are often *ad hoc* arbitrations wherein no specific arbitration institute is specified; for more on the use of the UNCITRAL Rules in *ad hoc* arbitrations, see Webster 2010: 11–13), reads as follows:

> Any dispute, controversy or claim arising out of or relating to this contract, or the breach, termination or invalidity thereof, shall be settled by arbitration in accordance with the UNCITRAL Arbitration Rules.
>
> (UNCITRAL 2011: 29)

The American Arbitration Association (AAA)

The AAA has produced specialised procedures for use in financial disputes, along with model clauses (in both short and long form) which incorporate these rules. Additionally, in 1996 the AAA established a 'global component' – the International Centre for Dispute Resolution (ICDR) (American Arbitration Association 2014). As its name suggests, this division of the AAA is especially aimed at the resolution of international disputes. The ICDR has produced various model clauses covering arbitration, 'step' dispute resolution, mediation–arbitration, etc.

The China International Economic and Trade Arbitration Commission (CIETAC)

The CIETAC also has, since 2003, specific arbitration rules for use in financial disputes and a model clause which refers thereto.

The City Disputes Panel

The City Disputes Panel 'creates and supplies bespoke conflict management and dispute resolution solutions. [It] provide[s] services that are tailored to meet the needs of the City and the financial services industry, commercial corporations and all who do business with them, in the UK [United Kingdom] and internationally' (City Disputes Panel 2015). Therefore, as it is already specifically focused on financial disputes, its model clause refers generally to arbitration under its rules.

The European Centre for Financial Dispute Resolution

EuroArbitration is also an arbitration institute which specifically focuses on financial dispute resolution.

The Panel of Recognised International Market Experts in Finance (P.R.I.M.E. Finance)

P.R.I.M.E. Finance has developed both model clauses with and without an express option to include mediation in the alternative dispute resolution process. Furthermore, P.R.I.M.E. Finance has also created model arbitration agreements to be used as amendments to the 1992 and 2002 International Swaps and Derivatives Association (ISDA) Master Agreements, i.e. the ISDA-fied P.R.I.M.E. Finance Model Arbitration Clauses. These arbitration agreements are stand-alone amendments to the respective ISDA Master Agreements and refer to arbitration under the specific legal relationship created by a given ISDA Master Agreement. P.R.I.M.E. Finance provides these standard amendments in various forms to be used by parties in conjunction with specific choices regarding the seat of arbitration, referring to The Hague, Hong Kong, London, New York, Paris and Singapore.

Other guidance in drafting arbitration clauses

IBA Guidelines for Drafting International Arbitration Clauses

In 2010 the International Bar Association (IBA) adopted the 'IBA Guidelines for Drafting International Arbitration Clauses'. This document gives numerous general guidelines for the drafting of international arbitration clauses, along with explanatory commentary and examples of texts which could be inserted into international arbitration clauses. Of particular interest is the Guidelines' handling of drafting issues that arise when multiple parties are involved in an arbitral agreement and when an arbitration agreement covers more than one contractual agreement. The Guidelines also include 'recommended clauses', which can be extremely helpful in assisting drafters in avoiding the pitfalls that can be involved in drafting arbitration agreements to be used in complex legal relationships.

ISDA's model arbitration clauses

In 2013 ISDA released the '2013 ISDA Arbitration Guide', which provides information about a number of arbitral institutes. Additionally, the annexes to the Guide provide arbitration agreements that are specifically tailored to these institutes and for use in newly concluded Master Agreements which use the 2002 ISDA Master Agreement, and guidance for the alteration necessary for the arbitration agreements to be inserted into newly concluded Master Agreements that use the 1992 ISDA Master Agreement. A difference between the P.R.I.M.E. Finance clauses, mentioned above, and the ISDA clauses is that the ISDA model clauses are intended for use in *new* (1992 or 2002) ISDA Master Agreements, whilst the P.R.I.M.E. Finance ISDA Amendments, as their name suggests, are intended to be used to amend *existing* (1992 or 2002) ISDA Master Agreements.

Arbitration and the European Union's EMIR

Drafters of arbitration clauses for financial services contracts making use of ISDA Master Agreements should also be aware of the ISDA 2013 EMIR Portfolio Reconciliation, Dispute Resolution and Disclosure Protocol. 'EMIR' refers to Regulation (EU) No. 648/2012 of the European Parliament and of the Council of 4 July 2012 on over-the-counter (OTC) derivatives, central counterparties and trade repositories (European Union 2012). EMIR imposes dispute resolution requirements which are applicable to certain ISDA Master Agreements. ISDA's EMIR Protocol allows parties to these master agreements to amend the agreements to comply with the EMIR requirements.

As regards compliance with the dispute resolution requirements under EMIR, '[t]he Protocol provides a method for the identification, monitoring and resolution of disputes without overriding the existing dispute resolution methods that the parties may have agreed' (ISDA 2013). Although the Protocol provides for certain steps in resolving disputes and requires that parties have a specific process in place for disputes that are not resolved within five days, '[t]he Protocol does not prevent a party from handling a dispute in the way it considers best suits the circumstances nor does it free a party from strictly following any applicable dispute resolution process that it has previously agreed with its counterparty' (ISDA 2013).

Therefore, the EMIR Protocol should not affect parties' obligations under valid arbitration clauses included in ISDA Master Agreements.

However, as some ISDA Master Agreements will require adjustment through adoption of the ISDA EMIR Protocol, parties to ISDA Master Agreements who are adopting the Protocol may find it an opportune time also to adopt an arbitration agreement into the master agreement, something which can be quickly and easily accomplished by signing an appropriate P.R.I.M.E. Finance ISDA amendment at the same time as signing the EMIR Protocol. This is all the more so in light of Commission Delegated Regulation (EU) No. 149/2013 of 19 December 2012 (European Union 2013) (CDR), which further fleshes out the EMIR requirements as regards dispute resolution. In paragraph 31 of the introductory considerations, the CDR provides:

> Dispute resolution aims at mitigating risks stemming from contracts that are not centrally cleared. When entering into OTC derivative transactions with one another, counterparties should have an agreed framework for resolving any related dispute that may arise. *The framework should refer to resolution mechanisms such as third party arbitration* or market polling mechanism. The framework intends to avoid unresolved disputes escalating and exposing counterparties to additional risks. Disputes should be identified, managed and appropriately disclosed.
>
> (European Union 2013: 15, emphasis added)

Arbitration agreements contained in instruments other than contracts

Arbitrations can also arise where there is not direct contractual privity (i.e. no direct contractual contact, connection or mutual interest) between the parties. In practice, this is most frequently seen in the context of investment treaty arbitration, whereby a clause in an investment treaty concluded between two (or more) states provides that nationals of the one state can institute arbitral proceedings directly against the other state if an investment dispute arises. The clause in the investment treaty concerned is seen as an offer to arbitrate, which offer is accepted by the investor when it files for arbitration against the state concerned. In this manner, an arbitration agreement between the parties to the arbitration comes into existence. Therefore, where financial services transactions fall under the definition of an 'investment' within the meaning of a relevant investment treaty, financial services arbitration could be instituted, even though there may be no contractual relationship between the investor and the state.

An example of where financial services arbitration may arise in this context would be disputes related to sovereign debt, as in the arbitration in the matter of *Abaclat and Others v Argentine Republic* (ICSID Case No. ARB/07/5). Of note is the discussion of the specialised nature of international arbitral tribunals in Georges Abi-Saab's dissenting opinion to the decision on jurisdiction and admissibility in this arbitration (Abi-Saab 2011). In this regard, we note that parties to an arbitration, even an arbitration under an investment treaty, can unanimously agree to alter the terms of the arbitration agreement and could therefore, for example, decide to submit an investment dispute to a specialised body such as P.R.I.M.E. Finance, instead of a more generalised body such as the International Centre for Settlement of Investor Disputes (ICSID), which may be mentioned in the investment treaty.

Finally, we note that talks for an investment treaty between the European Union and the United States (US) (entitled the Transatlantic Trade and Investment Partnership or TTIP), were ongoing at the time of writing, and it is unclear whether financial services will fall under any arbitration agreement which may be included therein. More information on investment arbitration (in the context of TTIP) can be found in a Concept Paper of the European Commission (2015).

Description of the legal relationship to which the arbitration clause relates

The New York Convention, along with many national arbitration law systems, creates a framework for arbitration agreements which is based upon a specific 'defined legal relationship' (Born 2014: 294; see also Blackaby and Partasides 2009: 93–94). Because most arbitration agreements in the realm of financial services disputes are contained in specific commercial contracts, the fact that an arbitration agreement regards a specific legal relationship could be taken for granted. However, it must be noted that where multiple commercial agreements between parties are involved, it could be possible that a general arbitration agreement would come to light in which no specific commercial agreement was mentioned, but in which 'all disputes between the parties in the future' or similar language was included (Born 2014: 294).

In legal systems in which the validity of an arbitration agreement is based on its relation to a defined legal relationship, such a general clause runs the risk of being declared invalid. Although this is technically true, '[i]n practice, the "defined legal relationship" requirement has seldom been tested and has very little practical importance' (Born 2014: 294). Even though this may be so, practitioners active in the area of financial services dispute resolution are well advised not to take any risks in this area, and therefore drafters should assure that arbitration agreements for financial services contracts refer to a clearly defined legal relationship. Model clauses such as those from ISDA or P.R.I.M.E. Finance can help to solve this issue, as these clauses are relatively specific as regards the legal relationship involved and the types of claims which explicitly fall under the arbitration agreement.

Legal relationships arising from ISDA Master Agreements somewhat complicate the 'defined legal relationship' assessment, as relationships under ISDA Master Agreements relate to numerous distinct transactions between parties. Even though this is so, an arbitration agreement contained in, or attached as an amendment to, a 'framework agreement ' such as the ISDA Master Agreement is still considered to refer to a sufficiently defined legal relationship, as long as this is what the parties agreed.

If such a global dispute resolution provision exists, either in a stand-alone agreement (providing an arbitration mechanism for disputes in a series of related substantive contracts) or as a clause in a single umbrella agreement, then application of the clause to disputes arising under several contracts is not controversial: there is no reason that an arbitration clause in one contract cannot encompass disputes or claims under another contract, provided that this is what the parties agreed (Born 2014: 1370; for a discussion of multiple transactions between parties which do not fall under a 'framework agreement', but rather constitute successive contracts between the parties, see Gaillard and Savage 1999: 305–306).

Parties

Multi-party

Special considerations are involved when more than two parties could be involved in arbitral proceedings. The most important reason for considering the effect that a multi-party situation can have on arbitration agreements for financial services contracts is that, because arbitration is based upon the consent of the parties, generally only those entities that have specifically agreed to be bound by the arbitration agreement (i.e. the 'signatories') can be required to participate in arbitral proceedings (Born 2014: 1406; see also Park 2009 and Lamm and Aqua 2002). In the realm of financial services disputes, where the number of parties to commercial agreements can create drafting difficulties, issues associated with the multi-party context must be carefully considered.

Although handling such issues in depth is beyond the scope of this work, it is important that drafters of arbitration clauses for financial services contracts are aware of the fact that there are ways (albeit contested) in which companies related to the signatories of arbitration agreements can be brought into arbitral proceedings. Therefore, it is very important that drafters of arbitration agreements take such possibilities into consideration and factor in their preferences in this regard (either broadly, so that other companies such as parents and/or daughters may be brought in, or narrowly, so that the chance of this is reduced) and record these in their arbitration agreements.

We recommend that drafters of arbitration clauses for financial services contracts amend the chosen model clause to reflect their wishes whenever multiple parties (e.g. parent and daughter companies) may be involved in financial services disputes. The 'IBA Guidelines for Drafting International Arbitration Clauses', mentioned above, can be of assistance in this regard (it is of note that the International Chamber of Commerce (ICC) also recommends alteration of its model clause, in order to take multi-party considerations into account; see ICC 2015).

Multi-contract

Complications in drafting arbitration agreements for financial services contracts can also arise where the arbitration agreement is intended to cover multiple commercial agreements (also of note in this regard is the issue of 'continuing trading relationships'; for a discussion of these under the New York Convention, see Van den Berg 1981: 221–22). In order to resolve these issues, one can look to the relevant model clauses and arbitration rules. Although relevant procedural laws could also provide a solution, most jurisdictions lack specific provisions for multi-contract situations.

Contrary to most national procedural laws, the 'IBA Guidelines for Drafting International Arbitration Clauses' anticipate the difficulties associated with multi-contract situations and offer guidance. This guidance is broken down into two general rules: (i) 'The arbitration clauses in the related contracts should be comparable', and (ii) 'The parties should consider whether to provide for consolidation of arbitral proceedings commenced under the related contracts' (IBA 2010: 39–40).

One suggested way to achieve the desired outcome of streamlined arbitral proceedings between the parties is to adopt a stand-alone dispute resolution protocol. Such a protocol would then be specifically referenced in the various contracts between the parties and incorporated therein. Should such a stand-alone protocol prove infeasible, it is then suggested that the various contracts contain identical or complementary arbitration clauses and that it be provided that an arbitral tribunal constituted under any one contract has jurisdiction to resolve disputes arising under related contracts (IBA 2010: 39).

Another option for dealing with the complexities involved in multi-contract disputes would be (i) to use a model clause which takes multi-contract disputes into account, or (ii) to choose, and thereby incorporate into the arbitration agreement, rules of an arbitration institute which provide for the settlement of multi-contract disputes. Rivkin and others 2004: 607–608 suggest coordinating the drafting of multiple contracts involved, in order to provide for the resolution of multi-contract disputes; they suggest that this can be accomplished through either cross-referencing amongst the different contracts or drafting a single composite arbitration agreement.

Using a model clause which takes multi-contract disputes into account

The ISDA model clauses, for example, are tailored for ISDA Master Agreements and are designed to apply the (same) arbitration clause to the various transactions concluded thereunder. The P.R.I.M.E. Finance ISDA amendments are even more specifically tailored in this respect, and therefore provide a safe option for drafters. However, these standard model clauses do not specifically provide for other multi-contract situations. In order to cover other multi-contract situations and to provide for the multi-contract aspects involved in the specific situation, one could use the above-mentioned model arbitration clauses and then alter the chosen clause as necessary with the help of the 'IBA Guidelines for Drafting International Arbitration Clauses'.

Choosing rules of an arbitration institute which provide for the settlement of multi-contract disputes

As mentioned above, the parties may also incorporate rules of an arbitration institute that provide for the settlement of multi-contract disputes into the arbitration agreement. Most of the institutional rules relevant for financial services disputes, including those of P.R.I.M.E. Finance, do not specifically address multi-contract issues. As an exception to this statement, the ICC Rules do specifically address multi-contract situations. Article 9 of the ICC Rules, dealing with 'multiple contracts', reads as follows:

> Subject to the provisions of Articles 6(3)–6(7) and 23(4), claims arising out of or in connection with more than one contract may be made in a single arbitration, irrespective of whether such claims are made under one or more than one arbitration agreement under the Rules.

Also, Article 10 of the ICC Rules, on the consolidation of arbitrations, could be relevant in this respect.

Place of arbitration

Arbitration agreements for financial services contracts should specify a place (or seat) of arbitration. Different from where the hearings and/or other activities of the arbitration actually physically take place, the term of art 'place of arbitration' refers to the legal seat of the arbitral proceedings, an aspect which is very important because it determines which country's procedural (arbitration) law is applicable to the arbitral proceedings (see e.g. Blackaby and Partasides 2009: 184–85; for a different view, see Gaillard and Savage 1999: 635–36). Therefore, deciding on a place of arbitration should not be a consideration of where it might be most convenient and/or cost-effective for the parties to hold the hearings, but rather a conscious and reasoned choice of procedural law issue.

Drafters of arbitration agreements for financial services contracts should closely consider the procedural (arbitration) law of any country which might be a potential seat of arbitration. Additionally, for drafters unfamiliar with a particular country's procedural (arbitration) law, it may be advisable to consult an (international) arbitration practitioner within the jurisdiction in question. Along these lines, it should be noted that the ISDA-fied P.R.I.M.E. Finance model arbitration clauses and the ISDA model arbitration clauses provide clear guidance in this respect.

Choice of law as to the applicable substantive law

This section relates to the choice of an applicable substantive law, i.e. the law applicable to the commercial agreement itself, to be clearly distinguished from the applicable (procedural) law that applies to the arbitral proceedings. In order to avoid conflicts regarding which substantive law should apply to the agreement (e.g. whether the law of the place of conclusion, performance, delivery, etc applies), parties should specifically state which substantive law is applicable to their commercial agreements (see e.g. Blackaby and Partasides 2009: 114).

In the financial sector, parties most frequently (if not almost always) choose the laws of England or New York to be applicable to their agreements as these are 'the principal governing law jurisdictions for international financial transactions' (Henderson 2010: 821; see also Park 2006: 559–60). One could even speak of a trend in this respect. One can imagine many reasons why this is so, for example the experience of jurists in those jurisdictions with financial services transactions and legal certainty. Further, where a financial services transaction involves parties from two different countries where neither party is seated in the US or the UK, these legal systems can serve as a neutral playing field for the settlement of disputes. However, one can also imagine that two parties with no connection to England or New York might find it attractive to choose a different substantive law, especially where they both come from the same country.

In particular as regards the resolution of financial disputes, it is argued that the authority of the parties to determine the applicable substantive law should be only one of the factors the arbitrators will take into account, together with, inter alia, 'the requirements of international or pertinent national public order' (Dalhuisen 2015: 238). In this view, contrary to the mainstream view in international commercial arbitration, the arbitrators, when determining the applicable law, would not necessarily be bound by the parties' choice of law.

Number and appointment of arbitrators

Number of arbitrators

Parties are generally free to choose a number of arbitrators as they see fit. In practice, however, the number of arbitrators will usually be one or three. Parties will have to weigh the pros and cons of a given number of arbitrators in light of the specific circumstances of their commercial agreement. For example, having one arbitrator can lead to streamlined proceedings and reduced costs, although it should be noted that it is still more common to have three arbitrators in international arbitration (for a discussion of the considerations involved with the various possible numbers of arbitrators, see Blackaby and Partasides 2009: 247–51).

Appointment of arbitrators

There are many different methods for appointment of arbitrators in use in international arbitration. Amongst these are systems (i) in which each party appoints one arbitrator and then these two arbitrators together appoint a third arbitrator to chair the tribunal, or (ii) in which an arbitration institute provides a list of arbitrators from which the parties can remove undesirable candidates. For commentary on these and other methods of appointment, see e.g. Blackaby and Partasides 2009: 251–58 and Gaillard and Savage 1999: 452–83 (for national and international rules regarding the appointment of arbitrators) and 532–59 (for international practice regarding the appointment of arbitrators).

One of the most effective ways for drafters of arbitration clauses for financial services contracts to address the appointment of arbitrators is to incorporate institutional arbitration into the arbitration clause. In this manner, the arbitration rules of the arbitration institute chosen become part of the arbitration agreement and the appointment of arbitrators is arranged as set out in the chosen arbitration rules (see e.g. Born 2014: 831–32). Such an approach has the advantage of relying on tried and tested appointment procedures, which have probably already been shown to comply with any applicable procedural laws regarding the appointment process.

Although such procedural laws are not many in number as national arbitration laws usually favour party autonomy, there are constraints when it comes to assuring the fairness/equality of the appointment process. For example, under Dutch law, if one party to an arbitration agreement is given a privileged position in the appointment process, the other party can petition the court for an order appointing the arbitrators (Article 1028 of the Dutch Code of Civil Procedure (Staten Generaal en Koning van het Koninkrijk der Nederlanden 2001)); for commentary on this provision, see Meijer 2014: 1751–53 and Snijders 2011: 152–56; see also Van den Berg and others 1993: 39–40). In order to avoid the parties' autonomy in this respect being usurped by the courts, drafters of arbitration clauses for financial services contracts should make themselves aware of any requirements in the applicable procedural law. In this regard, utilising a standardised arbitration clause from a reputable arbitration institute can assure that all procedural law requirements are met.

Decision standard

'Decision standard' refers to the standard that arbitrators use in order to reach their decision. The two general standards seen in international arbitration are the rules of law and *amiable compositeur*. Both ideas will be explained below. The important point to make is that, if parties wish to deviate from the default decision standard found in the applicable national procedural law, they must specify in their arbitration agreement which decision standard will be followed.

When an arbitration agreement (or applicable arbitration law) refers to a decision standard based on the rules of law, it means that the arbitrators are bound to decide the case directly in line with the applicable substantive law, following all jurisprudence, etc from the courts. When parties choose *amiable compositeur* as the applicable decision standard, they express their desire that the arbitral tribunal not necessarily be bound by the applicable substantive law. Instead of having to stick to any applicable substantive rules of law, the arbitrator 'is free to give effect to general considerations of equity and fair-play' (Born 2014: 284; see also Blackaby and Partasides 2009: 228–29).

Language of the proceedings

Because financial services arbitration often involves parties from different linguistic backgrounds, it is important for parties to make a choice as regards the language that will be used for the arbitral proceedings (see e.g. Born 2014: 207–208). As the *lingua franca* in international business is now mainly English, it can be assumed that most arbitration clauses for financial services contracts will specify English as the language of arbitration. In this respect, there is little if any difference between arbitration of financial services disputes and general international commercial arbitration.

One point that must be made, however, is that having two languages for the arbitration should definitely be avoided. Drafters of arbitration clauses for financial services contracts should avoid such a situation at all costs. Examples of difficulties encountered are that it is hard (if at all possible) to find arbitrators who are fluent in (the legal and/or technical terms in) both languages, and that all documents in relation to the arbitration (including statements of claim, statements of defence, etc) would have to be submitted in both languages. These issues in turn result in increased costs and delays in the proceedings (Blackaby and Partasides 2009: 115).

Confidentiality

It is often stated that one of the advantages of arbitration is that proceedings can be kept confidential, something desirable, for example, to protect trade secrets or the reputation and/or goodwill of undertakings. This is often described as an advantage over court litigation because, contrary to arbitration proceedings, court litigation is generally a process categorised by public access to information regarding the proceedings. However, '[t]he confidentiality and privacy of international arbitration proceedings is a contentious and unsettled subject' (Born 2014: 2780; for a different view, see Gaillard and Savage 1999: 773–74, who maintain that '[i]t is generally considered that the arbitral award, like the existence of the arbitral proceedings, is confidential'). Therefore, drafters of arbitration clauses for financial services contracts should not take it for granted that arbitral proceedings will automatically be confidential. If the arbitration agreement refers to a specific arbitration institute's rules, drafters should learn whether those rules provide for confidentiality.

Additionally, drafters are advised to determine whether there are provisions regarding confidentiality in the applicable procedural law (mostly the arbitration law of the place of arbitration). As international conventions and most national laws are silent on the issue of confidentiality (Born 2014: 89–90), drafters of arbitration clauses for financial services contracts are advised (if desired) to state explicitly that any arbitral proceedings commenced under the arbitration agreement are to be strictly confidential. The 'IBA Guidelines for Drafting International Arbitration Clauses' may also provide guidance in this respect (see above).

Waivers

Although 'waiver' can refer to the loss of various procedural rights during the arbitral proceedings for lack of a timely objection or the waiver of an arbitration clause – which can occur when both parties participate in court proceedings regarding the dispute – 'waiver', in the international arbitration context, can also specifically refer to the parties' explicit renunciation of the right to make recourse to the courts against awards rendered in arbitration based on the arbitration agreement. The suggested addition to the UNCITRAL model clause clearly illustrates this (second) meaning: 'The parties hereby waive their right to any form of recourse against an award to any court or other competent authority, insofar as such waiver can validly be made under the applicable law'.

Such clauses can serve parties' interests in having a dispute finally settled through the arbitration process they have agreed upon, saving the parties considerable time and money in having to relitigate a dispute before a court. Where drafters of arbitration clauses for financial services contracts wish to make such a waiver, this must be either explicitly stated in the arbitration clause (by using, for example, wording such as that in the UNCITRAL model clause), or contained in the arbitration rules, which have been explicitly agreed upon in the arbitration clause and therefore incorporated into the arbitration agreement by the parties.

Additionally, the last half of the UNCITRAL waiver text points out another important concern regarding waiver of recourse against an arbitral award. Most national legal systems do not allow for waivers of recourse to the courts, or limit the waiver in that it cannot apply in certain situations, such as violations of public policy (Paulsson and others 2010: 103–104). Where parties desire to achieve full effect for waivers included in arbitration clauses for financial services contracts, they are well advised to agree upon an applicable (procedural) law that does allow for waiver of the right of recourse to the courts against the arbitral award.

Conclusion

It is hoped that this chapter can assist those in the financial services world in taking the first step towards enjoying the benefits arbitration has to offer: concluding a valid and well-drafted arbitration agreement. To that end, the discussion of arbitration clauses for financial services contracts in this chapter shows the importance of recognising common pitfalls in drafting arbitration agreements. Standard clauses provided by arbitration institutes can be an important tool in drafting arbitration agreements that are effective and result in internationally enforceable awards. However, the unique nature of financial services disputes means that standard arbitration clauses sometimes do not sufficiently address the needs and wishes of parties to such disputes. Therefore, drafters of arbitration clauses for financial services contracts are best advised to use the available instruments and models as the basis for their arbitration agreements and then, if necessary, carefully tailor those instruments and models to fit the specific circumstances of their situation.

Finally, a few words to help place this chapter in relation to the theme of this book. Above, the authors have advised on how to best draft a solid and effective arbitration clause so as to ensure that disputes arising out of financial relationships can enjoy the benefits arbitration has to offer over court litigation. In this way, the authors advocate the use of arbitration as a private method of dispute resolution, especially as far as financial transactions are concerned. However, this does not mean that the authors advocate a dispute resolution mechanism which completely escapes (the laws of the) public domain. On the contrary, the arbitration clause itself, as well as some if not many aspects of the arbitral procedure, will necessarily be covered by the arbitration law applicable in the chosen place of arbitration.

Additionally, arbitrators will apply either a national law or international law to the substantive dispute at hand, either as chosen by the parties or, if the parties have not made a choice, as determined by the arbitrators by applying relevant conflict of laws tenets. In this way, there really is a private system of adjudication that actually applies the laws from the public domain, to an extent blurring the public–private boundary. Along with the advantages offered by such a system, as mentioned above, arbitration also offers an advantage to public legal systems in general, as with a division of labour that places some matters before arbitrators instead of the courts, some of the enormous burden faced by many court systems can be somewhat reduced.

Also on the matter of the division of labour between courts and arbitrators, it must be noted that arbitration remains subject to the oversight of the courts, unless the parties have concluded a valid waiver of recourse to the courts, and even then such waivers may not be valid in most legal systems or may not be honoured in most legal systems if a serious violation of public policy is alleged to have taken place in the arbitral award or the proceedings leading up to its coming about. In the end, a careful balance exists between the freedom of the parties to take advantage of private solutions, and public policy concerns and fundamental rights which are safeguarded by the courts.

Acknowledgement

Parts of this chapter are based on Meijer, G J and Hansen, R H, 2015, 'Arbitration clauses for international financial disputes', in Golden, J and Lamm, C (eds), *International Financial Disputes: Arbitration and Mediation*, Oxford: Oxford University Press, but the chapter as a whole is specifically reworked and written for the present publication.

References

Abi-Saab, G, 2011, '*Abaclat and Others v Argentina*: Dissenting Opinion, Georges Abi-Saab' (28 October 2011) Washington, D.C.: ICSID.

American Arbitration Association, 2014, 'About the American Arbitration Association (AAA) and the International Centre for Dispute Resolution (ICDR)' www.icdr.org/icdr/faces/s/about (last accessed 3 October 2015).

Blackaby, N and Partasides, C, 2009, *Redfern and Hunter on International Arbitration*, Oxford: Oxford University Press.

Blanshard, E, 2013, 'The future of financial services arbitration', *Herbert Smith Freehills*

Arbitration Notes hsfnotes.com/arbitration/2013/10/01/the-future-of-financial-services-arbitration/ (last accessed 9 October 2015).

Born, G B, 2014, *International Commercial Arbitration*, Alphen aan den Rijn: Kluwer Law International.

Briner, R and Hamilton, V, 2008, 'The history and general purpose of the convention: the creation of an international standard to ensure the effectiveness of arbitration agreements and foreign arbitral awards', in Gaillard, E and Di Pietro, D (eds), *Enforcement of Arbitration Agreements and International Arbitral Awards: The New York Convention in Practice*, London: Cameron May.

City Disputes Panel, 2015, 'Welcome to the City Disputes Panel', www.citydisputespanel.org/index84d3.html?article=1&lang=english (last accessed 3 October 2015).

Cologne University Faculty of Law Institute for Banking, 2015, 'Model clauses', bankrecht.uni-koeln.de/79/content/155/model-clauses/en (last accessed 3 October 2015).

Dalhuisen, J, 2015, 'The applicable law in international financial disputes', in Golden, J and Lamm, C (eds), *International Financial Disputes: Arbitration and Mediation*, Oxford: Oxford University Press.

European Commission, 2015, 'Concept Paper [on] investment in TTIP and beyond – the path for reform: enhancing the right to regulate and moving from current ad hoc arbitration towards an investment court', Brussels: European Commission (6 May 2015) trade.ec.europa.eu/doclib/docs/2015/may/tradoc_153408.PDF (last accessed 3 October 2015).

European Union, 2012: Regulation (EU) No. 648/2012 of the European Parliament and of the Council of 4 July 2012 on OTC derivatives, central counterparties and trade repositories, [2012] OJ L201/1.

European Union, 2013, Commission Delegated Regulation (EU) No. 149/2013 of 19 December 2012 supplementing Regulation (EU) No. 648/2012 of the European Parliament and of the Council with regard to regulatory technical standards on indirect clearing arrangements, the clearing obligation, the public register, access to a trading venue, non-financial counterparties, and risk mitigation techniques for OTC derivatives contracts not cleared by a CCP [2013] OJ L52/11.

Gaillard, E and Savage, J (eds), 1999, *Fouchard, Gaillard, Goldman on International Commercial Arbitration*, The Hague: Kluwer International.

Henderson, S K, 2010, *Henderson on Derivatives*, London: LexisNexis.

IBA, 2010, 'IBA guidelines for drafting international arbitration clauses', London: International Bar Association.

ICC, 2015, 'Standard ICC arbitration clauses', Paris: International Chamber of Commerce www.iccwbo.org/products-and-services/arbitration-and-adr/arbitration/standard-icc-arbitration-clauses/ (last accessed 3 October 2015).

ISDA, 2013, 'ISDA 2013 EMIR Port Rec, Dispute Res and Disclosure Protocol', New York: International Swaps and Derivatives Association www2.isda.org/functional-areas/protocol-management/faq/15/ (last accessed 3 October 2015).

Karampelia, K, 2013, 'Cross-border disputes in the financial sector: a trend towards arbitration and the release of the ISDA arbitration guide', *Kluwer Arbitration Blog* kluwerarbitrationblog.com/blog/2013/10/24/cross-border-disputes-in-the-financial-sector-a-trend-towards-arbitration-and-the-release-of-the-isda-arbitration-guide/ (last accessed 3 October 2015).

Lamm, C B and Aqua, J A, 2002, 'Defining the party: who is a proper party in an international arbitration before the American Arbitration Association?', *International Arbitration Law Review*, 3, 84–92.

Meijer, G J, 2011, *Overeenkomst tot Arbitrage* (dissertation Rotterdam), Deventer: Kluwer.

Meijer, G J and Perera, C, 2012, 'P.R.I.M.E. Finance: a new dispute resolution facility for conflicts relating to complex financial products', *New York Dispute Resolution Lawyer*, 5(1), 74–76.

Meijer, G J, 2014, 'Vierde Boek: arbitrage', in Van Mierlo, A I M and Van Nispen, C J J C (eds), *Tekst & Commentaar Burgerlijke Rechtsvordering*, Deventer: Kluwer.

Park, W W, 2006, *Arbitration of International Business Disputes*, Oxford: Oxford University Press.

Park, W W, 2009, 'Non-signatories and international contracts: an arbitrator's dilemma', in Permanent Court of Arbitration (ed), *Multiple Parties in International Arbitration*, Oxford: Oxford University Press.

Paulsson, J, Rawding, N and Reed, L (eds), 2010, *The Freshfields Guide to Arbitration Clauses in International Contracts*, Alphen aan den Rijn: Kluwer Law International.

Rivkin, D W, Marriott, A L and Friedman, M W, 2004, 'Drafting and enforcement of arbitration clauses in the United States and England', in Fellas, J (ed), *Transatlantic Commercial Litigation and Arbitration*, Dobbs Ferry, NY: Oceana Publications.

Snijders, H J, 2011, *Nederlands arbitragerecht*, Deventer: Kluwer.

Staten Generaal en Koning van het Koninkrijk der Nederlanden, 2001, Artikel 1028 van het Wetboek van Burgerlijke Rechtsvordering, Stb. 2001, 58, 's-Gravenhage: Sdu Uitgevers.

UNCITRAL, 2011, *UNCITRAL Arbitration Rules (as revised in 2010)*, New York: United Nations.

United Nations, 1958, *Convention on the Recognition and Enforcement of Foreign Arbitral Awards* (New York Convention), New York: United Nations http://www.uncitral.org/pdf/english/texts/arbitration/NY-conv/XXII_1_e.pdf (last accessed 2 October 2015).

Van den Berg, A J, 1981, *The New York Arbitration Convention of 1958* (dissertation Rotterdam), Deventer: Kluwer Law and Taxation Publishers.

Van den Berg, A J, Van Delden, R and Snijders, H J, 1993, *Netherlands Arbitration Law*, Deventer: Kluwer.

Webster, T H, 2010, *Handbook of UNCITRAL Arbitration*, London: Thomson Reuters (Legal) Limited.

Afterword: remembering and speaking

Nicholas Dorn

In closing, rather than digging into the detail of the contributions to this edited volume, we want to view regulation through two different lenses, both of which concern the conditions under which regulation could sustain itself in a robust manner. The first of these lenses is historical and concerns memory. The collective memory of public regulators has been fallible before – as a little history from the US Federal Exchange demonstrates – and so the question arises of the conditions for such professional amnesia in the coming years. The second concern is a theme in both public and private regulation: the question of publicity. Public visibility of regulatory actions is necessary (if not sufficient) for regulation to have constitutive effects, that is to say, to steer the whole financial market as distinct from reacting to its parts. And yet, as regulation emerges from fire-fighting mode and seeks to find a new normal, the possibility arises that this may involve the (re)construction of the public policy equivalent of dark pools.

Public regulators are human, hence forgetful

The two biggest changes in the aftermath of 2007–2009 were the invention of prudential or preventative regulation, replacing the previous policy of clearing up after crisis; and a renaissance in private regulation which, having been put on the back foot by the crisis, is now definitely on the front foot again. Pre-crisis public regulation, which we might call pre-prudential, has been widely and authoritatively repudiated. However, the mode of public regulation may not have shifted fundamentally. More regulation, yes; different regulatory *modus operandi*, yes; but a transformation in the ways in which regulatory agencies function internally, in the sense of how they learn, and how they apply or disapply that learning? Maybe not.

Actually, we still know relatively little about regulators' conceptual skills in terms of learning and forgetting. In illustration of this point, we look briefly at a study of the US Federal Exchange (henceforth the Fed), as researched by Golub and others (2015). These authors examined a long run of minutes of meetings, covering the deliberations of the board of governors of the Fed. The minutes show that these key individuals, meeting and deliberating together in that particular institutional, cognitive and cultural context, considered it difficult to the point of being impossible to recognise bubbles, predict their bursting or intervene in a manner that would mitigate danger rather than heightening it. Rather, the prevailing sense was that a pragmatic course would be to deal with crises if and as they arise: 'post hoc interventionism', as expressed in the following quotation.

> Attributing the Fed's failures to free-market ideology, reliance on unrealistic models and regulatory capture is too simplistic – FOMC discussions are remarkably pragmatic and Fed policymakers and staff are highly sophis- ticated. Instead we argue that a combination of factors, most prominently confidence in 'post hoc interventionism' as the best policy response to bub- bles, and institutional routines that directed attention away from the crucial issues, were what blinded the Fed to mounting systemic risks in the pre-crisis period. Along with [Fed chairman] Greenspan's scepticism about the efficacy of regulation, these two considerations contribute significantly to our under- standing of the Fed's pre-crisis thinking.
>
> (Golub and others 2015: 684)

That conforms with what we know about pre-crisis regulation. The thinking was: let the markets get on with what is their business and then, if and as might be required, the public authorities will pick up the pieces. But how did they come to think that way? If we understood that process better then it might get us halfway to understanding the room for manoeuvre in regulatory thinking today. One ele- ment in the Fed's pre-crisis thinking seems to have been pragmatism, based on an acceptance that uncertainty about markets limits the extent to which regulators could have constructed knowledge about bubbles, for example. Uncertainty takes centre stage in what is now called prudential regulation, rather than being pushed aside as an unrewarding worry.

However, there lies the point: today's prudential regulation, concerned with grappling with uncertainty and with crisis pre-emption, theoretically *could have been attempted* in previous decades. Post hoc interventionism was not the only possible pre-crisis approach, so how and why did it come to the fore? The analysis of Fed documentation by Golub and others (ibid), taken alongside other material, sug- gests that the Fed was somehow unlearning or pushing aside some large and *poten- tially* highly relevant aspects of its acquired knowledge. In 1998 a highly levered hedge fund, Long Term Capital Management (LTCM), had collapsed – leading the then Fed's vice chairman to ask: 'How many more LTCMs are there?' (ibid: 14). Maybe none at that time; yet 10 years later the whole top tier of US banks and non-banks, including Bear Stearns, Lehman Brothers and American Insurance Group (AIG) had developed business models that were broadly similar to that of LTCM, in that they involved big bets with high leverage.

Thus, at the start of those 10 years, regulators were alerted to systemic risk, yet they then suspended active consideration of it, through adoption of a view that financial markets are so complicated that regulators were not able to second- guess them. Such a capacity to unlearn or at least to forget does not seem to be adequately captured by concepts commonly deployed within the literature – such as complacency, cultural closeness to the market, cognitive capture or revolving doors. Yes, all those were no doubt present. However, none of those concepts quite encapsulates or explains what may be a core competency, necessary for regulatory functioning: the unlearning, discarding and wiping of knowledge, in order not to be paralysed by its possible implications.

The suggestion made here is that a capacity for unlearning might be a core regulatory accomplishment – one continuing today, below all the surface noise, details, data, models and networking. Before the crisis of 2007–2009, regulators had unlearnt the potential for systemic crisis in finance. Today, shamefaced but newly vigilant, they have relearnt that. So, is now *everything* perfectly in vision, with nothing cognitively obscured?

Publicity and constitutive aspects of regulation

So far in this book we have managed to discuss diverse aspects of public and private regulation of financial markets without offering rigid definitions. This has certain advantages in avoiding doctrinal disputes or foreclosing on interesting avenues of enquiry. More positively, it provides a space within which chapter writers explore interrelations of public and private – always with an emphasis on one but also with an eye for how the other co-produces, supports or subverts the one. O'Brien, Pesendorfer and Christophers focus on public regulation, its ambition to remake markets and some evident limits to that endeavour. Wheeler, Cullen and Kerr and Robinson examine subversion processes – markets bite back, occupationally, culturally and politically. The contributions of Cherednychenko, Biggins and Scott, Dorn and Meijer and Hansen reverse the point of view, seeing private regulation as proactive and, indeed, as ascendant but not unconstrained.

Taken as a set, these discussions recast the question of regulatory roll-back (or regulatory recalibration, as EU Capital Markets Union has it). From a perspective protective of public regulation, it would be possible to see private initiatives pushing back against 'post crisis' command regulation, re-establishing previous conditions. However, as many of the above contributors show, there is a persistent element of invitation from public actors to private actors, albeit on a variety of terms. For example: 'we require, you kindly comply' (Cherednychenko); 'hey, sort yourself out, or else' (O'Brien); 'help us with this particular problem' (Biggins and Scott).

Moreover, there are other respects in which private actors are effectively autonomous. Consider for example how litigious and publicity-seeking hedge funds can steal the trumpet of public regulators and blow their own tune (Dorn 2016: Chapter 9 in this volume). Conversely, in some respects private actors can hide from public regulators, indeed also from others in the market. Departing somewhat from the spirit of the text of Meijer and Hansen (ibid: Chapter 10 in this volume), and entering into matters that are controversial (Zlatanska 2015), let us imagine a contract/transaction between two parties: one of high repute and wishing to keep things that way, the other of lesser repute but attractive for reasons of execution and/or price. In the event of any dispute arising, the executives of both parties may have reasons to arrive at a resolution as quietly and efficiently as possible – without drawing the attention of boards, shareholders (if any), other business partners, the wider market or media.

Privacy can serve all kinds of purposes, including providing a partial insurance policy in terms of risk-taking: if you like the trade and its possible pay-offs but you worry about possible blow-back, then you can strip out the public element of the latter by entering into an enforceable agreement to deal with any dispute behind closed doors. Redeploying trade vernacular, one can 'go dark' not only on transactions but also on relationships.

What might a side-by-side comparison of hedge funds and arbitration of disputes tell us, when viewed against the more general perspective of public and private regulation? One of the aspects of public law – which can also be found in some private law – is that it not only adjudicates issues but also promulgates the outcomes and the reasoning, thus building upon, extending or revising the corpus. Publicity reaches beyond the litigants to reach much wider strata of both private and public actors, reconstituting the rule of law. This is generally regarded as a public good, although the manner in which the public good may be identified and described differs somewhat between commentators (for international investor–state relations, see Hafner-Burton and others 2013: 2; for the common law, see Mulcahy 2013). Summarising, in forms of law and regulation that have publicity, public good is present (leaving aside questions of equity for the immediate parties). In forms of settlement that are shrouded, it is absent.

We can perhaps imagine a gradient of privacy (quite apart from the private or public origins or 'ownership' of regulation), with arbitration being quite high in privacy terms, in comparison with which hedge fund litigations have much publicity – both positions in relation to privacy/publicity being strategically chosen. Notwithstanding characterisations of hedge fund litigation as an 'asset class' (Harrison and Huntriss 2015), such litigation provides a marked counterpoint to private settlement, insofar as litigation and publicity are concerned. We do not have to accept hedge funds' self-serving and sometimes pompous claims, when these so obviously provide a front for private interests; yet paradoxically those claims may have a *relative* truth.

Where might rule-making and rule application by industry sectoral associations fit on such a privacy/publicity dimension? Arguably such regulators may be intermediate or middling in such terms. Without wishing here to get into detail on for example the International Swaps and Derivatives Association (ISDA: Biggins 2012, drawing on Wai 2002; Rauterberg and Verstein 2013: 22–24), it is evident that, even if determinations in cases of uncertainty or conflict are made behind closed doors, the headline result has to be promulgated, just as the model contract has to be public. For things to be otherwise would be to defeat the association's purpose.

Alongside these considerations about private regulation, *public regulation* also varies in the extent to which its processes are publicly visible. For example, publicity is generally low in meta-regulation, middling in command regulation if pursued

		Visibility of modi vivendi		
		Public	Intermediate	Private
Origin/ownership	Public	Exceptional enforcement situations	Post-crisis prudential command	Meta-regulation
	Private	Hedge fund litigation	Sectoral associations	Arbitration

Figure I Public visibility of varieties of public and private regulation

actively and high in exceptional conditions of enforcement. As a summary of some vicissitudes of publicity over various forms of public and private regulation, see Figure 1. (Incidentally, and in passing, this offers a definition of public and private regulation, as together constituting a field of governance that varies along the two dimensions of origin and publicity.)

To be clear, what is under discussion here is the question of tendencies – both in terms of origins/ownership of regulatory regimes and in terms of privacy/ publicity. If an impression of categorisation or classification is given by the text or implied in Figure 1, then that is unfortunate. It is a risk taken, however, in order to summarise the analytical point, that public/private may be understood in two senses or along two dimensions. Of course, privacy is hardly ever absolute (there are always people who talk, sometimes surprisingly much) and publicity typically does not emanate as God-like rays of enlightenment (intermediaries reframe and cherry-pick information, information recipients do likewise and some potentially interested recipients may not pick up at all on some news).

Similarly, the origins and ownership of regulatory regimes are not totally either public or private. It has become a commonplace that public regulation can be imbued with private interests, sometimes right from the start (Dorn 2014). Moreover, and more interestingly, international sectoral associations may not be very distant from their effectively 'home' state (which in ISDA's case is the US).

From the perspective of the state under whose jurisdiction a transnational private regulator is headquartered, unique possibilities emerge. This juris-dictional reach provides a state with legal and regulatory power over a trans-national private regulator. Control over the home of a transnational private regulator is thus a largely unacknowledged source of international regulatory power. A nation that seeks a certain character of regulation for the world's derivatives markets may well find that its best chance of achieving harmo-nised international regulation of that market is through leveraging control over a transnational private regulator.

(Rauterberg and Verstein 2013: 47)

Indeed, the ostensibly 'private' nature of sectoral associations requires as much critical unpacking as the ostensible 'public' nature of state regulation. This has been demonstrated by several chapters in this book, which have also focused upon cognitive, cultural and communicative aspects of public and private regulation. In an attempt to unpack these issues further, the present chapter has proposed memory and privacy/publicity as analytical tools for the future.

References

Biggins, J, 2012, 'Targeted touchdown and partial liftoff: post-crisis dispute resolution in the OTC derivatives markets and the challenges for ISDA', *German Law Journal*, 13(12), 1297–328.

Dorn, N, 2014, *Democracy and Diversity in Financial Market Regulation*, Abingdon: Routledge.

Goldbach, R, 2015, 'Asymmetric influence in global banking regulation: transnational harmonization, the competition state, and the roots of regulatory failure', *Review of International Political Economy*, **(*), 1–41.

Golub, S, Kaya, A and Reay, M, 2015, 'What were they thinking? The Federal Reserve in the run-up to the 2008 financial crisis', Review of International Political Economy, 22(4), 657–692.

Hafner-Burton, M, Steinert-Threlkeld, Z and Victor, D, 2013, 'Transparency of investor-state arbitration', Cornell Law School http://www.lawschool.cornell.edu/cornell-IL-IR/upload/Transparency-in-Arbitration-2.pdf (last accessed 3 October 2015).

Harrison, N and Huntriss, F, 2015, 'Hedge funds and litigation: a brave new world', *Capital Markets Law Journal*, 10(2), 135–41.

Mulcahy, L, 2013, 'The collective interest in private dispute resolution', *Oxford Journal of Legal Studies*, 33(1), 59–80.

Rauterberg, G and Verstein, A, 2013, 'Assessing transnational private regulation of the OTC derivatives market: ISDA, the BBA, and the future of financial reform', *Virginia Journal of International Law*, 54, 9–50.

Wai, R, 2002, 'Transnational liftoff and juridical touchdown: the regulatory function of private international law in an era of globalization', *Columbia Journal of Transnational Law*, 40(2), 209–74.

Zlatanska, E, 2015, 'To publish, or not to publish arbitral awards: that is the question . . .', *Arbitration: The International Journal of Arbitration, Mediation and Dispute Management*, 81(1), 25–37.

Index

For Product Safety Concerns and Information please contact our
EU representative GPSR take@pasadehandels.com.La for Ic Laacks
Verlag GmbH. Kaniningerstraße 21, 50331 München, Germany